Fiction, Crime, and Empire

2007

Fiction, Crime, and Empire

Clues to Modernity and Postmodernism

Jon Thompson

University of Illinois Press
Urbana and Chicago

To Suzanne with love

© 1993 by the Board of Trustees of the University of Illinois
Manufactured in the United States of America
1 2 3 4 5 C P 5 4 3 2 1

This book is printed on acid-free paper.

Library of Congress Cataloging-in-Publication Data

Thompson, Jon, 1959–
    Fiction, crime, and empire : clues to modernity and postmodernism
/ Jon Thompson.
        p. cm.
    Includes bibliographical references and index.
    ISBN 0-252-01976-8 (cl). — ISBN 0-252-06280-9 (pb)
    1. English fiction—History and criticism. 2. Crime in
literature. 3. Detective and mystery stories, English—History and
criticism. 4. Detective and mystery stories, American—History and
criticism. 5. Spy stories, English—History and criticism.
6. Postmodernism (Literature) 7. Imperialism in literature.
8. Modernism (Literature) I. Title.
PR830.C74T46 1993
809.83′872—dc20   92-38701
                                                                CIP

Contents

Acknowledgments

The time, energy, and good humor of many people went into the making of this book. Without them, it would never have been written—although a much inferior one would have been. For help along the way, I am happy to thank Granger Babcock, Sara Baker, John Bassett, Suzanne Chester, Lucinda Cole, Daniel Fogel, Carl Freedman, Eamon Halpin, Melynda Huskey, Prabhakara Jha, Ger Killeen, Gantam Kurdu, Robert Lane, Patrick McGee, Richard Moreland, James Morrison, James Olney, Jérôme de Romanet, Robin Roberts, Lewis P. Simpson, Richard Swartz, and Nathaniel Wing. I am especially indebted to Carl Freedman for supporting all my work and for generously undertaking the thankless task of directing the earlier, dissertation version of this book, and to Patrick McGee, who, among other things, helped me to rethink its architecture and argument. I would also like to thank two earlier teachers of mine at University College Dublin, Declan Kiberd and Seamus Deane, for first helping me to realize that there are more than thirteen ways of looking at a blackbird. For her patience and taste in critical writing, I would like to thank Ann Lowry of the University of Illinois Press. For his rigorous and helpful readings of this book, I am indebted to Bruce Henricksen and the other, anonymous outside reader for the University of Illinois Press. And for saving me from numerous embarrassments, I owe a debt of gratitude to my copy editor, Rob Schneider. Lastly, I would like to thank my mother, who taught me how to read, and my father, who taught me what could be done with the lessons of reading.

Introduction

Ours is a culture fascinated by crime. By any estimate, most contemporary films concern crime—whether theft, murder, rape, forgery, blackmail, extortion, influence peddling, or any of the myriad forms of political corruption. Every fall the three major American television networks (not to mention cable TV) launch their new line of programs, many of which take crime as their primary subject. Although most of these tend to focus on the violent lives of police or private investigators, the genre has broadened over the years to include the exploits of secret intelligence teams and the role of legal advocates in the defense and prosecution of crime.

Indeed, this culture industry is now international: American programs are telecast around the world, creating in effect a global television culture, a culture sustained to a considerable extent by fictions of crime. Americans are also major consumers of foreign exports: many English programs dealing with crime have enjoyed success in America.[1] Whether foreign or domestic, these programs are fictions of crime. (I have not included crime motifs in television in this brief inventory, but it is fair to say that they add a dramatic element to almost every genre, ranging from soap operas—where adultery and other sexual crimes add a salacious touch—to westerns, to adventure, and even to science fiction.) But there are also other types of television programs that present "fictions," or ideologically coded accounts, of "real-life" crime. The most obvious example of this type of programming is the evening news, a substantial portion of which is devoted to covering the most sensational crimes of the day. "Coverage" in this sense is a euphemism inasmuch as scheduling constraints, popularity ratings, and advertising pressures tend to lead to a distortion and dramatization—in effect, a fictionalization—of the commercial networks' representation of crime stories.[2] Similarly, television "newsmagazines" specialize in, among other things, lurid "investigations" of crimes, criminals, or criminal patterns supposedly sweeping the nation. Talk shows, likewise, seek to exploit the American fascination with crime by interviewing criminals, victims, or the police—sometimes simultaneously.

This interest in crime is nothing new; within Anglo-American culture it is as old as English fiction. Indeed, the English novel has its roots in fictionalized accounts of criminal confessions, such as the *Newgate Calendar* (1773). Daniel Defoe's *Moll Flanders* (1722) marks the beginning of the full-scale crime novel; the story is purportedly told in the first person by Moll Flanders, a flamboyant character who, out of necessity, resorts from time to time to prostitution and theft. William Godwin's *Caleb Williams* (1794) represents the first sustained attempt to use the detective-fiction genre as a means of criticizing society. While Godwin's analysis proceeds from an anarchist premise—the notion that although humankind is inherently good, laws and institutions are inherently repressive and should, therefore, be eliminated— his fiction inaugurated a way of evaluating society that has since become a convention of crime fiction. These eighteenth-century fictions of crime, however, are not sensational in the sense that we would use the word. Indeed, the modern meaning of "sensational" came about only in the nineteenth century in conjunction with (and because of) the rise of a mass culture based on the newspaper. In chapter 3, I examine the effects of this sensationalism in more detail; suffice it to say here that printed sensationalized accounts of crime are still a staple of contemporary mass culture, especially in quasi-factual magazines specializing in the accounts of victims of violent criminals.

Clearly, then, these various fictions of crime are deeply rooted in our culture, but what do they mean?[3] Although sensationalism accounts for part of their interest, it cannot explain it entirely, if only because a good deal of the mass culture focusing on crime is not sensational—as the formal English novel of detection of Agatha Christie, Dorothy Sayers, and Margery Allingham demonstrates. One theme of this book is that fictions of crime offer myths of the experience of modernity, of what it is like to live in a world dominated by the contradictory forces of renewal and disintegration, progress and destruction, possibility and impossibility.[4] The capacity of crime fiction to evaluate different historical moments in the experience of modernity is not an accidental feature; rather, it is a dominant convention of the genre. Although literature has contained themes of detection at least as far back as *Oedipus,* detective fiction (in many ways the paradigmatic crime-fiction form) is relatively recent. It is thus possible to draw a distinction between detective fiction and literature containing themes of detection. One historical shift in particular signals the arrival of a new social experience upon which modern crime fiction depends—that is, the transition in Western countries from a judicial process centered on confession and torture to one centered on a trial by evidence. As Ernst Bloch has noted, the judicial process of trial by evidence produced the modern detective figure:

Why, then, is the narrator who fishes in murky waters such a recent phenomenon? Above all, why does the detailed hunt for evidence appear at such a late date? The reason is that earlier legal procedures did not depend on it. Justice was dealt out in cash, so to speak, whether or not extorted. Because the *trial by evidence demanded* that evidence be sufficient for both the initial arrest warrant and the trial, criminal investigators arose with the detective in the foreground. Signs of all kinds, footprints, false alibis and the inferences arising therefrom, have now become as important as the old, often too-sweeping, *cui bono.* Prior to the middle of the eighteenth century there were absolutely no evidentiary trials, at least none that were deliberate. Only several eyewitnesses and above all the confession, which was called the *regina probationis,* could sustain a conviction—nothing else. Since it was seldom that enough witnesses were available, torture was instituted to elicit the *regina probationis,* and its painful question was the only refined one in Charles V's gallows justice. The result was that the accused was put off his guard through pain and made to say things—a torn web of lies at the cost of equally torn limbs—that no one but the perpetrator and the judge could know. The effect was unthinkable atrocity, the worthless extortion of guilt, against which the Enlightenment rebelled for both humane and logical reasons. Since then, evidence is necessary and must be produced; it is the basis for proof before the judge and jury in most cases. . . . To this extent, the depiction of the evidence gathering work of the detective is no older than the evidentiary hearing itself. (246–47)

Bloch's analysis positions detective fiction within the historical context of Enlightenment societies and their development of evidentiary trials: that sociojuridical evolution made possible that evolution in fiction. All the fiction analyzed here assumes the existence of societies at least nominally guided by Enlightenment values and judicial procedures.

Throughout this study, the term "crime fiction" is used to denote all the genres and subgenres that concern themselves with violation of the law, whether or not this violation actually took place, and whether or not this violation is sanctioned by the novelist. Any definition that in theory encompasses fiction as varied as *The Blue Room* (Simenon), *Crime and Punishment* (Dostoyevsky), *Lolita* (Nabokov), *The Big Sleep* (Chandler), *The Murder at the Vicarage* (Christie), *The Secret Agent* (Conrad), *The Spy Who Came in from the Cold* (Le Carré), *The Crying of Lot 49* (Pynchon), and *Briarpatch* (Thomas) will inevitably attract the charge of imprecision or irrelevance. But it seems preferable to use a broader, looser term to signify the generic similarities that these novels share than to engage in meretricious and debatable judgments about whether or not a given novel meets the requirements of this or that subgenre. This is not to say that all the conventions among the subgenres are identical; clearly they are not. It is possible, sometimes even desirable, to categorize genres according to dominant conventions. In practice, however, many of these single-convention categorizations are called into question by the presence of other conventions, which "should not," as it were, "be there," and which then have to be rationalized away. In my view, the attempt to construct rigid generic categories as a basis for determining literary merit tends not only to obscure the hybrid nature of genres, but also to reduce literary analysis to the passing of arbitrary judgments. This criticism is not meant as an indictment of genre theory as such but only as a criticism of the excessive formalism of critics whose work is marked by the attempt to identify a text with a genre on the basis of a single convention—the aim of this interpretive process then being the reading of the text in question exclusively in terms of the genre to which it has already been assigned. Indeed, the theoretical infrastructure of the present study depends on a theory of genre, but it is a theoretical orientation emphasizing the hybrid nature of genre fiction. (Conan Doyle's detective fiction, for example, is read as a hybrid of the adventure novel, sensational literature, and the ratiocinative detective story formula refined by Poe.) Ultimately, this theory of genre leads to a reconsideration of the question of literary value: among other things, I argue that the traditional dismissal of genre fiction cannot logically be sustained because *all* fiction is genre fiction; all fiction acquires an identity through its incorporation of genres (Bakhtin 288–89).

This approach differs from those adopted by most critics writing on the subject. Julian Symons's history of crime fiction, *Bloody Murder,* in many ways the standard literary history of crime fiction, is also an exercise in the evaluation of literary merit. This has the side effect of turning his study into a list of his favorite (and not-so-favorite) crime novels. But in one sense, this candor is refreshing given that these judgments are not passed off as anything more than personal opinion, well informed though it may be. Moreover, Symons's view of crime fiction is not handicapped by the widespread critical tendency to denigrate popular fiction (or the equally reprehensible tendency to uncritically valorize it); indeed, his readings demonstrate that crime fiction cuts across "high" and "low" culture. By contrast, John G. Cawelti's *Adventure, Mystery, and Romance: Formula Stories as Art and Popular Culture,* one of the finest academic treatments of popular fiction, is at the same time permeated by a sense of the literary inferiority of popular fiction. Cawelti attempts to establish a hierarchy of literary value based on a distinction between formulaic and nonformulaic writing. This tendency to reinforce standard literary hierarchies, even while seeking to do away with them, can also be seen in Michael Holquist's otherwise-interesting essay "Whodunit and Other Questions: Metaphysical Detective Stories in Postwar Fiction." In the course of distinguishing between modernism and postmodernism, Holquist sets up a familiar opposition between "art" and "kitsch" that he contends is the defining division of cultural production in the modernist period. He argues that this opposition breaks down in post-modernist fiction, particularly postmodernist detective fiction, which has a more metaphysical scope and is therefore able to shed its status as mere kitsch. Not all critics rely on this high/low distinction—despite its title, Dennis Porter's *The Pursuit of Crime: Art and Ideology in Detective Fiction* is a case in point—but the tendency to associate cultural inferiority with crime fiction is still common.

Rather than start from a position that assumes that literary value is the monopoly of this or that tradition, I examine the ways in which literary value itself is produced and how ideologies of literary value are then used to elevate certain forms of writing over others. My argument, developed in full in chapter 1, is that the dismissal of crime fiction and other popular forms of writing is based on one version of high-modernist aesthetics, which in turn depends on a number of unstable (and untheorized) oppositions: generic versus nongeneric forms of writing, literature versus popular literature, realism versus modernism, and so on.[5] Paradoxically enough, many of the techniques and forms of popular literature have been appropriated by high literary forms—a process the Russian formalists referred to as "the canonization of the junior branch." In the high-modernist period of the early twentieth century, this process of assimilation of popular culture was regularly accompanied by high modernism's very conscious attempt to define itself in opposition to popular culture. (By "popular culture" I mean primarily all the cultural practices produced for a mass audience for the purposes of entertainment; I am less concerned therefore with the sense of popular culture that is used to refer to those largely localized practices whose ideological function is to affirm the identity of a subculture or marginalized group.) This project of self-definition on the part of high modernism frequently involved the stigmatization of popular culture.[6] Along with other forms commonly associated with popular culture, crime fiction became the "illegitimate progeny" of high modernism: born out of the same experience of urban modernity that gave its impetus to the great modernist fictions of Virginia Woolf, James Joyce, Franz Kafka, and Thomas Mann, the fictions of crime produced by Edgar Allan Poe, Arthur Conan Doyle, Dashiell Hammett, and others were accorded a second-rank status by a faction of writers and critics who saw in them an erosion of high-modernist aesthetic standards, as well as a threat to the select definitions that modernism was acquiring. It should be emphasized that discriminations about literature per se are not the problem. What is problematic, however, is the way in which these discriminations are frequently used as the basis for making judgments about the universal literary merit of a given work. Evaluations of literary merit, I argue, are always relative: they are always historically made judgments, influenced by contemporary values and ideologies.

My approach has been most influenced by Raymond Williams, Mikhail Bakhtin, and Antonio Gramsci, writers whose theories of culture, I believe, allow for a much more conjunctural, flexible understanding of the relations between high and low culture than that permitted by those who see mass culture as aesthetically inferior. In this respect, Bakhtin's theory of the novel as a hybridization of preexisting genres, drawn from both high and low culture, has been especially useful. For Bakhtin, the provenance of a given genre is less important than the articulations it makes about society. In my textual readings, I use Bakhtin's emphasis on the aestheticized political articulations made by popular culture as a way of analyzing different cultural formations. These readings are contributions toward an increased sense of the interactions of high and low culture; or, more accurately, they allow us, as Raymond Williams once put it, to see culture as "a whole way of life." These textual readings, however, do not limit themselves to analyses of "high" and "low" culture; instead they also seek to engage the politics of culture in which these narratives participated.

One of the chief aims of this study, then, is to develop a historical poetics of fiction that might enable us to see how cultural practices, such as crime fiction, interact with what Gramsci calls hegemonic values, beliefs, and ideas. Hegemony in this sense is not to be equated with rule by coercive means. Instead, it refers to the process in democracies in which a dominant class or class alliance struggles for intellectual, moral, and political ascendancy by winning the consent of subordinate groups and classes. Hegemony, then, is secured not so much by brute force, by terrorizing the subaltern classes, as it is by accommodating their alternate or opposing values in a terrain dominated by those of the ascendant class. Within this theoretical framework, mass culture plays a crucial role in that it exists as a vital part of the public sphere in which the struggle for the consent of subaltern groups takes place. Mass culture becomes one of the crucial arenas for the resistance, acceptance, or incorporation of hegemonic values.[7]

This theory of hegemony thus allows for a rethinking of ideology as impure, made up of dominant and subordinate (oppositional) elements. In my study, this emphasis has not only allowed for the analysis of fiction within its cultural and historical contexts, but it has also enabled an understanding of mass culture as always ambiguously related to dominant values. Whereas many critics—whether New Critics, New Historicists, Marxists, or post-structuralists—have tended to read mass culture as mere commodified versions of dominant ideologies, I have sought to develop a historical poetics more sensitive to the complex formal and ideological character of fiction, and in particular one that would allow for an articulation of mass culture beyond the battlefield positions of apologist or critic.[8] By using theories from the work of Williams, Bakhtin, and Gramsci in conjunction with post-structuralist insights, I relate the formal structures of the novels to the hegemonic relations of which they are a part; my assumption in doing this is that this method not only enlarges our sense of the formal composition of popular fiction, but also enlivens our sense of the contributions texts make to the politics of culture. One final note on my theoretical method: although in later chapters I take up in more detail the uses and abuses of postmodernist theory, I want to acknowledge a general debt to post-structuralism, especially the later work of Michel Foucault. For an example of my use of post-structuralist theory, see chapter 2. For a more critical evaluation of post-structuralist premises, see chapter 8 and the conclusion.

As this book's subtitle suggests, my inquiry is carried out within the chronological framework of what Marshall Berman has called "the experience of modernity."[9] Berman divides modernity into three major phases. The first runs from around 1500, the approximate date of the advent of the world market, to 1789, the date of the French Revolution. This period is marked by the initial disorientations in the life of communities that characterize the modern age. The second phase runs from 1790 to the end of the nineteenth century. To Berman, this is the age of revolution and of the emergence of a modern public: "This public shares the feeling of living in a revolutionary age, an age that generates explosive upheavals in every dimension of personal, social, and political life" (17). The third phase consists of the twentieth century, in which modernity, paradoxically, becomes problematic ("conceived in numerous fragmentary ways, [it] loses much of its vividness, resonance, and depth"), yet as a social process intensifies: "In the twentieth century, our third and final phase, the process of modernization expands to take in virtually the whole world and the developing world culture of modernism achieves spectacular triumphs in art and thought" (17). What is compelling about Berman's account is not so much his fairly standard periodization, but his conception of modernity as "a paradoxical unity" that for him characterizes, to a greater or lesser extent, this process of modernization in all of its phases. Although Berman doesn't dwell on the concept of imperialism, it is implied that its expansionist dynamic is the driving force behind modernization:

> There is a mode of vital experience—experience of space and time, of the self and others, of life's possibilities and perils—that is shared by men and women all over the world today. I will call this body of experience "modernity." To be modern is to find ourselves in an environment that promises us adventure, power, joy, growth, transformation of ourselves and the world—and at the same time, that threatens to destroy everything we have, everything we know, everything we are. Modern environments and experiences cut across all boundaries of geography and ethnicity, of class and nationality, of religion and ideology: in this sense, modernity can be said to unite all mankind. But it is a paradoxical

unity, a unity of disunity: it pours us all into a maelstrom of perpetual disintegration and renewal, of struggle and contradiction, of ambiguity and anguish.
To be modern is to be part of a universe in which, as Marx said, "all that is solid
melts into air." (15)

One governing thesis of this study, then, is that crime fiction's intrinsic
interest in society—in the law and in the violation of the law—inevitably
involves an exploration of the experience of modernity, of what it means to
be caught up in this "maelstrom of perpetual disintegration and renewal, of
struggle and contradiction, of ambiguity and anguish." Much of this tension,
energy, and conflict comes from the British and American investment in the
imperial enterprise. In projecting an image of an individual within imperial
societies, or their social norms, this genre offers fictions of what modern
experience is like. Hence, the fiction examined in this study also explores
the experience of empire, and the laws, written and unwritten, that help to
define, regulate, and maintain it. And it is precisely because these fictions
challenge "high" and "low" cultural boundaries, because they occupy an
ambiguous position—a position both marginal (in canonical terms) and
central (in ideological terms) in the production of culture—that these narratives also challenge many of the ways in which the experience of modernity
is understood. Too often crime fiction, especially detective fiction, is regarded
as purely escapist, as providing the reader with comfortable and reassuring
myths of modernity. In some cases this is true, but it is no more true of crime
fiction than of any other genre: every genre contains domesticating elements,
elements that naturalize, reassure, and confirm the reader's beliefs and
expectations. What this cliché overlooks is the extent to which crime fiction
dramatizes the contradictory experience of modernity. In this sense, crime
fiction is not escapist but hermeneutic: it explores what it means to be
caught up in the maelstrom of modernity.

This study is not comprehensive; it does not pretend to analyze all the
subgenres or traditions of crime fiction. And it is not a literary history of
crime fiction, although it certainly has implications for literary history.
What I have attempted to do is to use my analyses of crime fiction as a basis
for intervening in contemporary critical debates. Accordingly, in this study I
use crime fiction as a point of departure for three related inquiries: a
reconsideration of some of the categories that we use to describe and
understand literature (realism, modernism, postmodernism); the articulation
of the relationships between fiction and the dominant ideological values in
historical periods dominated by the struggle to extend or maintain empires,
from the first half of the nineteenth century to the second half of the
twentieth; and last, the exploration of the possibilities and limitations of
fiction itself as a type of social praxis.

Modernism is construed here as the *institutionally* and culturally dominant field of literary practices containing residual (realist) as well as emergent (postmodern) elements.[10] Hence, while my readings move among "realist," modernist and postmodernist texts, my overall contention is that these modes of representation are part of a larger field of writing practices that, for lack of a better word, have still to be designated as porously modernist. Thus each of the historical divisions adopted in this study—the late-nineteenth-century age of high imperialism, the post–World War I and the post–World War II periods of imperial decline—cannot be understood as defined by a single mode of representation.

My analysis of crime fiction begins late in the time frame identified by Berman as modernity, at the point at which mass culture began to manifest itself. In America this occurred in the first half of the nineteenth century with the rise of the mass-circulation magazines that Edgar Allan Poe despised— and to which he contributed, among other things, his detective stories.[11] In England, mass culture began to be a major social phenomenon in the second half of the nineteenth century, which, not coincidentally, marks a crucial time in the life of both Great Britain and America in terms of the importance played by mass culture in the dissemination of imperial values. In chapter 3 I read Conan Doyle's detective fiction in light of its relations to both mass culture and imperialism; or, more accurately, I read his detective fiction in light of its relations to a late Victorian mass culture *of* imperialism. In chapters 4 and 5, I examine the emerging spy novel in terms of its response to this culture of imperialism. *Kim,* I argue, offers a valorization of empire, while Conrad's *The Secret Agent* offers a more critical interpretation of empire in terms of the changes it has brought about within English society itself. *The Secret Agent* is also seen in relation to modernism; Conrad's novel makes use of a dominant ideology of modernism in order to fashion a new kind of novel—the ironic spy novel.

The second moment of modernity represented here is the post–World War I period—in literary terms, the age of high modernism. In chapter 1, I analyze modernism as both a historical phenomenon and a critical concept. The historical context of modernism is seen as a response to the experience of the metropolis. As a critical concept, modernism is assessed by examining the ways in which influential readers and critics have sought to define modernism by distancing it from popular culture. My evaluation of these dismissals is used to pave the way for a more broadly based theory of modernism, which is developed most fully in chapter 6, in which I explore the structural, conventional, and epistemological similarities between modernism and detective fiction, and in chapter 7, in which I offer analyses of the American hard-boiled school (exemplified by Hammett) and the formal English novel of detection (exemplified by Christie). In this theory of modernist culture, a "residual" evaluative realism is absorbed into the dominant field of modernism. Chapter 7 then examines how these literary strategies portray—or betray—the hidden cracks in the facade of order and stability in the pre–World War II empire nations of Britain and America.

The third and last moment in the experience of modernity I explore is the post–World War II period, often referred to in literary and critical theory as postmodernism or postmodernity. In brief, my notion of postmodernity is complex, but crucial for my study, since this period or mode of representation accords the artifacts of mass culture a more significant and positive role in the constitution of culture than high modernism. In brief, my notion of postmodernity does not jettison what I have identified as the experience of modernity, but is seen as an emergent formation containing elements both continuous and discontinuous with earlier stages of modernity. In chapter 8 I analyze the post–World War II antiheroic spy novel as an evaluation, in a quintessentially popular form, of a culture that is simultaneously postmodern and postcolonial. I then use this reading as a basis for analyzing what I contend are problematic aspects of contemporary postmodern theory, particularly Baudrillardian postmodernism. Following this discussion, in the conclusion I explore two central issues: first, what it means to refer to crime fiction as postmodern, and second, the extent to which fiction offers a dynamic model for understanding, and even transforming, historical reality.

One final note on the structure of the book. *Fiction, Crime, and Empire* is organized chronologically. In one sense this is awkward, since I deal with both British and American fiction, and my argument concerning attitudes toward the British or American Empire gets buried for a time with almost every shift in authors. Yet this chronological progression seems preferable to a predominantly thematic structure inasmuch as it allows for a clearer sense of the parallels between the British and American experiences of empire, and gives an overall sense of the cumulative effects of that experience on the cultures of both nations. One conclusion of this book is that postmodern culture is born out of the experience of imperialism, both the old-style colonial imperialism and the newer cultural imperialism exercised by Western nations over developing countries; and whether it affirms or resists those imperialisms, postmodern culture is still tied to that legacy.

Notes

1. I have in mind the BBC productions of Le Carré's espionage novels and the ongoing PBS "Mystery Theatre" series that features mystery or crime programs made in the United Kingdom.

2. For more on the way in which "free market" forces shape the media, see Edward S. Herman and Noam Chomsky's *Manufacturing Consent.*

3. The sense in which I use the word "culture" is an important one for this study since the concept is repeatedly invoked. In general I rely on Raymond Williams's materialist conception of culture, laid out in *Marxism and Literature.* Williams contrasts his sense of the material basis of culture to Marx's superstructural sense of culture: "Instead of making cultural history material, which was the next radical move, it was made dependent, secondary, 'superstructural': a realm of mere ideas, beliefs, arts, customs, determined by the basic material history. What matters here is not only the element of reduction; it is the reproduction, in an altered form, of the separation of 'culture' from material social life which had been the dominant tendency in idealist cultural thought. Thus the full possibilities of the concept of culture as a constitutive social process, creating specific and different 'ways of life,' which could have been remarkably deepened by the emphasis on a material social process, were for a long time missed, and were often in practice superseded by an abstracting unilinear universalism" (19). My application of Williams's theory of culture consists primarily of the attempt to see the symbolic system of language itself as material, as a dialogic response to different contexts or ways of life, but responses that simultaneously enable the production of those ways of life. For a more elaborate articulation of this materialist conception of culture, see Williams's *Sociology of Culture.*

4. As will be evident shortly, I am consciously echoing the rhetoric and argument of Marshall Berman's eloquent book *All That Is Solid Melts Into Air.*

5. Unless otherwise qualified, in this study I use "modernism" to refer to the literary formation and "modernity" to refer to the social experience of modernization.

6. I am aware of the debate in cultural studies over the meaning and desirability of the terms "popular fiction" and "mass fiction," "popular fiction" usually being taken to emphasize the notion of a literature created by a people to establish their own autonomous identity. By contrast, "mass fiction" usually denotes an emphasis on the ascendancy of the values not merely of the culture industry, but also of dominant social and cultural ideologies. As I explain in the introduction, I try to negotiate this standoff by using Antonio Gramsci's notion of hegemony, which permits an articulation of both emphases within the same text. Accordingly, throughout the book I use the terms almost interchangeably, with the context determining the dominant meaning.

7. For more on Gramsci's theory of hegemony, see his *Selections from the Prison Notebooks.* For some fascinating readings of this theory, especially in relation to popular culture, see Tony Bennett *et al., Popular Culture and Social Relations.*

8. I do not believe that it is possible to read fiction in a morally and politically neutral way. Hence, the readings that follow are sometimes critical, but the criteria that underwrite those criticisms are, I hope, clear. Thus, there is no pretense of objectivity, but there is an attempt to make the readings as rigorous as possible without equating literary value with a political position.

9. Berman's rich, magisterial argument is contained in *All That Is Solid Melts Into Air.* Berman's reading of modernity has greatly influenced my own, as any reading of subsequent chapters will reveal.

10. The terms "residual," "dominant," and "emergent" are Raymond Williams's and are theorized more explicitly in *Marxism and Literature*. It almost goes without saying that although modernism is *institutionally* dominant, there is a great deal of realist writing that is widely read and enjoyed, despite its less-glamorous, low-culture status.

11. For more on this, see Richard Ohmann's "Where Did Mass Culture Come From? The Case of Magazines" (in his *Politics of Letters*). Ohmann's essay provides an invaluable discussion of the origins of mass culture in America.

Preliminary Mappings: Modernism and Genre Fiction   1

> For it goes without saying that nothing concerning art goes without saying, much less without thinking. Everything about art has become problematic; its inner life, its relation to society, even its right to exist.
>
> —*Theodor Adorno,* Aesthetic Theory

> Mass culture has always been the hidden subtext of the modernist project.
>
> —*Andreas Huyssen,* After the Great Divide

The Problem of Modernism

Since nothing goes without saying in relation to modernism either, this chapter articulates what I take modernism to be and the ways in which it relates to genre fiction. As a historical phenomenon, modernism emerged out of a specific set of socially recognizable circumstances and so acquired a varied but identifiable range of formal characteristics and ideological preoccupations. Exactly what these formal characteristics and ideological preoccupations were—or are—has been the subject of a large debate in modernist studies. In my view, much of this debate has mistakenly centered on rigidly defining these characteristics and preoccupations. This "will to definition" is problematic from a number of points of view.

Perhaps the most prominent irony associated with the desire to define modernism once and for all is that when it comes to dealing with modernism, a body of writing famous for its extreme ambiguity, little ambiguity is tolerated. Often, a quasi-mathematical degree of exactitude in matters of definition and classification is sought, as is evidenced by the large number of definitions of modernism (with the defining characteristics sometimes numbered, as if to give them the status of corollaries), comparative tables (usually intended to distinguish modernism from other cultural formations), and other schemata that abound in studies of modernism.

This attempt at rigid definition also fails to take into consideration the history of the term itself. The term "modernism" itself is relatively new; indeed, it did not come into general use until about 1960 (Alan Sinfeld, *Literature, Politics and Culture in Postwar Britain,* 191). Part of the difficulty with the term is that from the beginning it was used to designate both the largely European modernism that flourished in the first few decades of the century and the largely American post–World War II modernism (what many people now refer to as "postmodernism"). Thus the original formulation was always somewhat ambiguous, and this initial ambiguity has only fueled the more recent controversy surrounding the term, that of the distinction between modernism and postmodernism, if indeed there is one.[1]

The central question in this regard is whether any phenomenon as complex as modernism can ever be satisfactorily defined. Friedrich Nietzsche remarked in *On the Genealogy of Morals* that "only that which has no history is definable" (516). If one accepts the premise that modernism has a history, then it follows that it cannot be neatly defined. Nietzsche's epigram, however, does not suggest the worthlessness of historical categories per se; it only asserts the impossibility of defining them. What follows, then, is not so much a definition of modernism as it is an analytical description of a number of contexts in which it is possible to see the history of modernism and in which key characteristics of modernism are delineated in relief, as it were.

Another problem with modernism is that the term has always been used selectively to designate what is modernist. At one level, this selectivity stems from the ways in which various generations and artistic movements have opportunistically used the term to advance a certain poetics or praxis: at various times, modernism has been equated with symbolism, imagism, surrealism, futurism, expressionism, and formalism (Raymond Williams, "When Was Modernism?" *New Left Review,* 49). Sometimes drawing on the artistic appropriation of modernism, sometimes contesting it, critics and schools of criticism have also appropriated modernism, most often in order to advance a certain version of it. If it is by now almost a truism that canons are produced by critics and schools of criticism, then it is virtually impossible to conceive of a definitive, nonexclusionary version of modernism that satisfactorily comprehends the literature and art of the past century (or, in some versions, the past century-and-a-half). It is therefore more accurate to speak of *modernisms.*[2]

To suggest the diversity of modernisms, or more accurately the different modes of representation within modernism, I will focus on what I take to be its two dominant traditions. The first is the largely canonical tradition of modernism, which tends toward experimentalism, seemingly eschews referentiality, and is frequently seen as self-referential. James Joyce is often cited as one of this tradition's primary practitioners. The second tradition of modernism has been somewhat overshadowed by the first. It is more continuous with the techniques of the nineteenth-century classical-realist tradition and is often seen as more oriented toward social analysis. It is often regarded as less experimental, less self-referential, and less autotelic. Though the names of many famous twentieth-century writers can be found on its rolls (Ford Madox Ford, Jean Rhys, Ralph Ellison, Graham Greene), it is the mode of representation most often associated with genre fiction and popular fiction in general.

Although there are very real formal differences between these two traditions, their differences obscure a more fundamental similarity. Despite appearances to the contrary, especially in the case of experimental modernism, both traditions are oriented "outward," toward social critique. Each tradition employs different techniques, but they share a common objective: the critical evaluation of modernity. Indeed, one could go so far as to say that the objectives of social evaluation from the classical-realist tradition continue into modernism, but those objectives no longer necessarily find the same forms; rather, through the interaction of changing social pressures and creative individual reactions to those pressures, new forms emerge.

Historicizing Modernism: Modernism and the Metropolis

If there is no single definitive version of modernism, then there is no getting around the fact that the following discussion of modernism is itself selective. This is inevitable, since modernism is *overdetermined,* produced by a multiplicity of historical factors. Nevertheless, I have emphasized the relations between modernism and the metropolis because it seems to me that this connection, above all, encapsulates the decisive shifts in the experience of time, space, technology, and culture that produced the phenomenon now identified as modernism. This historicization does not try to reduce art to being a mere reverberation of socioeconomic or cultural life. Instead it suggests that modern art exists as a response to a particular historical context and to a large extent embodies in its forms that historical context; in doing so "we thus restore to it its concrete richness as a complex, contradictory, polyvalent, historical act" (Fredric Jameson, *Marxism and Form,* 378). History inscribes itself into texts as a range of practices, but those practices can be—and often are—then rewritten. To say that art is both an artistic and political practice does not reduce or diminish it; instead, it is a way of restoring to art its full complexity both as a formal object and as a voice (or assemblage of voices) engaging in a cultural dialogue.

Indeed, when contrasted to the realism of the nineteenth-century novel, one of the chief characteristics of modernism (with the exception of F. R. Leavis's version) is the explosion of new or hybrid forms, techniques, styles, and modes of representation. These breaks or new syntheses in form represent creative responses to related transformations in technology, social organization, and politics that effectively restructured nineteenth-century society and life. As Raymond Williams points out, these changes in artistic form, often articulated first in avant-garde movements, have to be seen in the context of the revolution in cultural production that occurred in the late-nineteenth-century industrialized world:

> Any explanation of these changes and their ideological consequences must start from the fact that the late nineteenth century was the occasion for the greatest changes ever seen in the media of cultural production. Photography, cinema, radio, television reproduction and recording all make their decisive advances during the period identified as modernist, and it is in response to these that there arise what in the first instance were formed as defensive cultural groupings, rapidly if partially becoming competitively self-promoting. ("When Was Modernism?" 50)

Similarly, in "The Work of Art in the Age of Mechanical Reproduction," Walter Benjamin argues that the age of mechanical reproduction necessarily produced a new kind of modern art, one liberated from the bonds of tradition and thus able to become "an agent of collective self-emancipation" (Eugene Lunn, *Marxism and Modernism,* 154). Though there are a number of weaknesses in Benjamin's theory of the decay of aura, it does offer a valuable theoretical framework for historically situating the emergence of modernism. His analyses of the relations between the art object and technological reproduction, the internalization of technological practices within art, the cognitive shift away from seeing art as an embedded artifact of a religious tradition, and the emergence of art as a more overt form of political praxis all represent ways of seeing modernism as, inevitably, a form of cultural politics.

According to Benjamin, the limited means of artistic reproduction in the premodern age reinforced a cultic loyalty to the notion of originality, allowing the artwork to become subservient to the demands of ritualistic and religious practices. These practices ensured an adherence to the idea of the work's "authenticity": "The presence of the original," Benjamin declares, "is the prerequisite to the concept of authenticity" (220). For Benjamin (at least in this essay), the authenticity of the work of art ratifies the tradition of which it is an example, and affirms the values of that tradition: "The uniqueness of the work of art is inseparable from its being imbedded in the fabric of tradition" (223). These mutually informing connections between the artwork's originality, authenticity, and religious or cultic use and tradition are all distilled in Benjamin's famous theory of "aura": "We define the aura of the latter as the unique phenomenon of a distance, however close it may be" (222). "Aura," that is, defines the relationship between the art object and tradition as one of "uniqueness and permanence" (223); at the same time, the work's aura defines a sense of the inviolable distance between the art object and its audience such that the audience is compelled to see the art object in terms of its affirmation of cultic tradition and, by extension, all unliberated traditions.

Benjamin suggests that all of these relations are disturbed by the advent of modern methods of technological reproduction. The reproduction of art on a mass scale effectively decenters the relations between the art object, its audience, and tradition in such a way that the function of art is transformed into one that is not based primarily on religious or cultic practices. This reconfiguration of the relations between art, its tradition, and its audience, however, is only one aspect of a larger process. Benjamin contends that the arrival of this new technology represents nothing less than a historical shift in perception: "During long periods of history, the mode of human perception changes with humanity's entire mode of existence. The manner in which human sense perception is organized, the medium in which it is accomplished, is determined not only by nature but by historical circumstances as well" (222). Clearly, for Benjamin, the most recent of these revolutionary changes in human consciousness is due to the technology of the modern age.[3]

One of the most important consequences of this historical shift in perception traced by Benjamin in "The Work of Art in the Age of Mechanical Reproduction" is the "contemporary decay of the aura":

> It rests on two circumstances, both of which are related to the increasing significance of the masses in contemporary life. Namely the desire of the contemporary masses to bring things "closer" spatially and humanly, which is just as ardent as their bent toward overcoming the uniqueness of every reality by accepting its reproduction. Every day the urge grows stronger to get hold of an object at very close range by way of its likeness, its reproduction. Unmistakably, reproduction as offered by picture magazines and newsreels differs from the image seen by the unarmed eye. Uniqueness and permanence are as closely linked in the latter as are transitoriness and reproducibility in the former. To pry an object from its shell, to destroy its aura, is the mark of a perception whose "sense of the universal equality of things" has increased to such a degree that it extracts it even from a unique object by means of reproduction." (223)

This loss of the aura of an artwork, the detaching of artifact from tradition that takes place via technological reproduction, represents a profound shaking off of traditional constraints and initiates the possibility of rewriting the present, signaling the potential for a new era of human emancipation. For Benjamin, these utopian possibilities exist by virtue of the ways in which technologies of reproduction can be harnessed both to transform existing works of art and to produce new art forms. Eugene Lunn describes the qualitative changes in artistic production emphasized in Benjamin's essay in the following manner: "Montage and radical juxtapositions—in both technologically reproducible art and the work of dadaists and surrealists— were historically conditioned by the masses' attempt to overcome spatial, temporal, and social distances, such as those between high and low (economically and culturally), past and present, there and here" (*Marxism and Modernism,* 152).

Modern art forms such as the cinema and the experimental novel gave a privileged place to techniques such as montage. This new sense of space expressed in montage offered the potential to "defamiliarize" or "make strange" existing senses of time, space, and perspective. For Benjamin, modern art telescopes or condenses the oppositions that inform premodern art. Hence the relationship between technology and human subjectivity figured in modern art is a dialectical one. This is evident not only in Benjamin's historicization of modern art vis-à-vis the technologies of reproduction emerging in the late nineteenth century, but also in the dynamism of his model: "the desire of contemporary masses to bring things 'closer' spatially and humanly" suggests the possibilities of appropriating technology for human purposes and indicates the ways in which technology creates a context for the transformation of humanity.

Although Benjamin plays down the capacity of capitalism to limit the emancipatory possibilities of mass art, his essay stresses the fact that "the contemporary decay of aura" reveals the *political* basis of art: "But the instant the criterion of authenticity ceases to be applicable to artistic production, the total function of art is reversed. Instead of being based on ritual, it begins to be based on another practice—politics" (224). Deprived of its cultic status, the work of art is no longer seen chiefly as an object of veneration. (Indeed, for Benjamin "the doctrine of *l'art pour l'art*" (224) is nothing but the last version of the age-old attempt to theologize art.) Instead, art's capacity to defamiliarize reality, and its potential status as a means of mass communication, highlights its political potential.

"The Work of Art in the Age of Mechanical Reproduction" leaves open, however, the broader historical and political contexts within which these revolutions in art and technology were taking place. What was the "age" of mechanical reproduction? One clue can be found in Benjamin's suggestion that these new art forms emerged out of a predominantly urban context. The dominant form of modernism, "experimental modernism," grew out of metropolitan centers, that is, those largely European cities—London, Paris,

Berlin, Vienna, and, later, New York—that formed the commercial, administrative, and cultural centers of the great nineteenth- and twentieth-century empires. Raymond Williams has explored this connection with great subtlety in "The Metropolis and the Emergence of Modernism." He notes that modernism achieved and maintained its ascendancy, and to a considerable degree still remains hegemonic, largely because of its strategic positioning within the most influential cultural apparatuses of these empires—the galleries, theaters, museums, publishing houses, newspapers, magazines, and "intellectual institutions, formal and especially informal" (14). With the extension of an organized, global market, the modern culture of the metropolis attained a position of enormous influence within the economically developed, technologically advanced nations, but also outside them, transmitting that culture to a colonial or neocolonial world. For Williams, then, the modern is itself a part of a specific set of historical circumstances, producing what he calls "a new set of 'universals,' aesthetic, intellectual, and psychological, which can be sharply contrasted with the older 'universals' of specific cultures, periods, and faiths, but which in just that quality resist all further specificities, of historical change or of cultural and social diversity: in the conviction of what is beyond question and for all effective time the 'modern absolute,' the defined universality of a human condition which is effectively permanent" (14).

One key paradox of modernism is that its "universality" is rooted in the historically specific experience of the metropolis, the beginnings of which can be seen in the Romantic identification of the modern city as "crowd of strangers" (15). This identification of the city with alienation is an obvious component of the poetry of William Blake and William Wordsworth; for both, the sheer size and complexity of a city like London imply the loss of the intimacy characteristic of earlier, "knowable communities." This loss leads to two related forms of alienated perception: first, the perception of others as alien, and second, the consequent alienation of the perceiver; increasingly, there is "the now familiar characteristic interpretation of strangeness as 'mystery'" (16). Within the vastness and anonymity of the metropolis, the individual is seen as lonely and isolated within the crowd. In Romantic literature (and beyond), "a direct relationship is proposed between the city and a form of agonized consciousness" (16). In both Romantic and modern poetry, for instance, the city's vastness and inhumane systematization are frequently seen as the source and cause of this "agonized consciousness." There is an obvious line of filiation here running from Blake and Wordsworth to Eliot. This specific experience of isolation in the city is then extended to describe a condition of general alienation (16).

Significantly, this historical experience of the metropolis also provides the ground for detective fiction. In this context the figure of the modern

urban detective emerges in the late nineteenth century as a literary response
to the alienation and crime fostered by the metropolis. By virtue of a keen
rational intelligence, the detective is able to penetrate the "teeming, mazelike"
(18) complexities of an otherwise-unknowable city. The complexity of society is thus a precondition of most detective fiction. Detective fiction was not,
of course, the only mode of representation that emerged as a response to the
increasing complexity of metropolitan life. Statistics, similarly, began to be
used more and more as a means of understanding a bewilderingly complex
and populous society (18). Yet the pervasive sense of alienation registered in
Romanticism, realism, and modernism is not the only structure of feeling
found in this writing; there is also the opposite response, a way of viewing
the city not only as a place of misery and alienation, but as "the site
of new kinds of human solidarity" (18). This perspective tends to emphasize
"the vitality, the variety, the liberating diversity and mobility of the city"
(19). This energy of course informed early modernist writing and social
movements—perhaps most famously in the social experiments of the Paris
Commune—as much as the emphasis on alienation; indeed, Walter Benjamin's
writing, as we have seen, not only comments on this aspect of modernity,
but is itself informed by it.

It is a telling fact of modernism that many of its most famous literary and
artistic innovators were exiles or émigrés; this experience of alterity has a
direct connection with the characteristic modernist themes of strangeness,
distance, and alienation (21).[4] The presence of the metropolis vis-à-vis
modern literature was not only, or even primarily, a matter of thematic
preoccupation. It was also responsible for, or inspired, many of the *formal*
innovations for which modernism is famous. These innovations not only
show the productive effects of technological reproduction, they also point
toward the cultural matrix of modernity. Metropolises like London and Paris
became international convergence points because of the centripetal pressures of capitalism and imperialism. This is evident in the relationship
between art and technological reproduction, but modernism also "reflects"
the diverse cultural matrix brought about by the forces of capitalism and
imperialism that converged on large European cities and now converge on
metropolitan environments in North American cities like Los Angeles. As
the centers of empires, these metropolitan centers "had characteristically
attracted a very mixed population, from a variety of social and cultural
origins—and [with the cities'] concentration of wealth and thus opportunities of patronage, such groups could hope to attract, indeed to form, new
kinds of audience" (21). For Williams, however, "the decisive aesthetic effect
is at a deeper level": "Liberated or breaking from their national or provincial
cultures, placed in quite new relations to those other native languages or
native visual traditions, encountering meanwhile a novel and dynamic

common environment from which many of the older forms were obviously distant, the artists and writers and thinkers of this phase found the only community available to them: a community of the medium; of their own practices" (21).

One consequence of the establishment of a "community of the medium" by this diverse, heteroglot group of exiles was a concentration on language itself: being foreign or marginal meant that many modernists tended to see language not as natural or given, but as arbitrary or conventional. As the very medium of literature, language came to be seen as a medium that could be molded (22) in ways unthinkable or unacceptable to those who accept language as a natural medium. To a large extent the modernist fascination with the medium of representation is comprehensible in these terms. Indeed the different registers, dialects, languages, consciousnesses, and cultures existing within the metropolis offered modernist writers rich opportunities for literary experimentation, experimentation that was not purely self-referential but critical of social reality. Once established, these literary innovations in technique and form could be, and were, then appropriated and refashioned by those outside the metropolis, either in more provincial regions of the mother country or outside it altogether, in the underdeveloped world. Alongside the initial process of dissemination were the critical ratification and solidification of modernist practices—both, again, due in large part to the sheer cultural power of the metropolis (22). Although many modernist movements began as practices opposed to the values and social structures of the metropolis, the cultural dominance of the metropolis tended to transform those practices into a newly, if sometimes imperfectly, incorporated orthodoxy, even if that orthodoxy was not hegemonic within popular culture or other spheres of lived experience.

The historical experience of modernism, then, has to be seen in relation to a complex matrix of interrelated cultural factors, for which analytical designations—such as the range of social adjustments necessitated by the pressures of a relatively new metropolitan order, the experience of implosive technological change, and the political and cultural tensions involved in maintaining a global system of imperial conquests—exist as a necessary shorthand. Many of the tensions mentioned above articulated themselves in the brash new forms and styles that we have come to identify with modernism; often, however, these formal innovations were as much a response to historical absences as to historical presences.

In "Modernism and Imperialism" Fredric Jameson observes that imperialism brought about a series of conceptual changes that were ultimately caused by the structure of imperial rivalry. These social, political, and economic relations, he suggests, had ramifications in terms of representation, indeed in terms of consciousness itself. Jameson notes that for the first theorists of imperialism (Marx, Lenin, Hilferding, Bukharin), the concept of "imperialism" did not usually designate the relationship of metropolis to colony but "rather the rivalry of various imperial and metropolitan nation-states among themselves" (47). Now, of course, imperialism is thought of in very different terms—it is conceived of as a relationship of economic dominance, rather than one of military competition. Since World War II, imperialism has been associated with neocolonialism, decolonization, multinational capitalism, and transnational corporations (47). This relationship suggests that up until World War II, "the axis of otherness" (48) was defined by the imperial subject in relation to other imperial subjects, and thus consciousness tended to repress "the more basic axis of otherness" (48)—namely, the colonial subject. Jameson points out that the cognitive and formal effects of this worldview were immense. Because "colonialism means that a significant structural segment of the economic system as a whole is located elsewhere, beyond the metropolis, outside the daily life and existential experience of the home country, in colonies over the water whose life experience and life world—very different from that of the imperial power—remain unknown and unimaginable for the subjects of imperial power" (50–51), it becomes virtually impossible to grasp the way in which the imperial system functions as a whole (51). Not only then do the "radical otherness of colonial suffering and exploitation" (51) and the causes of that suffering become unknowable, but the "daily life and existential experience in the metropolis . . . can now no longer be grasped immanently" (51). Consequently, Jameson says, a "national literature will always have something missing about it, but in the sense of a privation that can never be restored or made whole simply by adding back in the missing component" (51).

The stylistic complexity of high modernism thus exists as an attempt to negotiate or resolve this historical impasse, an impasse defined by a fractured sense of space and community. The style of modernists writing out of the context of a colonialist metropolis is comprehensible as a kind of sleight-of-hand in which "an appearance of meaning is pressed into the service of the notation of a physical perception" (54). Style, that is, vainly attempts to bridge the unbridgeable gap between *this* and *that*. It "becomes the marker or substitute . . . of the unrepresentable totality. . . . Because in the imperial world system this [representation of metropolitan space] is now radically incomplete, it must by compensation be formed into a self-subsisting totality: something Forster uniquely attempts to achieve by way of his providential ideology, which transforms chance contacts, coincidence, the contingent and random encounters between isolated subjects, into a utopian glimpse of achieved community" (58). Whether or not Forster is really unique in this regard is questionable, but the connections Jameson draws between the formal composition of modernism and the historical experience of imperialism foreground modernism's relation to one of its occluded others. Not surprisingly, then, for Jameson, *Ulysses* comes to represent that which is not possible in modernist literatures from colonizing nations. Because it emerges out of a colonized culture, "space does not have to be made symbolic in order to achieve closure and meaning: its closure is objective, endowed by the colonial situation itself" (61).

Although Jameson, like Benjamin and Williams, emphasizes the fractured sense of space brought about by the implantation of the metropolis within the imperial world system and the effects this has on the style of modern fiction in particular, he sees that the formal innovations of modernism are only fully comprehensible when seen in the context of the metropolis. As I have already suggested, underlying each of these theories is an emphasis on the *political* dimension of modernism. Numerous critics have sought to identify a class basis for modernism. In "Modernity and Revolution" Perry Anderson argues that modernism itself is a response to the persistence of "forms of dynastic anciens régimes" (325) in Europe before World War I:

> Briefly I think the following: the persistence of the anciens régimes, and the academicism concomitant with them, provided a critical range of cultural values *against which* insurgent forms of art could measure themselves but also *in terms of which* they could partly articulate themselves. Without the common adversary of official academicism, the wide range of new aesthetic practices have little or no unity: their tension with the established or consecrated canons is constitutive of their definition as such. At the same time, however, the old order, precisely in its still partially aristocratic coloration, has afforded a set of available codes and resources from which the ravages of the market as an organizing principle of culture and society—uniformly detested by every species of modernism—could also be resisted. (325)

Although Anderson's account is problematic, especially in its adoption of the view that the ancien régime remained the dominant class in Europe up until World War I—haute bourgeois society had all but displaced the aristocracy, even as it sought to adopt aristocratic values and a quasi-aristocratic lifestyle[5] —once reformulated, it nevertheless suggests the antiestablishment character of at least the most famous tradition within modernism. Anderson's analysis of modernism also points to the way in which it tends to be internally divided between a longing for an aristocratic order, mythical or otherwise, and a desire for a more egalitarian, nonbourgeois order. Within Anderson's perspective, the former tendency often leads to the embracing of fascism or some version of right-wing politics (Ezra Pound, Wyndham Lewis, W. B. Yeats, Virginia Woolf, T. S. Eliot), while the latter often leads to sympathy toward some variety of left-wing politics (Bertolt Brecht, Ignazio Silone, James Joyce, George Orwell).

There are of course modernisms outside these political borders—there is, for example, the modernism that finds itself fascinated by and drawn to both forms of politics, as might be seen in the work of Joseph Conrad and D. H. Lawrence—but more important than the overt political divisions within modernism, however they are designated, is what those divisions suggest about modernism, for its largely antibourgeois character indicates that modernism exists as a critical response to modernity itself.

Historically, theories of modernism have tended to vacillate, in a contradictory fashion, between seeing it as aesthetically autonomous (self-referential, autotelic, or purely formal), or else as a subversion of social norms (Astradur Eysteinsson, *The Concept of Modernism,* 24).[6] However, in *Aesthetic Theory,* Theodor Adorno develops a theory of modernism that indicates the way in which modernism's "self-referentiality" can be read as a critical response to modernity. He overcomes the self-referential/subversive dichotomy in modernist criticism by suggesting that the refined formalism of high modernism is itself a mode of social criticism. Adorno's theory takes as its point of departure the formalism that is such a pronounced feature of high modernism: "The manner in which art communicates with the outside world is in fact a lack of communication, because art seeks, blissfully or unhappily, to seclude itself from the world" (7). For Adorno, this seclusion on the part of modern art is not an abandonment of the social world so much as it is a strategic response to it: "Even the most sublime work of art takes up a definite position *vis-à-vis* reality by stepping outside of reality's spell, not abstractly once and for all, but occasionally and in concrete ways, when it unconsciously and tacitly polemicizes against the condition of society at a particular point in time" (7). Modern art thus embodies a sociality that is compromised everywhere else. In an administered, commodified society, authentic critique is possible only outside that order:

> Nor is art social only because it derives its material content from society. Rather it is social primarily because it stands opposed to society. Now this opposition art can mount only when it has become autonomous. By congealing into an entity unto itself—rather than obeying existing norms and thus proving itself to be 'socially useful'—art criticizes society just by being there. Pure and immanently elaborated art is a tacit critique of the debasement of man by a condition that is moving toward a total-exchange society where everything is a for-other. This social deviance of art is the determinate negation of a determinate society. (321)

Within this purview, the "autonomy" of modern art becomes the necessary condition for its being a means of criticism; its formal purity exists as a "determinate negation of a determinate society." In other words, it exists as an admonition to a society in which use value has been debased by exchange value. Whereas Anderson emphasizes the politics of expression, Adorno emphasizes the politics of form. For Adorno, modernism is critical of society not by virtue of expressed statements contained within the text, but by formal indirection. Form is socially symbolic: "What makes art works socially significant is content that articulates itself in formal structures. Kafka is a good example here. Nowhere in his work did he address monopoly capitalism directly. Yet by zeroing in on the dregs of the administered world, he laid bare the inhumanity of a repressive social totality, and he did so more powerfully and uncompromisingly than if he had written novels about corruption in multinational corporations" (327).

The expression of social content in form is exemplified most dramatically for Adorno in Kafka's work, especially in the contrast between "stylistic sobriety" and "highly imaginary happenings" (327), a contrast that "brings what seems distant and impossible [presumably the administered world of monopoly capitalism] into menacingly close range" (327). The example of Kafka—for Adorno a key modernist—foregrounds the paradoxical nature of Adorno's theory in which the seeming autonomy of art brings about radical social critique: "Freedom from repression can be represented only by what does not succumb to repression; residual use value only by what is useless. Works of art are plenipotentiaries of things beyond the mutilating sway of exchange, profit and false human needs" (323). The formal difficulty and intricacy of modern art allow it to minimize its dealings with a society based on the imperatives of exchange value, but it cannot abjure them altogether. Art thus exists in a near-permanent double bind: "In its relation to society art finds itself in a dilemma today. If it lets go of autonomy it sells out to the established order, whereas if it tries to stay strictly within its autonomous confines it become equally co-optable, living a harmless life in its appointed niche" (337). Modern art thus exists in the precarious condition of continually resisting the reifying pressures of capitalism by self-consciously fashioning forms that defy any kind of easy consumption.

Powerful as Adorno's reading of modernism is, it is clear that his theory privileges one kind of modernism—experimental modernism—and quite explicitly denigrates other forms, especially those that continue to work in a realist vein. His rejection of the social-realist tradition as contaminated by the compromised values of an economically imperialistic world system—because it does not make the strategic withdrawal embodied in the formal triumphs of modernism—amounts to a programmatic dismissal of the achievements of modernists such as Willa Cather, Zora Neale Hurston, D. H. Lawrence, Nathanael West, Lewis Grassic Gibbon, Katherine Mansfield, Ford Madox Ford, and Jean Rhys. Their sin consists of a commitment to linguistic referentiality. And this list does not begin to take into consideration those writers who have been classified as "popular";

for Adorno, they are nonentities or worse—exemplars of a kind of political bad faith. This categorical dismissal is perhaps most disturbing in its implicit elitism: linguistic reflexivity is sanctified, while referentiality is stigmatized. In effect, this amounts to an almost-wholesale privileging of canonical writers over noncanonical ones, and in this regard Adorno merely ratifies the values of the administrative society that he criticizes so effectively elsewhere.

Thus, whereas Williams, Benjamin, and Jameson see that the metropolis has been, among other things, artistically productive in terms of its impact on the inner forms of modernism, for Adorno it is precisely this experience of deathly reification that modernism must fend off via its stylistic sorcery. Modernism itself is for Adorno a species of negative dialectics, negating the dystopia capitalism makes of the world. Despite the critical capacity he attributes to nonmimetic forms of modernism, at best it can engage in a perpetual endgame with society, one that it can never win since it is constantly fighting a rear-guard action against a totalizing system of commodification. Although modern art's self-referentiality enables its social critique, it also ensures the critique's marginalization. And though this marginalization endows modern art with a kind of heroism, the heroism of resistance, that heroism is also a form of defeatism since it can never effectively challenge what is seen as a monolithically powerful economic, political, and semiotic order.

At the same time, paradoxically enough, Adorno's theory of modernism oddly resembles Benjamin's. Both downplay at times the potential of capitalism to modify modernism's *telos,* whether that is seen as critique, as is the case with Adorno, or emancipation, as is the case with Benjamin. For if modernism became for a time a new orthodoxy, a new "universal," it also became commodified—quite literally it became a commodity. This need not mean that modernism automatically became emasculated, but it does suggest the necessity of seeing it in relation to mass culture. And it is this issue, and the related one of literary value, that I now want to explore in more detail.

Literature versus Popular Fiction?

Discussions of popular fiction often contain references to at least some of the following assumptions: Popular fiction is aesthetically inferior to canonical literature. Genre fiction is more limited than nongenre fiction. Modern literature is intrinsically different from popular literature. (In using the phrase "modern literature" or "modernism" I will be referring primarily to canonical modernism.)

In this section, I will focus on the assumptions that have dominated the perceived relationship between modernism and popular fiction. I want to do this not only because I believe that this approach opens up new ways of understanding connections modernism had—and to some extent still has—with other cultural formations, but also because it opens up new ways of understanding modernism itself as a mode of literary production that negotiates relationships between high and low culture.[7] This section is primarily theoretical; chapters 6 and 7 contain textual analyses intended to be an application and substantiation of these theoretical claims.

Consider, then, the reception of two famous writers of detective fiction, Agatha Christie and Dashiell Hammett. In 1980 UNESCO estimated that 400 million copies of Christie's books had been sold worldwide since she first published *The Mysterious Affair at Styles* in 1920 (Janet Morgan, *Agatha Christie,* 377). More recent figures put her worldwide circulation at well over 500 million, making her the most translated author in the English language and one of the most widely read novelists in the world. Though popular, Dashiell Hammett's work does not command the same global readership. Nevertheless, in most circles the work of both authors is generally regarded as subliterary, mere pulp, a disposable product whose inferiority can be inferred from its large sales. Admittedly, the situation is somewhat different with Hammett and other hard-boiled detective fiction writers, inasmuch as their style has always held a kind of existential chic for literary critics who go slumming in popular fiction; however, by and large, it is fair to say that Hammett is not accorded the same position within the canon as, say, William Faulkner or even F. Scott Fitzgerald. The usually unspoken assumption behind the dismissal of crime fiction seems to stem from two beliefs: first, that when it comes to popular fiction, quantity and quality are mutually exclusive, and second, that crime fiction suffers from formulaic restrictions that true fiction or literature transcends. My purpose here is not only to challenge this argument, but also to show that the opposition inscribed in much modernist criticism between literature—usually meaning the canonical texts of modern literature—and popular fiction is itself untenable, and that a close examination of this argument inevitably leads to a radical rereading of modernism.

With the notable exception of feminism, most schools of contemporary literary theory have tended to accept established literary traditions without challenging the values and ideologies that underpin and produce them. Indeed, in literary traditions influenced by hermeneutics, structuralism, post-structuralism, Marxism, and semiotics, as well as the more traditional, empirically based criticism of popular culture, canonical texts still hold sway. Although the issue of canonicity has attracted more attention in recent years, many critics and critical schools still habitually separate an autonomous high literary culture from a popular or low culture, and on that basis either implicitly accede to established literary canons or explicitly construct ones that can be valorized. This fetishization of what are actually overlapping cultural formations and not separable entities frequently leads to a distorted understanding of the extent to which the techniques, forms, and ideologies of popular fiction shaped modernist literary production and vice versa. In his analysis of "residual, dominant and emergent" forces, Raymond Williams offers a way of going beyond the paralyzing dichotomies and value judgments that inform many of the debates on popular culture. In allowing us to articulate the residual relations of realism to the *institutionally* dominant cultural field of modernism, his theory of cultural formation also enables us to theorize literary modernism as incorporating a much wider cultural space than avant-garde production; indeed, it is my contention that the detective fiction produced in the age of high modernism is part of a larger culture of modernism that includes popular culture and is not limited to institutionalized high art. The modernism of popular crime fiction is not, of course, identical to high modernism; in my view it is more obviously dedicated to linguistic referentiality and is more overtly concerned with an evaluation of social reality, but it is, nonetheless, shaped by social and cultural forces of modernity, and it makes use of the techniques and ideologies of modernism to respond to the experience of modernity. (As case studies, in chapter 7 I examine two roughly contemporaneous subgenres of detective fiction: the formal English novel of detection, typified by the work of Agatha Christie, and the American hard-boiled novel of detection, typified by the work of Dashiell Hammett.)

The relevance of Williams's theory of cultural formations to all of this is that it allows us to see that each subgenre uses, in different proportions and for different ends, the residual literary strategies of realism in conjunction with the institutionally dominant techniques and ideologies of modernism. This approach enables a revisionist reading of modernism: whereas most theorists and critics tend to see the transition to modernism in terms of a rupture with the realist tradition of fiction, Williams's work on cultural formations and realism allows us to see the continuation of realist strategies within modernism. In addition, Williams's approach effects a shift away from literary value to an understanding of the full historical complexity and richness of cultural practices, which are comprehensible only in terms of their relation to other literary, cultural, and social practices. I will return to this point shortly, but for the moment it is important to emphasize that for Williams, there is no actual division between high and low culture; there are only ways of seeing culture in this way. For him, that is, both popular and high culture are part of one cultural process that uses similar techniques, forms, and ideologies. Modernism, then, can be seen as an ideology of literary production, often radically at odds with the doctrines espoused by its apologists.

Literary Value versus Reading Subjects

The attack on popular fiction is nothing new. But modernist critics upped the stakes by defining modernism in antithetical terms to popular culture, and popular fiction in particular. Indeed, the dense, complex, allusive, and self-referential style that is so often taken to be characteristic of high modernism in the fiction of James Joyce, Virginia Woolf, and Gertrude Stein was widely seen in contrast to the more straightforward, realistic style of popular fiction. In the eyes of many critics, the latter style suffered in comparison not only because it lacked a dense verbal texture, but also because in popular fiction—science fiction, thrillers, adventures, westerns, and romances— it was used more to describe outward event and action than to explore the subtleties and nuances of "centers of consciousness." This dismissal was especially acute in relation to crime fiction because the genre relied so heavily on realist modes of representation. In this connection it is interesting to note that critics, not novelists, were harshest in their dismissal of popular fiction. Many high modernists were fascinated by popular fiction, and some, like Faulkner, actually wrote what was considered to be pulp fiction. It may be that many modernists sensed connections and similarities between the modernist project, which was culturally recognized, and the work of popular writers, which was not. At any rate, this must remain speculative. What is not speculative, however, is that modernism's relationship to mass culture has often been characterized by what Andreas Huyssen in *After the Great Divide* has called "an anxiety of contamination": "Ever since the mid-19th century, the culture of modernity has been characterized by a volatile relationship between high art and mass culture. Indeed, the emergence of early modernism in writers such as Flaubert and Baudelaire cannot be adequately understood on the basis of an assumed logic of high literary evolution alone. Modernism constituted itself through a conscious strategy of exclusion, an anxiety of contamination by its other: an increasingly consuming and engulfing mass culture" (vii).

This process of exclusion has not been as uniform within modernism as the examples of Flaubert and Baudelaire suggest. But to some degree, modernists have sought to define a particular version of modernism by asserting what it is *not.* Accordingly, they have helped to shape a tradition by elevating certain literary and artistic qualities and by excluding and denigrating others. The question of quantity versus quality therefore is not susceptible to resolution by adducing examples in which popular fiction can be shown to meet the standards set by modernist fiction—not merely because counterexamples can always be offered but, more important, because this strategy leaves the premises of the modernist case unexamined. It is not, in other words, sufficient to say that popular fiction is as good as canonical fiction because this leaves the aesthetic premises of high modernism in the position of dictating what is and is not good literature. This essentially defensive posture leaves the criteria of high modernism firmly in place. Instead of displacing the modernist hierarchy, this posture defers to it, and ultimately confirms it.

When F. R. Leavis declared in the first sentence of *The Great Tradition* that "the great English novelists are Jane Austen, George Eliot, Henry James and Joseph Conrad—to stop for the moment at that comparatively safe point in history," he was clearly attempting to identify an incontestable tradition of great novel writing in English. Now, several decades later, it is evident that the problems associated with this kind of project are considerable. A major difficulty is that Leavis's Great Tradition is radically selective; indeed, it stands as one of this century's most overt examples of the selectivity of canon formation. Leavis himself seems to have realized this; by originally omitting Dickens and then later adding him to the pantheon, Leavis was forced to acknowledge, albeit implicitly, that the Great Tradition was subject to revision, and hence not God-given and eternal.

It may be objected that Leavis is not a modernist at all, but an antimodernist; however, I think it is more accurate to regard him as a conservative modernist. The list of modern writers approved by Leavis's periodical *Scrutiny,* after all, included Conrad, Eliot, James, and Lawrence—all modern writers who were themselves conservative or who, more important, could be interpreted as fulfilling the criteria of *Scrutiny* conservatism, which found in these writers a density and allusiveness of language devoted to counteracting the cultural and linguistic degradations of an industrialized mass society. Although Leavis originally opposed the aristocracy and its cultural apparatuses, eventually he came to think that the only redemption for society existed in a highly educated elite that would sustain the embattled values of past civilizations now in danger of being warped by philistinism. The job of the critic, then, was to cultivate a sensitivity to the cultural values lost everywhere else. In its vitality of language and creative energy, literature was seen as one of the last outposts of culture, and for Leavis, the critical task came down to identifying it as such. Yet in doing these "close readings" the critic was not to stray from the text into history or into the conceptual structures that created those texts, for that would be to lose sight of the critic's primary task—that of rigorously scrutinizing and judging literature, and on that basis distinguishing the great from the good. In his attention to the text, in his rejection of history as a way of understanding the formal composition of the text, and in his attempt to locate in the structure and organization of the text an aesthetic coherence lacking in industrial civilization, Leavis resembles nothing so much as a member of that other conservative school, the New Critics. By abstracting literature out of its social context, and by valorizing the notion of the text "in itself," both schools sought to locate different versions of a preindustrial pastoral in literature. Because of this ideological agenda, for Leavis and for most of the New Critics, it became necessary to distinguish sharply between literature and nonliterature.

Yet Leavis, like other critics who adhere to a literature/nonliterature mode of criticism, begins and ends by begging the question. There is no universally acceptable, coherent set of criteria that will allow readers to make that distinction. There is, as Terry Eagleton puts it, no ontological basis for deciding what is literature and what is not; there are only functional reasons for doing so. Using a term like "literature" does not describe the "fixed being" of a complex range of writing practices so much as it signifies in a casual and informal way a kind of writing that someone values for one reason or another (Eagleton, *Literary Theory,* 9). This is not a fancy way of saying that one man's meat is another man's poison; it is instead a recognition that literature, strictly speaking, is a relative term and that excluding other writing practices on the basis of aesthetic preference alone is a conventional or ideological operation.

Still, it must be admitted that the problem of value in literary theory cannot be dispensed with so easily. It could be argued that on purely formal grounds the mystery novels of Ruth Rendell or Patricia Highsmith are equivalent or even superior to Anita Brookner's Booker Prize winner, *Hotel du Lac,* and that the exclusion of genre writers from the consideration of the judges is only further evidence of the widespread prejudice of the literary establishment against genre writing and, indeed, is evidence of its inability to value the distinctive qualities and artistic achievements of genre fiction. Many modernist critics would concede as much—and then go on to point out that there is a world of difference between James Joyce and Arthur Conan Doyle, and further suggest that Joyce opened up ways of using and seeing language that Conan Doyle did not. Though this might be true, the argument is not as comprehensive as it might first seem. Tony Bennett has addressed this issue by conceding that there is a difference between the writing of, say, Joyce and Conan Doyle, but he argues that we cannot attribute value to one form of writing or another on this basis: "However, such purely technical assessments of the formal effects of different practices of writing do not, of themselves, offer grounds for valuing the one above the other" ("Marxism and Popular Fiction," 243). The fundamental reason that such discriminations are invalid is that they rest on the assumption that value inheres in the text, that it is an inalienable essence of the text. In actuality, literary value is largely a function of reading subjects who relate to texts in determinate ways: "Texts do not *have* value: they can only *be valued* by valuing subjects of particular types and for particular reasons, and these are entirely the product of critical discourses of valuation, varying from criticism to criticism" ("Marxism and Popular Fiction," 244).

The question of the value of different writing practices, then, ultimately relates more to the valuing reader than to the text in isolation; given this, the question of value does not have to be the primary consideration in the analysis of writing. Looked at in this way, literature, and in particular modern literature, is not a uniquely privileged body of texts whose common factor resides in some indefinable difference from popular fiction; instead, it signifies a wide range of writing practices differentiated by their strategic deployment of particular narrative strategies, modes of representation, registers of discourse, literary devices, conventions, forms, and so on. This fluid, mobile, more conjunctural theory of literature clearly is more suited to the study of popular fiction—and, of course, to the study of those forms of fiction that have been canonized. One of the implications of this theory is that all writing practices use a common pool of literary and linguistic resources. Consequently, it becomes theoretically impossible to maintain a stable, objective distinction between generic and nongeneric forms of writing, even though, of course, booksellers market and display their books according to these categories. In "Discourse in the Novel" Mikhail Bakhtin develops the notion of literature-as-genre by contending that all forms of writing are mutations of different genres—"genre" understood generally to mean "a horizon of expectations."[8] For him, every new form of writing is merely an extension of the possibilities of a known genre or a creative synthesis of two or more already-existing genres. So, for example, *Madame Bovary,* that most modern of novels, a novel that is taken to be at the furthest remove from genre fiction, can also be regarded as a particularly fine example of a genre that flourished in the nineteenth century—the novel of adultery. As Ken Worpole puts it: "What are *Madame Bovary, Anna Karenina,* and *Middlemarch* other than particularly brilliantly written examples of the 'novel of adultery' (female adultery), another favorite 19th century genre that is as strong in the melodramatic tradition as it is that of the 'serious' novel?" (*Reading by Numbers,* 20). In a sense, every novel owes its existence to a genre, and as Worpole's comments suggest, the study of both "serious" and "popular" novels can benefit from this less rigid, more fluid conception of the relations between high and low culture.

Before considering the effects that other dismissals of popular culture have had on more established versions of modernism, I wish to clarify one point. As I have been arguing, there is no essential set of characteristics that we can point to in order to arrive at an objective description of modern literature. Despite this, the academy and the literary establishment in general continue to use and to rely on, both explicitly and implicitly, many of the oppositions that I have been concerned to destabilize: literature/nonliterature, genre/nongeneric forms of writing, high/low culture, literary/nonliterary fiction. Although these oppositions do not have, in my view, any objective validity, it is necessary to acknowledge that they retain a social importance inasmuch as they designate the various ways in which existing literary institutions organize and value a multiplicity of writing practices.

Trashing Popular Fiction: Critical Pastimes from Leavis to Lukács

In this century popular culture has been denigrated by critics and theorists on both the left and the right. F. R. Leavis (again) led the way with *Mass Civilization and Minority Culture* (1930). Leavis is a crucial figure for any exploration of the history of culture in the Anglo-American world because of the sheer influence of his views. As one might surmise from the book's title, his theory is that although in every age culture is kept and preserved by a sensitive elite, in the twentieth century the rapid growth of a mass civilization threatens to swamp this embattled minority. As is well known, Leavis's argument is basically an updated version of Matthew Arnold's *Culture and Anarchy* (1869), and Leavis traces the disintegration of cultural values that has taken place since Arnold's day by noting that whereas Arnold despaired of the *Daily Telegraph* as the most popular newspaper in the late Victorian era, more than half a century later, it is tabloids such as *News of the World* that have the largest circulation. For Leavis, the contrast between the two newspapers is an index of the cultural depravity that has overtaken modern life. As he says in the first sentence of the book, "For Matthew Arnold it was in some ways less difficult" (3). For Leavis, mass production and standardization are not just newfangled American ways, but facts of life in Britain, too; he assigns them primary responsibility for the accelerated philistinism and the related decay of traditional values he sees about him in Britain: "It seems unlikely that the conditions of life can be transformed in this way without some injury to the standard of living (to wrest the phrase from the economist): improvisation can hardly replace the delicate traditional adjustments, the mature inherited codes of habit and valuation, without severe loss, and loss that may be more than temporary. It is a breach in continuity that threatens: what has been inadvertently dropped may be irrecoverable or forgotten" (6–7).

One would be mistaken, however, to conclude that this argument has advocates only on the right side of the political spectrum. Leavis, like the theorists of the Frankfurt school, sees very little hope for liberation from the "triumph of the machine" (31). In Max Horkheimer and Theodor Adorno's *Dialectic of Enlightenment,* the language is a little different, but the basic charge is the same: modern life and culture are debased by the onslaught of an all-encompassing, superficial mass civilization. Their rhetoric, like Leavis's, is infamously programmatic:

> Films, radio and magazines make up a system which is uniform as a whole and in every part. Even the aesthetic activities of political opposites are one in their enthusiastic obedience to the rhythm of the iron system. The decorative industrial management buildings and exhibition centers in authoritarian countries are much the same as anywhere else. The huge gleaming towers that shoot up everywhere are outward signs of the ingenious planning of international concerns, toward which the unleashed entrepreneurial system (whose monuments are a mass of gloomy houses and business premises in grimy, spiritless cities) was already hastening (120).

Or more explicitly:

> Under monopoly all mass culture is identical, and the lines of its artificial framework begin to show through. The people at the top are no longer so interested in concealing monopoly: as its violence becomes more open, so its power grows. Movies and radio no longer need to pretend to be art. The truth that they are just business is made into an ideology in order to justify the rubbish they deliberately produce (121).

The notion that popular culture is a degraded art form, or, as Horkheimer and Adorno would have it, a mass-produced replica of a dominant ideology, is a ubiquitous one in literary studies. There have been, then, elements on both the left and the right that have concurred in seeing popular culture as distinct from high culture: both traditions have contended that popular culture lacks the achieved greatness of genuine art and exists as a disposable form of entertainment that embodies the "false consciousness" of the age. Whereas high or true art transcends the ideologies of its time, popular art is deeply scored by them. Within Marxism this notion of popular culture as pure ideology has been especially widespread. Louis Althusser, the French structuralist Marxist whose theories are the inspiration for many ideological critiques of mass culture, follows in the tradition of the Frankfurt school in making such a distinction. To put his case in schematic, somewhat figurative terms, for Althusser, literature exists midway between science (represented by Marxism and psychoanalysis) and ideology. Although complex, his notion of ideology is not fundamentally dissimilar to Marx's notion of "false consciousness." In addition, as is indicated by his "Letter on Art in Reply to André Daspre," in which he distinguishes between "art" and "authentic art"

(222), Althusser assumes that there is a fundamental, objective distinction between literature and popular fiction—an assumption that, as we have seen, is deeply flawed. But there is another problem with this formulation. As Tony Bennett has observed, within this triangle of literature, science, and ideology there is no place for popular fiction except the degraded sphere of ideology ("Marxism and Popular Fiction," 251). As with Lukács, for Althusser popular fiction is apparently not important enough to warrant any attention in the first place. (I will return to Lukács shortly, but for the moment suffice it to say that there is another approach, the cultural materialism of Raymond Williams, Mikhail Bakhtin, and Antonio Gramsci.) Although this approach takes a much more sympathetic view of popular fiction than many varieties of Marxism, the anti-mass-culture tradition within Marxism has been extremely influential, especially in its theorization of modernism. It is thus ironic that in this respect certain traditions on both the left and the right have confirmed each other's dismissal of popular fiction, and have developed theories of modernism identical in their rejection of it.

Evaluative Realism and Modernism

Modernism itself is not so guilty of what Andreas Huyssen calls the "anxiety of contamination," that is, the desire to see itself as totally different from popular fiction. Rather, the attempt to purify modernism is largely made by interested readers who want to construct modernist canons amenable to their own moral or political agendas. To be sure, there are examples of this "anxiety of contamination" in modernist works. In T. S. Eliot's "The Waste Land" and Ezra Pound's "Hugh Selwyn Mauberley," popular culture exists as an index of the degradation of the modern age. But on the other hand, there is *Ulysses,* which revels in the language and forms of popular culture. Contempt for popular culture is certainly not a universally shared aspect of modernism. Yet among some critics, writers, and readers, the presence of popular culture has occasioned an anxiety about the purity of modernism. This anxiety has most often manifested itself in the attempt to distance modernism from the modes of representation taken to be typical of popular fiction. In practice this has meant drawing a distinction between the "classic" realist tradition of fiction that flourished in the nineteenth and early twentieth centuries and the putatively different culture of official modernism.

Very often this has led to an accentuation of the differences between modernism and realism, to the extent that modernism has represented itself as coming into being by means of a rupture with realism. To be sure, modernism succeeded in problematizing representation. After modernism it becomes increasingly difficult to maintain that art reflects reality in any direct or unmediated way, especially if one equates realism with a mode of representation that defines itself as a way of unmediated "natural seeing." Modernism's emphasis on the medium, that is, reminds the reader that the reality of literature is *made*.

At least one tradition of modernist representation—what I referred to earlier as the less experimental, mimetic tradition of modernism—did not abandon the realist tradition, as many modernist apologists suggest, but instead adapted and shaped realist strategies of representation in order to evaluate society. My usage of the term "realism" is highly specific, and differs from casual connotations of the word. By "realism" I do not mean a mode of representation that pretends to merely reflect a reality "out there." Nor do I mean a single style; instead, I refer to a method of social representation with many styles. In "Realism and the Contemporary Novel" (in *The Long Revolution*) Raymond Williams develops this theory of realism by arguing that its function is in some sense to equate with reality, but not by claiming to mirror it. For Williams realism is a mode of registering experience that is fundamentally evaluative: "When I think of the realist tradition in literature, I think of the kind of novel which creates and judges the quality of a whole way of life in terms of the qualities of persons" (278). Thus Williams is a long way off from claiming that realism is a styleless, transparent way of writing, the type of writing that Roland Barthes criticized in *Writing Degree Zero*. Williams agrees that realism is a form of *écriture,* a highly conventionalized way of writing that encodes certain ideological values. But he differs from Barthes in that he maintains that art is not only perception but communication, and that reality is not just the vision of the monad or individual: "But art is more than perception; it is a particular kind of active response, and a part of all human communication. Reality, in our terms, is that which human beings make common, by work or language. Thus, in the very acts of perception and communication, this practical interaction of what is personally seen, interpreted and organized and what can be socially recognized, known and formed is richly and subtly manifested" (288). This theory of referentiality in art was anticipated in the work of Volosinov and Bakhtin on language.[9] In their work they acknowledge that language does not reflect reality in any direct way; rather, language speaks about it, engages in an evaluative discourse about it.

Perhaps their most explicit statement on the subject is contained in an essay entitled "Discourse in Life and Discourse in Art": "First of all, it is perfectly obvious that, in the given case, the discourse does not at all reflect the extraverbal situation in the way a mirror reflects an object. Rather the discourse here *resolves the situation,* bringing it to an *evaluative conclusion,* as it were. Far more often, behavioral utterances actively continue and develop a situation, adumbrate a plan for future action, and organize that action" (Volosinov, *Freudianism,* 100). The view that the discourse of realism is not reflective but evaluative seems to me extremely useful. First of all, it displaces the terms of the realism debate by shifting attention away from the vexed question of the veracity of realism to the social and moral imperatives registered in and through discourse. Second, the emphasis on the communicative function of realism—the fact that through the interchange of discourse, reality is produced and made socially recognizable—means that realism need not be rejected as a naive medium, a pseudo-objective version of reality. Third, this formulation allows us to see that realism is movable—that realist strategies of representation can be combined with other modes of representation. Using Williams's theory of cultural formation, it is now possible to read realism as defined above as a residual, but still flourishing, element within the institutionally dominant modernist mode of representation. Far from modernism inventing itself anew, less purely self-referential forms of modernism took over, adapted, and problematized realist strategies of representation, all the while integrating them with modernist ideologies, forms, and techniques. This is particularly true of the mixed forms of modernism found in popular culture.

This notion of realism in modernism requires a rethinking of received ideas of modernism, many of which, as I have argued, depend on some notion of a break with realism. The most famous—or infamous, depending on one's point of view—attempt to analyze the relations between realism and modernism is Georg Lukács's. In *The Meaning of Contemporary Realism* Lukács attempts to establish a border between realism and modernism. Although Lukács's argument is notoriously programmatic, it represents only the most extreme version of the widespread attempt to distinguish realism from modernism. Indeed, his arguments about modernism have been extraordinarily influential. As Astradur Eysteinsson notes in *The Concept of Modernism,* "His views are representative not only because his approach to modernism has assumed a central place in much sociological and Marxist criticism, but also because of his strong ties with traditional bourgeois humanism, the critical branch of which has often reacted with great reserve, if not hostility, to modernism" (28–29). Though most modern critics question Lukács's unconditional rejection of modernism, few challenge his characterization of high modernism's formal and ideological structures; indeed, that characterization is now commonplace in modernist studies.

Lukács argues that realism represents the highest form of literary achievement. For him realism is the achieved artistic balance between objective reality and subjective consciousness. Realist characters typify the characteristic social and economic forces of a given era without ceasing to be richly individualized; they enact a dialectical synthesis of the psychological and the social. Lukács's theory of realism enables him to develop also a theory of naturalism and modernism, both of which for Lukács represent a fall from grace. Naturalism and modernism are the "decadent progeny" of realism; each represents a fragment or aspect of the perfectly realized, many-sided synthesis of realism. Naturalism fetishizes objectivity, but in doing so it yields a false and superficial objectivity. Modernism, on the other hand, fetishizes subjectivity. In emphasizing only individual psychology, modernism neglects the objective forces of history and remains lost within the solipsistic perspective of the individual. Lukács's quarrel with modernism stems from the fact that the modernist, unlike the realist, is incapable of making an objective critical assessment of contemporary reality.

There is a curious tension at the heart of this theory. On the one hand, Lukács wants to maintain that realism is an essential component of all writing; on the other hand, his valorization of realism and the rigidly analytical, a priori definition he gives it compel him to read naturalism and modernism negatively, as only fragments of the integral whole that is realism. And yet Lukács is surprisingly flexible in his judgments about other forms and historical eras: Shakespeare, for instance, is admitted into the ranks of realists. Thus Lukács has to do some wrenching from time to time in order to make recalcitrant authors or facts fit his scheme. Joyce is another case in point; many of Lukács's criticisms of his work seem limited at best and flat-out wrong at worst. For example, he claims that "Joyce uses Dublin, Kafka and Musil the Hapsburg Monarchy, as the locus of their masterpieces. But the locus they lovingly depict is little more than a backcloth; it is not basic to their artistic intention" (*The Meaning of Contemporary Realism,* 21). As I have argued elsewhere, this is not true of either Joyce's early work in *Dubliners* or his later work.[10] This tension between Lukács's desire to assign to realism an essential role in representation and his unwillingness to find realism in modernism, or to find it there only in distorted form, is inscribed in the title of his essay "Franz Kafka or Thomas Mann"—Kafka being the bad modernist and Mann being the good modernist by virtue of his "critical realism." (For Lukács, the only acceptable form of modernism is a form of realism.)

The underlying logic of Lukács's argument is that to a greater or lesser extent realism constitutes an essential part of literary representation, but the narrow way in which he has defined what he regards as postrealist literature pulls him in the opposite direction and compels him to deny this logic, indeed to dismiss these forms. Given that Shakespeare has been admitted to the pantheon, on Lukács's own terms Joyce could be, too, and with fewer logical contortions. And given that he has conceded that realism is not restricted to a single style—there is little stylistic similarity between Shakespeare and Balzac, after all—it does not make much sense to exclude other modes of social representation radically different from the nineteenth-century classic-realist style, like modernism, for instance; yet this is what Lukács does. Lukács sees modernism as an ideology, but, paradoxically, he accepts this ideology more or less at face value. He does not see it as being at odds with modernist literary texts, which are a good deal less consistent in their technique, ends, and worldview than Lukács's taxonomy might suggest. The irony is that although Lukács sees modernism as an ideology, he does not see it, as every ideology inevitably is, as self-contradictory. Modernism for him has a metaphysical consistency, even if that consistency is warped in its worldview.

Conclusion

Despite their formal differences, both the allegedly "self-reflexive" and the more overtly referential forms of modernism engage in social criticism. Lukács's attempt to purify realism by stigmatizing self-referentiality finds its mirror image in Adorno's attempt to purify modernism by purging it of referentiality. In the case of modernism, it is clear that this desire for purity leads to a refusal to acknowledge the multiplicity of modernisms. Given that Lukács and Adorno are agreed on the triviality of mass culture, it is ironic that it is now in the anarchic, quasi-populist world of mass culture—in advertisements, videos, TV, magazines, movies, and popular fiction— that one now finds some of the purest forms of avant-garde modernism competing for attention with the purest forms of classical realism. The terrain of the debate has shifted from the academy and relatively small avant-garde circles to the more brazenly commercialized world of popular culture. If it is true, as Huyssen suggests, that "mass culture has always been the hidden subtext of the modernist project," then what we are witnessing, among other things, is the working out of the logic of modernism in mass culture. In the near-global domain of mass culture, modernism is not superannuated but revivified. The real threat facing art is neither referentiality nor self-referentiality; various audiences have affirmed their sense of the artistic and social value of both traditions. Rather, the threat—and a real possibility for mass-cultural art—lies in the ways in which art is used in societies saturated by the mindless values of consumerism and the qualitatively blind imperatives of capitalism. The constant social challenge confronting modern art is to avoid transforming its critical edge into just another easily consumed and easily forgotten commodity. If art can do this, then it has the potential to rewrite those values and imperatives.

Notes

An altered version of parts of this chapter appeared in my essay "Realisms and Modernisms: Raymond Williams and Popular Fiction," in *Views beyond the Border Country: Raymond Williams and Cultural Politics,* ed. Dennis L. Dworkin and Leslie G. Roman (London: Routledge, 1993).

1. I might add that the dual reference of the term is less problematic for those who, like myself, see modernism and postmodernism as largely continuous formations.

2. In certain instances, stylistic imperatives will dictate the use of the singular, "modernism"; however, the multiplicity of modernisms should always be understood as an implicit sense.

3. In "Leskov the Storyteller" Benjamin adopts the opposite view, viewing the breakdown of the "traditional" relationship between art and audience as tragic, but the dominant tone in that essay is elegiac.

4. For more on this aspect of modernism, see Terry Eagleton's shrewd but sometimes reductive study, *Exiles and Emigrés.*

5. For a sympathetic and searching analysis of Perry Anderson's theory of modernism (and of Anderson's critique of Marshall Berman), see Alex Callinicos's *Against Postmodernism,* especially pages 38–48.

6. Eysteinsson's book, especially pages 39–49, has strongly influenced my reading of Theodor Adorno's work here.

7. Hereafter, I will use low (or popular) and high culture as terms to designate the ways in which culture has traditionally been categorized. These terms, that is, should *always* be understood as being within quotation marks. My usage of these terms should not be understood as acceptance of these modes of valuation. These terms do not have any ontological meaning in my view, but they do have a political significance inasmuch as they reveal the ideological values that permit the division of culture into different spheres.

8. This shorthand way of referring to genre as a "horizon of expectations" is not, as far as I know, Bakhtin's, but is instead a formulation by Caryl Emerson and Michael Holquist in their glossary entry for "genre" in their translation of *The Dialogic Imagination.* "Discourse in the Novel" is an essay in the same book.

9. I have in mind *Marxism and the Philosophy of Language, Freudianism: A Marxist Critique,* and *The Dialogic Imagination.* The first two works appear in print in their English editions under the name of V. N. Volosinov, but there is a growing consensus that they were at least coauthored, if not in fact written, by Bakhtin. Because of this, and because of Bakhtin's emphasis that language is not owned by one writer or another but is accentuated by the intentions of all writers, it seems to make more sense to refer to the coauthorship of the first two texts mentioned above.

10. See my article "Joyce and Dialogism: The Politics of Style in *Dubliners,*" in *Works and Days* 5:2 (1987).

Part I

The Emergence of the
Modern Detective Hero

The Power of Knowledge:
Poe's Detective Fiction and
the Ideology of Rationalism

> Perhaps, too, we should abandon a whole tradition that allows us to imagine that knowledge can exist only where the power relations are suspended and that knowledge can only develop outside its injunctions, its demands, and its interests. Perhaps we should abandon the belief that power makes people mad and that, by the same token, the renunciation of power is one of the conditions of knowledge. We should admit, rather, that power produces knowledge (and not simply by encouraging it because it serves power or by applying it because it is useful); that power and knowledge directly imply one another; that there is no power relation without the correlative constitution of a field of knowledge, nor any knowledge that does not presuppose and constitute at the same time power relations.
>
> —*Michel Foucault,* Discipline and Punish

Poe and the Disciplinary Society

Poe's most famous detective stories, "The Murders in the Rue Morgue," "The Mystery of Marie Roget," and "The Purloined Letter," as well as his less famous ones, such as "The Gold Bug" and "Thou Art the Man," are rightly celebrated for inaugurating a number of subgenres in detective fiction. "The Murders in the Rue Morgue" introduced the famous amateur detective Chevalier C. Auguste Dupin, and was the first of the "locked-room mysteries," which present the puzzle of a corpse in a room that appears to be sealed; "The Mystery of Marie Roget" was the first of the "armchair detection" stories, in which the detective figure solves the mystery at one remove from the crime by sheer analytical brilliance rather than by firsthand examination of the scene or of the suspects of the crime; and "The Gold Bug" was the forerunner of the code story, which has as its main interest the solution to a cipher.[1] Although this concentration on Poe's formal achievement conveys the enormous impact he made on an area of fiction—effectively transforming motifs of suspense and detection found in romantic and Gothic fiction into what we now recognize as the conventions of the detective-fiction genre—this emphasis also tends, at least implicitly, to situate these texts within an abstract realm, distanced from the historical conditions that produced them. My thesis is that far from being merely abstract, intellectual puzzles devoid of social interest, Poe's detective stories embody a specific vision of knowledge structurally similar but ultimately antithetical to the dominant mode of knowledge fueling the social transformations in the early decades of nineteenth-century America, and that this conception of knowledge becomes a crucial element in subsequent detective fiction. Furthermore, I want to suggest that this vision of knowledge plays a crucial role in determining the style of these stories.

Poe's stories of detection were part of what might be called an emergent nineteenth-century culture of knowledge. Once transformed into new technologies and disciplines, these nascent forms of knowledge generated new forms of power and social relationships. Impelled by the same drive for knowledge that fueled the nineteenth-century American scientific and industrial revolutions, Poe's stories are part of the development of what Foucault terms a "disciplinary society," that is, a society transformed by the extension of technologies of observation and control in schools, factories, the military, and prisons. Within the disciplinary society, this drive toward the acquisition of knowledge is achieved by the development of practices, institutions, and technologies devoted to surveying and controlling individuals. Foucault's chief paradigm for the disciplinary society is the "panopticon," a circular prison arranged around a central watchtower in which surveillance is exercised on completely visible prisoners by unseen guards. Though I do not want to suggest the eradication of human will in this disciplinary society, Foucault's notion of the panopticon offers interesting possibilities for understanding the narrative structure of Poe's detective stories.

The relevance of this conception of power-knowledge to my argument, then, is not that Poe recreates a disciplinary society in his detective fiction; rather, it is that in the person of Chevalier C. Auguste Dupin, Poe creates a figure whose omniscience is comparable to that of a panopticon. There is some similarity here with the classic English realist novel, in which the narrator typically enjoys a position of omniscience, but there is also a shift in narrative structure. Here it is not the narrator who is omniscient, but a character. The narrator in detective fiction is often the less astute but still-indispensable assistant to the master sleuth—the classic example, of course, being the ever-faithful Dr. Watson. The chief significance of Foucault's notion of the disciplinary society for Poe's detective fiction, then, is that it articulates a desire for a complete form of knowledge, a desire that ultimately becomes a structural element of the genre. This desire for knowledge is not an immutable feature of detective fiction but changes with the transformations in the genre.[2] At the same time, however, Poe's stories reject the empirical, "scientific" mode of knowledge that was doing so much to revolutionize existing technologies and industry, recasting them into a modern industrial, capitalist, and democratic mold.[3] In fictional terms, Poe's rejection of empiricism as an adequate means of understanding reality translates into a certain aloofness, a definable distance that the detective hero assumes in relation to society: Dupin not only represents values antagonistic to democracy, but his rationalism is repeatedly valorized over the narrow empirical values of the police, which, Dupin makes clear, are also held by the inferior democratic masses.[4] For Poe, rationalism and empiricism represent ways of understanding the world that are linked to different social formations—rationalism to the superior capabilities and values of the aristocracy, empiricism to the creation of a democratic, industrializing society built on philistine values. Through Dupin's rationalism, Poe indirectly criticizes the values of democracy and the narrow empirical methods that were doing so much to industrialize American society, always implicitly contrasting these values and mechanical methods to the ennobled lifestyle and aims of the aristocracy.

It is worth noting that the critical stance of Poe's detective hero in relation to society subsequently becomes a standard convention in detective fiction. Detective heroes after Dupin may or may not have aristocratic pretensions, but, like Dupin, typically they are outsiders. This convention, especially pronounced in the American "hard-boiled" tradition, often provides the basis for an exploration of social and moral problems. Accordingly, in what follows, I will focus on Poe's most famous detective stories, those featuring Dupin as protagonist, as they highlight most dramatically the related issues of knowledge and power crucial to the genre.

Dupin's Romantic Rationalism and American Manifest Destiny

As an initial formulation, Poe's stories of detection may be defined as fantasies, even wish-fulfillment fantasies, of knowledge and power. They are, to be sure, masculine wish-fulfillment fantasies inasmuch as Dupin represents a gendered accession to knowledge.[5] They embody a consciousness specific to an age of intense "scientific" investigation in which knowledge is power in radically new senses, without sacrificing older traditions of exclusivity. Yet for Poe, as for many of his Victorian successors, knowledge is not acquired empirically, through the observation of outward appearances alone; rather, it is gained when observation is combined with intuition or deductive forms of reasoning. This is the meaning of the abstract philosophical introduction to "The Murders in the Rue Morgue," in which "calculation" (mere observation) is repeatedly disparaged in favor of "analysis":

> But it is in matters beyond the limits of mere rule that the skill of the analyst is evinced. He makes, in silence, a host of observations and inferences. So, perhaps, do his companions; and the difference in the extent of the information obtained lies not so much in the validity of the inference as in the quality of the observation. The necessary knowledge is that of *what* to observe. Our player confines himself not at all; nor, because the game is the object, does he reject deductions from things external to the game. (3)

This brief meditation on the epistemological possibilities and limitations of the (game-playing) subject also reveals something of Poe's worldview. Essential to it is an emphasis on the duplicity of appearances: any good player will make acute observations, but what sets the superior player apart is his incorporation of "things external to the game." Throughout the introduction to "The Murders in the Rue Morgue," games are presented as both examples and evidence. As examples, they are adduced to support the narrator's contentions that the analyst's power remains superior to the weaker ability of the plodding empiricist in the most intellectual of sports— draughts, chess, and whist. But the metaphor is also evidence of a particular ideology founded on the desire to believe that the multiplicity of life can be reduced to a gamelike structure in which variety is restricted to a finite number of possibilities and mutability is frozen within the unchanging laws of the game.

This essentially rationalistic ideology differs radically from the Manifest Destiny ideology, dominant in the early part of the nineteenth century, which proclaimed America's God-given right to extend its territory throughout North America. By contrast, Poe wanted to locate a pastoral idyll in the South, and, failing that, at least to create in his fiction and poetry an aesthetic world regulated by a combination of exoticism and control unfurnished by contemporary American society. In any event, Poe's worldview had little to do with the contemporary belief that Americans had a divinely sanctioned obligation to conquer the American continent, a belief that was impelling "almost half of "Yankeedoodledum" . . . [to keep] on the move toward the setting sun" (William Miller, *A New History of the United States*, 162).

Indeed, Larzer Ziff has noted that Poe's work figuratively opposes this ideology of expansionism: "In closing down access to wide nature in the world of his fiction, Poe was taking a social stand, asserting that art, growing from the imagination, is confined to the pure products of the mind and has no commerce with the collective destiny of the people" (*Literary Democracy*, 70). Within the context of his detective fiction, this withdrawal from a "wide nature," this desire to reduce life to convention, to formalized rules is in effect a fantasy of power in which knowledge plays a dominant role. (It might also be argued that Poe's desire to reduce reality to knowable conventions parallels his attempt to elaborate a theory of aesthetics in mathematical terms.) The superior knowledge of the analyst, in this case the estimable Dupin, pierces the bewildering array of surface appearances to find the actual source of the crime. The analyst, as Poe says, "disentangles" ("The Murders in the Rue Morgue," 2). Knowledge simplifies, clarifies chaos. Poe's lack of enthusiasm for the American imperial enterprise and scorn for what he regarded as a flaccid belief in democratic values find their correlative in the alienated figure of Dupin, whose intense, analytical, antiempirical mind effortlessly resolves the most difficult of mysteries into neat formulas possessing knowable patterns of cause and effect. In this respect Dupin symbolically fulfills Poe's unrealized desire to dominate. Whereas Poe's fortunes were dominated largely by a society embracing values radically different from his, Dupin, though similarly alienated, is dominant. He appears to be above circumstance. Society's most heinous or vexing crimes find their solution in his hands. In principle there seems to be no mystery incapable of resolution; Dupin's power of analysis is almost preternatural. This is why I refer to Poe's stories as fantasies of power and knowledge: In them, reasoning is exalted so much that it loses any claim to verisimilitude. In them, knowledge confers power upon the subject. What is valorized in Poe's detective stories, then, is not rationalism per se, but a romanticized version or ideology of rationalism in which reason, or more properly "analysis," figures as the highest mode of apprehension.

The contrast between the empowered mind of Dupin and the inferior mind of the police is nowhere sharper than at the beginning of "The Purloined Letter," in the initial dialogue between Monsieur G——, the Prefect of the Parisian police, and Dupin. The narrator begins the dialogue by addressing the Prefect:

> "And what is the difficulty now?" I asked. "Nothing more in the assassination way, I hope?"
>
> "Oh no; nothing of that nature. The fact is, the business is very simple indeed, and I make no doubt that we can manage it sufficiently well ourselves; but then I thought Dupin would like to hear the details of it, because it is so excessively odd."
>
> "Simple and odd," said Dupin.
>
> "Why, yes; and not exactly that, either. The fact is, we have all been a good deal puzzled because the affair is so simple, and yet baffles us altogether."
>
> "Perhaps it is the very simplicity of the thing which puts you at fault," said my friend.
>
> "What nonsense you do talk!" replied the Prefect, laughing heartily.

"Perhaps the mystery is a little too plain," said Dupin.

"Oh, good heavens! who ever heard of such an idea?"

"A little too self-evident."

"Ha! ha! ha! ha! ha! ha! ho! ho! ho!" roared our visitor, profoundly amused, "oh, Dupin, you will be the death of me yet!" (125–26)

The purloined letter is of moment precisely because it gives Minister D——— power over royalty, power that, once exercised, is lost.[6] Blackmail is the quintessential form of knowledge-as-power. This knowledge-power relation is roughly analogous to Dupin's relation with the Prefect of the police. Just as Minister D——— enjoys ascendancy over the queen by virtue of his knowledge of the contents of the letter, so too does Dupin enjoy ascendancy over the Prefect by virtue of his confidence as to the letter's location. At this stage, Dupin has not been informed of any of the particulars of the case, yet already he knows that the Prefect is in error. Dupin immediately discerns that the solution to the mystery of the letter's whereabouts lies in its being put in an obvious place, not in its being concealed. This omniscience, what Poe calls "analysis" in "The Murders in the Rue Morgue," clearly represents an idealized version of ordinary analysis; indeed, Sherlock Holmes would be hard-pressed to come up with the solution to the mystery as rapidly as Dupin. And though it could be argued that Dupin blackmails the Prefect—he extorts Fr 50,000 for the return of the letter—the most important analogue between the relationship of Dupin and the Prefect and that of Minister D——— and the queen is that in both cases knowledge gives its possessors power over their less clever victims.

What is striking about the passage above, however, is not merely Dupin's supernatural acumen, but the tone in which he addresses the Prefect. Dupin's superciliousness derives as much from his consciousness of his superior social position as from his sense of intellectual superiority. Indeed, for Poe, the two are one: Dupin's hauteur is the result of genius, but it is equally the result of being a member of the aristocracy.

It is not surprising, then, to find that the figure of Dupin arose out of a nineteenth-century American subculture that prized, or liked to think of itself as prizing, aristocratic values. Chevalier C. Auguste Dupin exists as a projection of the aristocratic ideals found in the antebellum South. These ideals, taken mainly from English Romantic literature, particularly the work of Lord Byron and Sir Walter Scott, were fashioned into cultural myths of the South, and formed the basis for Poe's aesthetic theories. As an aristocratic man of letters (and science), a gentleman of grace and wit, Dupin embodies the refined aestheticism that Poe developed out of British Romanticism. As Michael Allen has noted, "Poe came to his first magazine, the *Southern*

Literary Messenger, after growing up in a South that was extending an aristocratic code from the original Virginia gentry to the whole region to consolidate it against Northern pretensions. This process was considerably assisted by British literary and cultural sources, and the British conservative attitudes to the 'many' and to the 'trade' of writing fitted well into this milieu of cultural conservatism" (*Poe and the British Magazine Tradition*, 133).

Dupin's supercilious tone, then, ultimately derives from Poe's investment in the southern valorization of an aristocratic code. In this way, as in so many others, Poe established the convention for much detective fiction; this tone, this lofty way of speaking, can be heard in the voices of many subsequent detective figures—most obviously in Sherlock Holmes, but also in Lord Peter Wimsey, Hercule Poirot, and, more recently, Adam Dalgliesh.

None of these sleuths, however, matches Dupin's omniscience. Dupin's powers of ratiocination are such that phenomena capable of being understood are capable of being controlled. Individuals may behave stupidly, irrationally, perversely, or even maliciously, as in "The Purloined Letter," but through Dupin, social disorder becomes order, the unknowable becomes knowable. Dupin's analytical capability represents a fantasy of power, a fantasy for a kind of Nietzschean superman. Poe differs from Nietzsche, however, in that for Poe disorder is not systematic but individual, aberrational. The chief role of Dupin's ratiocinative genius is to rectify what in the larger scheme of things are temporary aberrations from the norm. Nowhere is it suggested that crime may have a social cause or a class character; for Poe it is an abstract puzzle, an intriguing deviation from an otherwise smoothly running social mechanism.

If the conventions of detective fiction offer unique possibilities for exploring social and political relations, then, given Poe's role in the shaping of the genre, it is ironic that these sociopolitical concerns are marginalized, present most tellingly in the knowledge-power connection that is such a vital part of the narrative structure of his detective stories. Poe's emphasis on the ratiocinative abilities of Dupin and his lack of interest in depicting the workaday world in the detailed fashion of the realist novel imply a certain vision of society. In "The Murders in the Rue Morgue," "The Purloined Letter," and, to a lesser extent, "The Mystery of Marie Roget," society exists as a backdrop for Dupin's disembodied intellect. Or, to put it in another way, society exists as a mere aspect of Dupin's character, and this, as we shall see shortly, has a profound effect on the style of these stories.

The Political Unconscious; or, Negating Society

Up to this point, I have been focusing chiefly on the image of society projected by Poe's narratives of detection, and have argued that it represents a fantasy of wish-fulfillment. I would now like to suggest that this fantasy is only one element in a larger drama of political tension, and, at the same time, I would like to develop my theoretical sanction for this appropriation of Freudian theory.

Although Poe's stories do not render the complex, interlocking social, personal, and working relationships often found in the realist novel, they nevertheless register—indeed they cannot help but register—some repressed anxieties about society. Following some of Fredric Jameson's work on what he has most recently termed "the political unconscious," I want to suggest that there is an economy of both wish-fulfillment and repression within the narratives I've been discussing. In "Reification and Utopia in Mass Culture" Jameson argues that "to rewrite the concept of a management of desire in social terms now allows us to think repression and wish-fulfillment together within the unity of a single mechanism, which gives and takes alike in a kind of psychic compromise or horse-trading, which strategically arouses fantasy content within careful symbolic containment structures which defuse it, gratifying intolerable, unrealizable, properly imperishable desires only to the degree to which they can again be laid to rest" (141). In these narratives what is incompletely repressed is the "unrealizable" desire to be rid of society as an affective experience. In one sense, this is only the flip side of Poe's desire to completely dominate society. To dominate it totally is to abolish it as an entity that makes claims on the individual. This represents a reversal of the conventions of the classic realist novel: In *Madame Bovary, Middlemarch,* and *Sons and Lovers,* it is society that determines the boundaries of individual possibility, of what can and cannot be achieved—ultimately, what course of action the protagonist will take. In Poe's detective fiction this sense of the determinative power of society over the protagonist is almost entirely absent. Instead, Dupin's analytical prowess enables him to dominate society. Yet his power of analysis is in itself an instrument of alienation, for the price he pays is an Olympian detachment from ordinary life. Dupin, it appears, is incapable of relating to others in any way other than through his rarefied mode of analysis. Consequently, social intercourse can only be understood in abstract terms. Life as emotion, as felt experience, is conspicuously absent, except when Dupin's triumphant resolution of the mystery is at hand. The perverse, nocturnal life of Dupin and the narrator is indicative of this isolation from any larger human community.

This fantasy of a completely self-sufficient, pure rationalism results in a reified vision of society lacking in the human conflict that enriched the nineteenth-century tradition of realist fiction. Paradoxically, Poe, one of the genre's most important inaugurators, takes crime, the most social of phenomena, and drains it of its social character. In Poe's detective fiction, crime is not a social problem but an analytical one. The effects of this vision have been immense, particularly in the ratiocinative fiction of Christie, Allingham and Sayers, to mention just a few. Within this tradition, fascination with the power of knowledge is almost always associated with a lack of interest in the interaction between the individual and society. In this sense, detective fiction, at least in the ratiocinative tradition, uses the conventions of the classic realist novel but also breaks with them, largely as a result of its deification of the ratiocinative detective hero or heroine.

Within the context of Poe's oeuvre, however, the stories of ratiocination form a part of a larger polarization of logic and feeling. Although his detective stories represent a fantasy of the intellect unencumbered by society or feeling, much of his other fiction depicts the insufficiency of the intellect in the face of inadequately repressed or even overwhelming fears and desires. In this context, "The Fall of the House of Usher" can be taken as an allegory of the rational mind's inability to contain fears originating in the unconscious. From the very beginning, the narrator struggles, through the use of reason, to exorcise the gloominess and horror hanging over the House of Usher. Roderick Usher, as he himself recognizes, has almost succumbed to madness by the time the narrator arrives: "In this unnerved—in this pitiable condition—I feel that the period will sooner or later arrive when I must abandon life and reason together in some struggle with the grim phantasm FEAR" (181). The narrator manages to escape the ruin of reason; Roderick Usher, however, does not: he dies facing it. My point, however, is not that the narrator escapes with his reason intact while Usher dies in a maddened frenzy, for the narrative problematizes this simple opposition between madness and reason: Usher's private madness ultimately becomes generalized, indeed oppressive to both Usher and the narrator. In "The Fall of the House of Usher" reason cannot confer order on life; Roderick Usher is thus the antithesis to Dupin.

This tension between intellect and feeling is related to the struggle within the nineteenth-century consciousness to synthesize the two. In Victorian literature, ratiocinative genius eventually comes to be seen as sterile and lifeless. George Eliot's Casaubon and Dickens's Gradgrind are tragic and parodic versions of this overdependence on ratiocination, which in the Victorian era and later is considered primarily a masculine faculty. In *Middlemarch,* for example, the sterile rationalism of Casaubon is explicitly contrasted with the sustaining affections of Dorothea. John Stuart Mill's *Autobiography,* probably the most famous example of this split, describes in minute detail the debilitating emotional and psychological effects of this valorization of the rational mind, and the succor Mill received from literature and from his wife, Harriet.

The strain of this division can easily be seen in Poe's oeuvre: if some of his work exists as a fantasy of the self-sufficiency of the ratiocinative mind, detached from society and bonds of empathy—and, ultimately, beyond the demands of historical necessity—much of his other fiction negates that fantasy by luridly dramatizing the instability of reason. In both cases, society exists only as a background or as a projection of the protagonist's psyche. Poe's profound ambivalence toward reason and his more active desire to efface society "as a community binding the individual to others" (Ziff, *Literary Democracy,* 76) are connected impulses, as Elliot Gilbert has observed: "Poe's experience paralleled that of the nineteenth century, which was also preoccupied with the idea of order, with the desire to subdue and control the universe through the application of reason. What the age discovered, however, in its quest for order and control—and what it powerfully symbolized in the detective—was not man's ability to achieve that order but his inability to do so" (31). This is, I think, an acute observation on the continuity between Poe's worldview and nineteenth-century Anglo-American culture, detective fiction in particular, but it remains too general. What must still be specified are the cultural tensions of the antebellum American South that Poe incorporated or, rather, transformed in his fiction, including his detective fiction.

The Detective and the Garden

In *The Dispossessed Garden* Lewis P. Simpson argues that the dominant image of paradise in the literary imagination of the South was realized exclusively in terms of a plantation society founded on the master-slave relationship. Over a period of time, slavery was gradually assimilated to the myth of the new world as a redemptive garden. This metaphoric association of the plantation with a pastoral order, Simpson argues, was further complicated by the Western pastoral tradition, ultimately Hebraic in origin, of the plantation as the natural locus for the cultivation of the life of the mind (182). The difficulty for the southern writer, then, was the difficulty of reconciling the brutal, morally repugnant reality of slavery to this pastoral ideal. To be sure, harmonizing slavery with the values of the pastoral tradition presented no real difficulties to the ingenuity of some southern writers. Poe's desire to banish society as an affective community, as a social entity capable of regulating the fate of the individual, relates to this tension in southern culture, partly because every contemporary form of social organization was distasteful. Rejecting both the industrialized, mammonistic society of the North—and what he saw as its insipid egalitarianism—and the tensions inherent in the South, Poe could locate no satisfactory existing social archetype. Although Poe's relationship with the South is admittedly more problematic than his primarily hostile relation to northern society—since he saw himself as an apologist for slavery and for southern values in general—nevertheless his work displays an acute awareness of the tensions of plantation society, an awareness symbolized in "images of diseased nature, poisoned gardens, ruined castles, depraved humanity, and above all, in the image of a mysterious blight moving across the landscape and rotting the seed of all lovely, young life."[7]

Poe's work thus reveals a much more ambivalent attitude toward the South than many of his public statements might suggest, partly because his self-appointed position as defender of the South against northern condescension did not encourage an open admission of the problems of southern society. Undoubtedly, too, Poe did not want to acknowledge, perhaps could not acknowledge even to himself, the real basis of southern society, because this would have amounted to an acknowledgment of the contamination of the pastoral idyll, which was Poe's plantation version of the Coleridgean notion of a "clerisy"—an endowed class of southerners devoted to the cultivation and diffusion of learning. Because of Poe's overt distaste for industrialism, his latent awareness of the problems of southern society, and his fascination with repressed or partially repressed desires and fears, his work gravitates toward a dissection of the individual psyche. Any predominantly realistic or mimetic mode of representation would involve social description; instead, Poe's dominant literary technique is a protomodernism that constantly refers back to the enlarged consciousness of the alienated individual in which external reality is dissolved into intensified or even hyperactive mental states.

This alienation from what Raymond Williams calls a "knowable community" is evident in the style of Poe's prose.[8] Its syncretic, artificial quality—that dense, orotund reworking of romantic prose so despised by Mark Twain—attests to his remoteness from the idioms of everyday speech. If Poe's style is legitimately associated with a southern tradition of verbose rhetoric, that rhetoric is qualitatively different from the more immediate, distinguishable, and genuinely colloquial speech patterns of specific speech communities. By drawing on the resources of a highly refined, highly educated, highly generalized tradition of rhetoric, Poe's style attempts to transcend the boundaries and pressures, both social and linguistic, of a "knowable community." His style, then, can be seen as a way of mediating the conflict in his fiction, especially pronounced in his detective stories, between reason and society. Poe's detective fiction testifies to his faith in the self-sufficiency of the ratiocinative consciousness; his style, in its submerging of everyday speech, reinforces this testimony by asserting the autonomy of that consciousness from society. Poe's style thus attempts to build a world elsewhere, removed from the perceived social and cultural failures of American society.[9]

Mass Fiction and Chevalier C. Auguste Dupin

Of the many ironies of Poe's career, one of the most striking concerns Poe and his audience. Poe's relationship with his audience was curious: The founder of an emerging form that would become most popular in mass culture, Poe despised the democratic values that provided the ideological basis for the existence of this new fiction.[10] From time to time Poe expressed a less elitist attitude toward popular literature and the mass audience that read it, but these more benign judgments were, in the main, aberrations from his vain, lifelong hope for an aristocratic, predominantly southern literary community that would both produce and consume a rarefied, aesthetically superior national literature. The last question I want to explore here, accordingly, is this: How does Poe's ratiocinative fiction respond to the contradictions of its literary production?

To begin to answer this question it is necessary to identify the general professional conditions within which writers in Poe's time had to work. For most American writers in the first half of the nineteenth century, literary production was an extremely difficult business. The undeveloped state of the American publishing industry made the publication of nonmainstream American fiction a precarious enterprise at best. The centralization of publishing within a few urban centers; a disparate national audience; an extremely volatile market; the lack of finance capital—all these elements combined to make high risk and low profit the norm in printing American fiction. Predictably enough, publishing concerns preferred to ensure their profits by reprinting the works of proven English and Continental best-sellers—Sir Walter Scott, Charles Dickens, Eugène Sue, Bulwer Lytton—for which they paid no royalties. If they did publish the work of American writers, they tended to stick to known genres such as moralistic or sentimental fiction. Magazines thus remained one of the few outlets for American writers like Poe or Hawthorne, who were not writing sentimental or realistic fiction (J. Clark, *Working Class Culture,* 245).

Most reviewers of Poe's *Tales* (1845) were not hostile; with the exception of a few English newspapers, they were generally receptive.[11] Yet Poe's critical reception was not matched by his popular appeal; apart from a few popular hoaxes, his work never gained a popular audience. The chief problem with Poe's fiction was not that it was rejected by a conservative class of literary mandarins, but that Poe's tastes, values, and aesthetic principles were at odds with the literary tastes of a newly literate, expanding middle class. A new moralistic, popular, highly commercialized mass-circulation journalism was displacing the more middlebrow, self-conscious literary publication. Indeed, Ross Chambers sees this new commercial reality figured in "The Purloined Letter" itself: "Poe's 'The Purloined Letter' includes, at the centerpoint of the text, a moment in which Dupin exchanges the letter for a fat check from the Prefect of Police—a manifest enactment of the exchange value of fiction ('letters') in the economic marketplace and a reminder that economic forces form part of the situation that Poe's fiction makes meaningful" (*Story and Situation,* 8).

The "exchange value of fiction," as Michael Allen notes in *Poe and the British Magazine Tradition,* brought about a new type of publication, the mass-circulation magazine: "Popular literary articles and tales were 'packaged' in the modern way with material of the kind most of the consumers wanted: sentimental love tales, gossip, recipes, popular songs, and fashion news, and plates; and the latter material guaranteed the circulation (131). Although Poe was a capable editor of two mass-circulation magazines—*Burton's Gentleman's Magazine* and *Graham's Magazine*—his idiosyncratic style and subject matter were ill suited to the lighter tastes of this newly formed mass audience. As Allen points out, "The 'shudders' of moral perversity, putrescent corpses, living burials, apocalypse, plague, and ruin with which he was still working were instinctive enough. They were attuned, however, not to the love-adventure-sentiment staple of the popular magazine fiction of the 1840's but to the morbid Byronic and Gothic stock-in-trade of the previous generation, which Poe had absorbed in his youth and still found congenial" (166).

Another reason for Poe's failure to appeal to this new mass audience was that his learning, aestheticism, and aristocratic attitudes caused him, in spite of his best efforts, to condescend to his readership. As Allen notes, his tales of ratiocination, his burlesques, and even his parodies depend on an appeal to an intellectually superior, select group of readers capable of catching the clues, subtle allusions, and indirect, often caustic references that characterize his fiction.

The answer, then, to the question of how Poe's detective fiction responded to the anomalous situation of an antidemocratic writer writing for a mass audience with decidedly republican views is complex; however, within Poe's stories of ratiocination there is a strategy of neutralization that aims not so much at negotiating this tension as at eliminating it. In his detective stories Poe shows his distaste for democratic values by inversion, parody, or satire, techniques with which he was more than adept, but also by creating a new form that valorized a different and superior epistemology. The epistemology of Poe's detective fiction takes the ideology of commonsense empiricism everywhere evident in this young, pragmatic, productive country and, in a disdainful act of one-upmanship, attempts to expose the ideology as a crude and limited way of problem solving. This is, to be sure, a subtler strategy than the one he employs in his satires, where commonsense empiricism is also the target. Dupin, the quasi-aristocratic rationalist, consistently seeks to expose what to him are the shoddy assumptions involved in empirical thinking. In "The Purloined Letter" he criticizes the mechanical empiricism typical of the prefect and, for that matter, most men: "They [the Prefect and his cohort] consider only their own ideas of ingenuity; and, in searching for anything hidden, advert only to the modes in which *they* would have hidden it. They are right in this much—that their ingenuity is a faithful representative of that of *the mass;* but when the cunning of the individual felon is diverse in character from their own, the felon foils them, of course" (132). Dupin's acute faculty of reasoning, superior to the mere calculating ability of the prefect and the unimaginative bourgeoisie in general, stands as an emblem of the superiority of the aristocracy to the leveling effects of democracy. Dupin's patrician intellect alone is capable of penetrating the mysteries of bourgeois society. Thus the aristocracy, of which Dupin is the proud descendant and representative in an otherwise-tarnished age, figures as the implied utopian resolution to the contemporary failures of industrial democracy and the polluted agrarianism of the South.

This is not to say that Poe was an abolitionist; on the contrary, he was an apologist of slavery.[12] But again, Poe's work, like that of many other southern writers, is marked by the struggle to reconcile slavery with the idealized notion of society as a pastoral idyll. Poe, it seems, could ratify slavery, and the society founded on it, only when its more brutal aspects were etherealized, transformed into a form of benevolent paternalism. This contradiction was rooted in the South's self-image. Southern culture saw itself as the genteel guardian of literary and cultural values threatened by the utilitarianism and crassness of the industrial North, yet this self-representation of southern society as the locus of refinement and learning was called into question by the decidedly antipastoral nature of slavery.

Dupin, then, not only embodies the aesthetic fastidiousness of southern culture, but he also represents an aristocracy of the mind, an idea deeply rooted in the pastoral ideal of the antebellum South. Dupin *is* an aristocrat. But more important, he possesses an aristocratic mind superior to the police, muddling democrats that they are. As Dupin says, the police have only "ordinary intellects" useful only in "ordinary occasions" (133). Through Dupin, Poe suggests that intelligence, or at least the faculty of analysis, is class-based: only an aristocrat could understand with Dupin's completeness, for the police possess merely an ingenuity that is "a faithful representative of that of *the mass*" (132). Poe's reworking of the pastoral ideal in the figure of the aesthetic yet supremely rational figure of Dupin thus enables him to produce a model of southern culture, a model that implies the cultural poverty of the democratic masses.

Dupin and Poe's representation of Parisian society exist together, then, as an attempted resolution of real social contradiction. Dupin, the empowered aristocrat, presides not only over a society drained of the tensions of the decaying South and the industrializing North, but ultimately over an urban agglomeration that ceases to have any affective force whatsoever. Society is effectively neutralized, deprived of its determinative power. Interestingly, Dupin's rationalism, the rationalism responsible for this valorization of this individual over society, replicates the ideology characteristic of aristocratic European formations that recognized only social equals as members of society: in English, this history is preserved within the semantic history of the word "society," which in the eighteenth century signified "active fellowship" and "company" before gradually evolving into a description of a general system or order (Raymond Williams, *Marxism and Literature*, 11). There is no general society to speak of in these stories because there are no equals to Dupin; the narrator's inferiority is emphasized at the beginning of "The Murders in the Rue Morgue," in the famous passage in which Dupin appears to read his mind; in subsequent stories the narrator's intellectual inferiority is never in question. Ultimately, his function consists of narrating his mentor's more prodigious mental exploits.

Poe's longing for a prebourgeois, settled aristocracy untainted by iniquity is one of the legacies he left to the genre of detective fiction, and persists to this day in the work of Margery Allingham, Agatha Christie, Ngaio Marsh, and Dorothy Sayers, novelists who added to this legacy by bringing an analysis of manners to the genre; indeed, it might be said that this longing is still one of the hallmarks of the ratiocinative tradition of detective fiction. Poe's main legacy to the adolescent, popular-fiction industry of his day, then, was his definition of detective fiction as oppositional, as antagonistic to contemporary values, mores, ways of thinking and seeing. To be sure, Poe wrote in the name of an idiosyncratic, radical conservatism, shaped by an unrealizable social fantasy; nevertheless, by articulating values alternate to those dominant in nineteenth-century America, he helped to define a genre rich enough in novelistic possibilities to be reworked by writers as ideologically and stylistically different from himself as Dashiell Hammett, Raymond Chandler, and Ross Macdonald.

Notes

1. I am indebted here to Julian Symons's discussion of Poe's detective fiction in *Bloody Murder: From the Detective Story to the Crime Novel,* pages 36–37, in which he points out the subgenres of detective fiction that Poe inaugurated.

2. This change can be seen in the contrast between Poe's and Conan Doyle's detective fiction. In "From Semiotics to Hermeneutics: Modes of Detection in Doyle and Chandler" William Stowe argues that while Poe and Conan Doyle share a semiotic model of detection, Chandler develops a hermeneutics of detection: "He [Chandler] achieved his ambition by moving away from semiotics toward hermeneutics, away from the methodological solution of 'mysteries' toward the philosophical understanding of mystery" (382).

3. In *A New History of the United States* William Miller writes that this period of American expansionism was accompanied by widespread corruption: "The growth of cities, regional specialization in agriculture, expansion of the transportation network, the development of markets for American manufacturers and the relation of all these to everyday politics and life lent a vigor and unity to the northern spirit probably unmatched in this epoch anywhere on earth. One consequence of expansiveness was the hunger for wealth at any price and a deterioration of business morality" (201).

4. Michael Holquist makes a similar point in "Whodunit and Other Questions: Metaphysical Detective Stories in Postwar Fiction": "It was to this powerful impulse toward the irrational that he opposed the therefore necessarily potent sense of reason which finds its highest expression in 'The Murders in the Rue Morgue' and 'The Purloined Letter.' Against the metaphors for chaos, found in his other tales, he sets in the Dupin stories, the essential metaphor for order: the detective" (156). I stress, however, that it is not so much reason that is incorporated in these stories but an ideology of reason.

5. For an interesting discussion of the way in which science has been specifically gendered as male in the West, see Ruth Bleier's "Lab Coat: Robe of Innocence or Klansman's Sheet?" in *Feminist Studies/Critical Studies.*

6. As is well known, "The Purloined Letter"'s fascination with identity, signification, and power has made it a seminal text for psychoanalytic criticism. For some of the most famous psychoanalytic readings of Poe's story, see John P. Muller and William J. Richardson, eds., *The Purloined Poe: Lacan, Derrida and Psychoanalytic Reading.* My reading, by contrast, focuses on "The Purloined Letter" as a socially symbolic drama of nineteenth-century American social, political, and cultural tensions.

7. The quotation is from Charles L. Sanford's essay "Edgar Allan Poe," reprinted in Eric W. Carlson, ed., *The Recognition of Edgar Allan Poe: Selected Criticism Since 1829.* Sanford uses this summary of the dominant imagery in Poe's work to emphasize what he sees as Poe's "pain of loss" due to his failure to locate an Edenic society. It seems as likely that this blighted imagery exists as a specific response to the tensions within the plantation society of the South.

8. In *Politics and Letters* Williams defines a "knowable community" as a knowledge of "an effective range of social experience [understood] by sufficiently manifest immediate relations" (247).

9. I am echoing the title (and argument) of Richard Poirier's *A World Elsewhere: The Place of Style in American Literature*.

10. For more on Poe's antidemocratic views, see Arthur Hobson Quinn's biography *Edgar Allan Poe*, especially page 94: "He was never a democrat in any sense. His reference in *Tamerlane* to 'the rabblemen' is characteristic."

11. In a review in the *New York Daily Tribune* on July 11, 1845, Margaret Fuller declared in no uncertain terms that "Mr Poe's tales need no aid of newspaper comment to give them popularity; they have secured it" (I. M. Walker, ed., *Edgar Allan Poe: The Critical Heritage,* 176). Evert Augustus Duyckinck eulogized in a similar manner: "Few books have been published of late which contain within themselves the elements of greater popularity. This popularity it will be sure to obtain if it be not for the operation of a stupid prejudice which refuses to read, or a personal enmity which refuses to admire" (Walker, 187).

For the purposes of the present argument, it is important to recognize that American and English reviewers, even those unsympathetic to Poe's fiction in general, tended to be more predisposed to his stories of ratiocination. An unsigned notice in the *Spectator,* which deplored Poe's fiction as being "of a magazinish kind" (Walker, 180), may be taken as a fair example: "To unfold the wonderful, to show what seems miraculous is amenable to almost mathematical reasoning, is a real delight of Mr Poe; and though he may probably contrive the mystery he is about to unravel, this is not always the case as in the tale of the murder of Marie Roget; and in all cases, he exhibits great analytical skill in seizing upon the points of circumstantial evidence and connecting them together" (Walker, 180).

12. In a review published in the *Southern Literary Messenger* Poe declared of slavery that: "Nothing is wanted but manly discussion to convince our people at least, that in continuing to command the services of their slaves, they violate no law divine or human, and that in the faithful discharge of their reciprocal obligations lies their true duty. Let these be performed, and we believe (with our esteemed correspondent Professor Dew) that society in the South will derive much more of good than of evil from this much abused and partially-considered institution" ("The South Vindicated," 275). Incidentally, this paternalistic attitude toward slavery forms the basis for the relationship between William Legrand and his freed slave Jupiter in the "The Gold Bug," another of Poe's detective stories.

The Adventurous Detective:
Conan Doyle and Imperialism | 3

I had called upon my friend Sherlock Holmes upon the second morning after Christmas, with the intention of wishing him the compliments of the season. He was lounging upon the sofa in a purple dressing gown, a pipe rack within his reach upon the right, and a pile of crumpled morning papers, evidently newly studied, near at hand. Beside the couch was a wooden chair, and on the angle of the back hung a very seedy and disreputable hard felt hat, much the worse for wear, and cracked in several places. A lens and a forceps lying upon the seat of the chair suggested that the hat had been suspended in this manner for the purpose of examination.

—Arthur Conan Doyle, "The Adventure of the Blue Carbuncle"

The Sherlock Holmes Myth

It is difficult to think of Sherlock Holmes as a mere literary character. Ever since his first appearance in *A Study in Scarlet* in 1888, and the subsequent, more successful series of stories that appeared in *Strand Magazine* between July 1891 and June 1892, Holmes seems to have led an almost larger-than-life, autonomous existence from his literary creator. Indeed, Conan Doyle so much resented the popularity of Holmes that in "The Final Problem" he killed him off. Even Conan Doyle, however, could not assassinate the redoubtable Sherlock Holmes. Eventually his contribution to the Holmes myth would include four full novels, five collections of short stories, and an immensely successful play, predictably called *Sherlock Holmes*. Since he was "killed" by the evil Professor Moriarty at the Reichenbach Falls, Holmes has outlived—and continues to overshadow—his creator in films and novels. One of the more notable recent examples of Holmes's enduring popularity is Nicholas Meyer's novel *The Seven Per Cent Solution,* in which Holmes and Freud together solve a mystery. To this day, the deerstalker hat, the magnifying glass, and the meerschaum pipe are the totemic symbols of what can only be called the Sherlock Holmes myth.

Few other myths centered on a single character in modern popular culture has been so familiar, so ubiquitous, so pervasive within the English-speaking world and, in many cases, outside it. Many explanations have been advanced to explain the popularity of the Holmes myth, most of them resting on the character of Holmes himself. Holmes, it is argued, represents a qualitatively different type of detective hero.[1] Whereas C. Auguste Dupin was a disembodied intellect, and Wilkie Collins's Sergeant Cuff a mere eccentric, Holmes is the first truly complex, fully rounded, psychologically interesting detective hero. Sherlock Holmes was a new type of hero, or at least an interesting amalgam of older detective figures. It possible to see him as a synthesis of the ratiocinative qualities of Dupin and the eccentricities of Cuff. Yet this explanation does little to explain the popularity of a complex cultural phenomenon. One index of the popularity of Conan Doyle's stories was that they quickly doubled the circulation of *Strand Magazine* from 200,000 to 400,000 (Ken Worpole, *Reading by Numbers,* 48). But the question remains: Why did English and American audiences in the 1890s and thereafter take to Holmes with a fervor matched in recent times only by the Beatles? Clearly the complexity of Sherlock Holmes's character cannot entirely account for this. After all, there were many contemporary literary characters with more complex psychological portraits who were not attracting comparable readerships.

To some extent, Conan Doyle's formal success was due to his refinement, following Poe, of a new, quintessentially popular genre, featuring a single detective hero within an open-ended, continuous form responsive to public fears, hopes, and anxieties. But the success of this form, and of the Sherlock Holmes myth in general, depends on a particular use of language, a realistic style notable for its vivid, precise detail:

> It was a September evening, and not yet seven o'clock, but the day had been a dreary one, and a dense drizzly fog lay low upon the great city. Mud-colored clouds drooped sadly over the muddy streets. Down the strand the lamps were but misty splotches of diffused light which threw a feeble circular glimmer upon the slimy pavement. The yellow glare from the shop-windows streamed out into the steamy, vaporous air, and threw a murky, shifting radiance across the crowded thoroughfare. There was to my mind something eerie and ghost-like in the endless procession of faces which flitted across these narrow bars of light—sad faces and glad, haggard and merry. (*The Sign of Four,* 98)

This use of a rich, referential language focusing on the primary qualities of objects enables Conan Doyle to produce a convincing, wholly "realistic" environment. Indeed, the London of Sherlock Holmes is almost as famous as Holmes himself. Nevertheless, it is only a representation, a fictional construct of late-nineteenth-century London, and, as I shall argue, remarkable as much for what it excludes or domesticates—class conflict, racism, imperialism, even women—as for what it includes. This is not to deny its efficacy as a representation, for the popular image of a timeless, fog-shrouded London is largely due to Conan Doyle. But it does suggest that the Holmes myth was at least originally produced by a particular way of writing that created the illusion of a fascinating, intricate, and believable society. There is, that is to say, nothing more solid, more "realistic," and more fictional than 221B Baker Street. What perhaps appears at first glance to be a purely formal device—style—reflecting an objective reality is, on closer inspection, a crucial element in the production of the Holmes myth. This myth, in other words, is not simply a myth of an eccentric but brilliant detective, but a myth of knowledge and, ultimately, a myth of society. To address the question, then, of the success of Conan Doyle's detective fiction, it is necessary to examine both his formal achievement and the ideological character of his work, for, as the example above demonstrates, its appeal lies in its powerful combination of formal innovation and ideological statement.

Sensationalism, Adventure, and Imperialism

Conan Doyle did not, of course, invent the formal realist style, but he did develop one that drew on the resources and conventions of the sensational literature flourishing in Victorian England. Unlike Poe's detective fiction, Conan Doyle's style grew out of a culture of a mass-circulation, popular fiction, a great deal of which was devoted to sensational subject matter. These popular mass-circulation newspapers and periodicals were an established fact of life by the 1890s: *Tit-Bits, Answers, Pearson's Weekly,* and others offered a staple diet of scandal, lurid crime, upper-class intrigue, melodrama, adventure, and sin. These periodicals were immensely popular and sold in the hundreds of thousands. This boom was facilitated by a number of factors, both social and technological; the most important of these were the abolition of the newspaper tax in 1855, the repeal of the paper duty in 1861, and the introduction of the rotary and typesetting presses. None of these changes would have mattered, however, if there had not been substantial improvements in literacy as the century wore on. Ironically, the huge sales of religious and devotional material in the early part of the nineteenth century did much to spread literacy and to create the general conditions in which sensational literature could flourish (Richard D. Altick, *The English Common Reader,* 348–64 *passim*). In short, as Ken Worpole notes, "The 1880s were a new period in the development of mass-publishing, just as the 1830s had been. Mass literacy was almost an accomplished fact; compulsory education had been in existence for a decade; the major cities were in a new era of expansion and the advent of the railways had brought not only a new form of communication but a new literature to go with it" (*Reading by Numbers,* 19).

Sherlock Holmes was an integral part of this "era of expansion." His popularity was directly related to the tremendous growth in the 1880s of the popular media oriented to a readership different in taste and size from the basically middlebrow literary audience for which Poe wrote. Conan Doyle's detective fiction appealed not only to a wider readership—the urban masses that traveled to and from work in commuter trains—but also to an increased public interest in sensational crime. Public interest in crime was not new to Victorian England. Indeed, the English novel has its roots in crime literature, beginning with the "true confessions" of criminals printed in pamphlet form in the seventeenth and eighteenth centuries and continuing through moralistic crime stories such as the *Newgate Calendar* (1773). This topos developed into the criminal-as-protagonist novel, of which *Moll Flanders* (1772) is probably the most famous example in eighteenth-century English literature. But the degree of public interest in crime in the latter half of the nineteenth century was unprecedented. In *Deadly Encounters: Two Victorian Sensations* Richard Altick documents the craze, beginning in 1861, that set off this new era of sensationalism. Although the 1850s had seen a spate of highly publicized homicides within middle-class families, these paled in comparison with the public sensation created by two cases in July 1861, the "Northumberland Street affair" and the Vidil case. Both were remarkable for the mysterious circumstances and unanswered questions that surrounded them.

The "Northumberland Street affair" concerned an Army major, the alleged ensnarement of his beautiful mistress by an unscrupulous moneylender, and the desperate and bloody hand-to-hand fight that ensued at 16 Northumberland Street, a combat that ultimately cost the moneylender his life. The Vidil case also had many of the elements of a sensational melodrama. It concerned the failed attempt of Vidil, a French nobleman living in England, to kill his son in order to avoid giving him his inheritance. A number of things, however, distinguished these cases from the ordinary, garden-variety crime found in popular pamphlets. First of all, the protagonists were real-life individuals, not literary types. This, along with the fantastic and bizarre events surrounding the crimes, caused many contemporary commentators to exclaim at the degree to which life was outdoing art. And in the "Northumberland Street affair" the mixture of treachery, violence, and titillating sexual hints enthralled the public imagination. These already-present sensational elements encouraged newspaper accounts to further dramatize the cases by writing about them in the language of melodramatic and romantic fiction. The sensational aspect of the events, the newspapers' literary representation of both real and rumored events relating to the cases, and the rampant speculation in the newspapers on the guilt and innocence of the parties involved all conspired to make the thrills and chills of contemporary fiction tame in comparison.

But more than that, these two cases provided prototypes for a new literature focusing on the dark mystery within the sacrosanct realm of the middle-class home: one has only to think of the work of Dickens, Collins, Hardy, and of course Conan Doyle (especially in *A Study in Scarlet* and *The Sign of Four*) to see how deeply these sensational elements had penetrated into the Victorian literary consciousness. The Gothic novel contained many of these elements, but its locus was usually a fantastic and forbidding setting remote from the safety and comforts of the middle-class Victorian hearth. The "Northumberland Street affair" and the Vidil case helped to shift the locus of the sensational from the fantastic to the familiar. The sensationalism craze, the appetite for a literature full of mystery, lurid crime, and eroticism that these cases whetted, also helped to make respectable what had previously been dismissed as working-class pulp: "In sensational fiction, the principal ingredients of the despised street literature, stories that sold in penny and halfpenny slices, moved up-market, so to speak, finding their way into staid households and corrupting the imaginations of susceptible readers" (Altick, *Deadly Encounters,* 153). In taking the readers of "respectable" literature by storm, sensational fiction became somewhat more respectable itself, though Conan Doyle's own feelings of inferiority about the worth of the genre in which he made his reputation can be taken as a fair indication of the limits of the respectability of this upwardly mobile genre at the end of the century. It would be a mistake, however, to see Conan Doyle's work as purely sensational. The most sensational scenes occur in his early work, while his middle and late fiction becomes more domesticated, more ratiocinative: there is nothing in his later work, for example, that compares with his lurid description of the body of the murdered Enoch Drebber in *A Study in Scarlet.*

If it is true, as Mikhail Bakhtin suggests, that every new genre is a synthesis of older ones, then Conan Doyle's detective fiction may be defined as a complex reworking of three genres:[2] the genre of sensation, which I have already considered, the detective genre, and the adventure genre.

In late-Victorian society, these genres had a popular appeal that cut across class lines. Conan Doyle's general debt to the genre of detective fiction begins with his adoption, from Poe, of the eccentric, rationalistic detective hero as the protagonist, and includes many other elements, such as the use of "backward construction" as the dominant narrative pattern, the presence of the not-so-brilliant narrator assistant, and a number of plots reminiscent of Poe. But whereas Dupin is deductive in method, employing a form of reasoning that moves from generalized propositions to particular conclusions, and is essentially an armchair detective, Holmes's usual *modus operandi* is inductive. Holmes's reasoning usually begins with facts and reaches conclusions by making generalizations based on them. As he counsels in "A Scandal in Bohemia": "It is a capital mistake to theorize before one has data. Insensibly one begins to twist facts to suit theories, instead of theories to suit facts" (163). Holmes, of course, reasons deductively, too, but his desire to discover all the facts of the case makes him a much more physical, vigorous, dynamic detective than Dupin. And it is partly through this emphasis on Holmes's physicality, his strength and vigor, that we can see Conan Doyle's debt to the long tradition of adventure writing in English literature.

If we accept the definition of adventure put forward by Martin Green in *Dreams of Adventure, Deeds of Empire,* Conan Doyle's stories are adventure stories: "In general, adventure seems to mean a series of events, partly but not wholly accidental in settings remote from the domestic and probably from the civilized (at least in the psychological sense of remote), which constitute a challenge to the central character. In meeting this challenge, he/she performs a series of exploits which make him/her a hero, eminent in virtues such as courage, fortitude, cunning, strength, leadership and persistence" (23). Significantly, Conan Doyle's first set of Sherlock Holmes stories was entitled "The Adventures of Sherlock Holmes," and, although they usually do not take place in remote and exotic settings—the stories almost always begin in the domestic comfort of 221B Baker Street—they place their hero in harrowing circumstances in which he proves his "courage, fortitude, cunning, strength, leadership and persistence." At a formal level, the achievement of Conan Doyle's fiction can be described as a synthesis of elements of sensation, detection, and adventure within a single genre. From the tradition of sensationalism he derived the emphasis on the exciting experience, whether of terror, horror, or surprise; from detective fiction, the ratiocinative element; and from the adventure tradition, the fast-paced action that characterized nearly all of Conan Doyle's detective fiction. In one sense, his fiction can be described as an effective combination of the intellectual appeal of a puzzle with the thrills and chills of a penny pamphlet.

In another sense, though, this taxonomy is misleading, for Conan Doyle not only combined formal elements from these genres, he also combined and reworked the ideologies that these formal elements articulated. Underlying both the novels of adventure and detection is a belief in empiricism as a means of organizing and making sense of experience. What Conan Doyle did in his fiction, and this was vital to its success, was to yoke popular elements previously dominant in lower-class culture, but existing only in a diluted fashion in mainstream fiction, together with empiricism, which as an ideology existed almost exclusively within the middle classes. The result of this fusion was a popularization and naturalization of empiricism. By empiricism I mean not only the detached, quasi-objective method of interpreting phenomena, but also, more important, a way of thinking about the world, an ideology, which by definition excludes qualitative, ethical, even aesthetic considerations in favor of abstract quantification, domination, and use of resources, human or natural, in the name of progress or profit.[3]

This is not to say that Conan Doyle's fiction only contains "themes" that take empiricism as their subject or that it crusades on behalf of an empirical point of view. Rather, the case I am making is that the formal structure of these texts articulates an adherence to a particular ideology of empiricism, an ideology that, in conjunction with a general ideology of imperialism, determines the form of Conan Doyle's detective fiction.[4] I will return to the question of form when I analyze *The Sign of Four,* but first it is necessary to establish the relationship in Conan Doyle's fiction between empiricism and imperialism.

Sherlockian Empiricism and the Values of Empire

Sherlock Holmes is the quintessential empiricist. For him knowledge is attained by stripping phenomena of their social or emotive characteristics, reducing them to pieces in a puzzle. Of course this methodological ruthlessness, structurally identical to that of the scientist or the quantitative economist, accounts for much of his success as a consulting detective. And yet this famous aspect of the Holmes mystique also sets him apart as something of an eccentric, if not a freak, who is likable largely for his other, more attractive qualities. Dr. Watson accusingly makes this point in *The Sign of Four:*

> "You really are an automaton—a calculating machine!" I cried. "There is something positively inhuman in you at times."
> He smiled gently. "It is of the first importance," he said, "not to allow your judgement to be biased by personal qualities. A client is to me a mere unit—a factor in a problem. The emotional qualities are antagonistic to clear reasoning." (96)

Although it is manifestly untrue that "the emotional qualities are antagonistic to clear reasoning," it is typical of Holmes's character that he should think in this way. Holmes's acute empirical powers enable him to dominate the vast landscape of London, from its sordid back-alleys, hovels, and opium dens to the sitting rooms of royalty. Yet Holmes, like Dupin before him, does not inquire, as Marx and Freud did, into the underlying causes of things. Although Holmes is not lacking in compassion, he does display a notable lack of interest in social problems. In this sense, Holmes confirms Franco Moretti's judgment that "Detective Fiction, however, exists expressly to dispel the doubt that guilt might be impersonal, and therefore collective and social" (*Signs Taken for Wonders,* 135).[5] In this respect Conan Doyle is strikingly different from almost every contemporary Victorian literary figure—Carlyle, Arnold, Ruskin, Mill, Eliot, Dickens, Gaskell, the Brontës, Hardy, and others. Holmes and Dupin, as William Stowe points out, "do not, however, open themselves to questions from these clues, they do not allow the objects of their investigations to question their methods or the ideological assumptions that inform them, so they remain prisoners of method, brilliant technicians who can only go on repeating what they already do so well" (*Poetics of Murder,* 374–75). This point may be put somewhat more forcefully: Holmes does not move "away from the methodological *solution* of 'mysteries' toward the philosophical understanding of mystery" (Stowe, 382) because he cannot perform this type of analysis. As an analytical method, empiricism is structurally incapable of theorizing its implantation within the socioeconomic domain, precisely because it admits only observation and experimentation as truly knowable entities. Because most social problems are not susceptible to resolution through the narrow logic of empiricism, these problems fall outside the purview of Holmes's expertise.

In addition, as Horkheimer and Adorno have suggested in *Dialectic of Enlightenment,* the values of the Enlightenment are not merely an abstract form of power, but within capitalism become concrete in the quantification and subjection of human labor and natural resources to laws of profit. Although every capitalist formation is subject to its own distinctive combination of historical conditions and pressures, by definition all are geared to production for profit rather than production for use. The values of empiricism—the emphasis on quantification and utility over qualitative considerations—are the same ones that have come to structure and regulate capitalist economies. Within predominantly capitalist societies, then, these values assume a material power inasmuch as individuals are compelled to conform to the distinctive material pressures exerted on them.

Whether critics or advocates of capitalism, Victorian intellectuals by and large recognized the tremendous energy and transformative power of this integration of Enlightenment values within an economic system. Dickens saw this clearly. His public advocacy on behalf of the disenfranchised and the obvious sympathy for them in his fiction are instances of this, as is the recurring imagery of systemic entropy in his later fiction—society as a prison in *Little Dorrit,* the Court of Chancery in *Bleak House,* the dust-heap in *Our Mutual Friend.* Indeed, Gradgrind in *Hard Times* is a caricature of the unfeeling empiricist. Other Victorian examples include Mill's attempt to enlarge and reform the narrow utilitarianism that so crippled him; Carlyle's condemnation of the "cash-payment nexus"; the Brontës' acute awareness of the subordinate position of women in a class-ridden society; the contrast in Eliot's fiction between an (idealized) organic rural society and the tensions of contemporary England; and the displacement and alienation of Hardy's characters by the forces of rural capitalism. All these literary examples indicate the widespread Victorian reaction against different forms of rationalized capitalism, a reaction that cut across lines of class, gender, and ideology.

By contrast, Conan Doyle's detective fiction is distinctive in its valorization of empirical values and imperialism.[6] He was one of the great Victorian apologists of empire. Between 1893, the year of publication of "The Final Problem," and 1902, the year of publication of *The Hound of the Baskervilles,* the greater part of his energy was devoted to defending the interests of the British Empire. In 1900 he went to the Boer War and enthusiastically worked as a doctor in a field hospital at the front. After returning to England he wrote an impressionistic history entitled *The Great Boer War.* Shortly thereafter, in response to foreign criticism of English conduct in the war, he penned an influential defense entitled *The War in South Africa.* Nor did his efforts end there. In 1914, at the outbreak of World War I, with characteristic energy he quickly turned out a patriotic pamphlet, *To Arms!*

It should be no surprise, then, that Conan Doyle's fiction was shaped by these imperial values. The British Empire was the net result of the extension of the domestic relations of capitalism on an international scale, a process that, as Horkheimer and Adorno have reminded us, was justified and sustained by the abstracting, ethically blind quantitative emphasis on Enlightenment values. Within Conan Doyle's life and work, imperial and Enlightenment values were deeply intertwined, as suggested by his innovations in the form of detective fiction. In *Dreams of Adventure, Deeds of Empire* Martin Green points out that "adventure . . . is the energizing myth of empire" (xi), and he traces the dependence of the adventure genre on the long history of English imperialism, beginning in its modern form in the seventeenth century. Conan Doyle's work thus has a long history behind it. His particular genius was to take the tradition of adventure fiction—a tradition that includes Shakespeare, Aphra Ben, Defoe, and Scott—and to transform it into a recognizably new genre by combining it with other traditions, genres, and values.

The result, however, is not a fiction that engages the issues that one might expect of a genre drawing on these rich traditions, but one that pushes to the margins almost every potentially disruptive subject imaginable—racism, imperialism, class conflict, even women. Yet, as we shall see in *The Sign of Four,* the narrative strategies Conan Doyle uses to contain the threats these elements pose to the ideologies of empire define the limitations of his fiction and, one might even say, his vision.[7]

Ways of Not Seeing

Except for a few scattered references to the wound (sometimes located in the shoulder, sometimes in the leg) that Dr. Watson received in the Afghan war, and the references to India, the enormous national pressures involved in maintaining the empire are scarcely mentioned in *The Sign of Four;* indeed, the subplot of the Agra treasure within *The Sign of Four* is the most extensive treatment of colonial relations in Conan Doyle's oeuvre. Not that this is in any way obligatory, but it is demonstrative of a certain way of seeing, or, more accurately, a way of not seeing. In Conan Doyle's detective fiction, once individuals are designated as cultural "others" by virtue of being foreign, lower-class, or simply female, they are scarcely characterized at all or are only handled in the most stereotypical fashion. Typically, characterization is replaced by an assumption of inferiority. Similarly, whatever cameo roles Indians have in the Sherlock Holmes stories, they are invariably represented stereotypically, as unfathomable exotics of the East. Behind these stereotypes is the assumption that foreigners, especially dark ones, are only important enough to warrant a quick "snapshot" characterization. One notable example is Tonga, Jonathan Small's dwarfish native accomplice in *The Sign of Four* who remains a cipher throughout the novel. Conan Doyle interpolates a gazette's quasi-objective description of the Andaman aborigines as a way of characterizing Tonga: "They are naturally hideous, having large misshapen heads, small fierce eyes, and distorted features. Their feet and hands, however, are remarkably small. So intractable and fierce are they, that all the efforts of the British officials have failed to win them over in any degree. They have always been a terror to shipwrecked crews, braining the survivors with their stone-headed clubs or shooting them with their poisoned arrows. These massacres are invariably concluded by a cannibal feast" (128).

The attitudes expressed here toward the East are what Edward Said has termed "orientalist"; that is, they are part of a larger, culturally bound way of conceiving of the East as exotic, cruel, sensual, opulent, and barbaric such that these characteristics and values are used to naturalize and legitimize Western civilization and its domination over the East. As Said says, "Without examining Orientalism as a discourse one cannot possibly understand the enormously systematic discipline by which European culture was able to manage—and even produce—the Orient politically, sociologically, militarily, ideologically, scientifically and imaginatively during the post-Enlightenment period" (*Orientalism,* 3). Conan Doyle's representation of Tonga and of India in general in *The Sign of Four* is part of a larger, nineteenth-century way of conceiving of the East as a domain requiring the stabilizing influence of the West. "In the system of knowledge about the

Orient," says Said, "the Orient is less a place than a *topos,* a set of references, a congeries of characteristics, that seems to have its origins in a quotation, or a fragment of a text, or a citation from someone's work on the Orient, or some bit of previous imagining, or an amalgam of all these" (177). In *The Sign of Four* the Orient is reduced to "a congeries of characteristics," originating in sensational personal narratives (Jonathan Small's, for example) and fragments from an imperial text. The description of the Andaman aborigines expresses Said's Oriental *topos* in its classical form: The natives are seen as unmitigated savages, wild, barbaric, and cannibalistic. Although they are viewed as exotic, they are also seen as aesthetically inferior to Europeans (they are "naturally hideous"). In addition, they are impervious ("intractable") to the civilizing influence of the West. By contrast, the English are portrayed as being actuated by noble aims rather than vulgar, material ones. The persistently paternalistic tone of Conan Doyle's pseudoethnographic description suggests that these primitives need the civilizing touch of English culture to curb their innate savagery.

All of this is more comprehensible in light of the narrative structure of *The Sign of Four:* On a dreary, unpromising September day, a Miss Morstan calls upon a bored Sherlock Holmes and Dr. Watson in their rooms at 221B Baker Street. Miss Morstan proceeds to tell the following tale: Her father, Captain Arthur Morstan, was an officer in an Indian regiment, the Thirty Fourth Bombay Infantry. Because her mother died when Miss Morstan was a child, the young girl was sent to a boarding school in Edinburgh, where she stayed until she was seventeen. At that time, her father arranged to return to England to visit her. He arranged to meet her at a hotel—but mysteriously he disappeared. Now without both parents, Miss Morstan became a governess. Some years later she was contacted through the newspaper, and subsequently received a pearl in the mail at the same time every year from an anonymous donor. This went on for ten years, at which time she was instructed via a letter, again anonymously, to meet the letter writer outside the Lyceum theater in the evening. It is at this point that Miss Morstan has decided to seek out the help of Holmes and Watson, whom she wants as escorts to her mysterious assignation.

That evening the three of them are met and conveyed by cab to the south London home of Thaddeus Sholto. Thaddeus is one of two sons of Major John Sholto, who was a friend of Captain Morstan's. Thaddeus reveals that his father and Miss Morstan's father came into possession of the famed Agra treasure in India, and that when Captain Morstan arrived in England they met to divide up the treasure. Before they could do so, however, they fell to arguing about shares in the treasure, and as a result Captain Morstan died of "a paroxysm of anger" (103). Fearing recrimination and the discovery of the treasure by the public, Major Sholto secretly disposed of the body and claimed Captain Morstan's share of the treasure. As a result of the treasure and its bloody history, Major Sholto led a prosperous but haunted life. On his deathbed, he was about to reveal to his sons, Thaddeus and Bartholomew, the location of the treasure when he was transfixed by the sight of a malevolent savage face outside the window; consequently he died without revealing the location of the treasure. The only known part of the treasure is a chaplet, pearls of which Thaddeus periodically sends to Miss Morstan in order to ward off destitution.

The novel then shifts to Pondicherry Lodge in Norwood, the manor bought by Major Sholto with the ill-gotten treasure; the manor is currently occupied by Thaddeus's brother, Bartholomew. The foursome—Holmes, Watson, Miss Morstan, and Thaddeus Sholto—drives out to Pondicherry Lodge with the fresh knowledge that Bartholomew has just discovered the location of the treasure. Upon arriving, however, they discover that Bartholomew has been murdered and the Agra treasure taken. The novel now turns to Holmes's and Watson's search for the thief who has stolen Miss Morstan's birthright and presumably killed Bartholomew Sholto. This search culminates with a steam-launch chase on the Thames, in which the miscreant, Jonathan Small, is finally apprehended.

The end of the novel is given over to Jonathan Small's narrative of his involvement with the Agra treasure. His story: At the age of eighteen, he entered the military and was sent to India. Shortly thereafter, he lost his leg in an accident and was discharged from the army, and subsequently became an overseer for a European indigo planter. A short time later, the Indian Mutiny broke out; after witnessing the depredations of "the black fiends" (described in lurid detail), Small escaped to the fortress city of Agra. There he fell in with three Indians who gained possession, through murder, of the magnificent and ancient treasure.

After the Indian Mutiny dies down, Jonathan Small and his three Indian confederates are sentenced to life imprisonment on Blair Island in the Andamans for the murder of the merchant who was conveying the treasure to the fortress city of Agra. There Small meets Captain Morstan and Major Sholto, who are officer guards on the island. Small offers them a portion of the treasure, still hidden in Agra, in exchange for helping him and his Indian accomplices to escape. Morstan and Sholto agree, and oaths on both sides are sworn to honor the agreement—"the sign of four" being used to signify Small's and the Indians' agreement in the deal. Sholto is nominated to recover the treasure in Agra, which he does, but he also betrays the rest, including his friend Morstan, by fleeing with it back to England. In the name of the pact they signed, Small swears his revenge. Years later, he finally manages to escape from the Andaman Islands, taking with him Tonga, a native whom he befriended there. Eventually Small catches up with Sholto in England, but is unable to wreak his revenge upon him before Sholto dies. Although frustrated, Small bides his time until Bartholomew discovers the whereabouts of the treasure. As Bartholomew is recovering the treasure at Pondicherry Lodge, Tonga, mistaking Small's intentions, kills Bartholomew. The novel concludes with two revelations: first, that Small has thrown the treasure in the Thames rather than see anyone else profit from it; second, that Miss Morstan accepts Watson's offer of marriage. By the end of the novel, the reader witnesses Watson's intention to enter into the state of matrimony, and, in an ironic parallel, Small goes to prison. The mysteries of the Agra treasure and Bartholomew's murder are thus solved, and Holmes's empiricism, as usual, is vindicated.

From this précis it is relatively easy to see how Conan Doyle draws on and weaves together conventions from adventure fiction, detective fiction, and sensational literature. The dark and mysterious settings of the novel—from the Gothic atmosphere of Pondicherry Lodge to the gloomy warrens of under-class London—establish *The Sign of Four* as an adventure novel. Indeed, these settings confirm Holmes's heroic virtues—his mental acumen, his resilience, his courage, and so on. Inasmuch as the novel's mystery is rooted in the murderousness and treachery of the Indian Mutiny, Holmes's resolution of the compound mystery (What happened to Captain Morstan? Who killed Bartholomew Sholto? Where is the Agra treasure?) symbolically vanquishes the exotic but violent element of the Orient within Victorian England by means of his unemotional empiricism. Although a most un-English barbarism, in the person of Jonathan Small, manages to penetrate England, it is detected and controlled via Holmes's extraordinary physical and mental prowess. In this way Holmes is able to domesticate the fear of the Orient as represented by the Indian Mutiny at the same time that he is able to justify English imperialism in India.[8] By adopting conventions from adventure fiction, Conan Doyle is able to create a form that naturalizes and hence supports English domination over India. Part of the effectiveness of Conan Doyle's fiction in this respect comes from his use of sensational detail, particularly in his description of the Indian Mutiny itself. The net result is the demonization of the Orient and the implicit affirmation of "civilized" English norms. This dichotomy is evident in the following passage, in which Jonathan Small recounts his involvement in the Indian Mutiny:

> Well, I was never in luck's way long. Suddenly, without a note of warning, the great mutiny broke upon us. One month India lay as still and peaceful, to all appearances, as Surrey or Kent; the next there were two hundred thousand

devils let loose, and the country was a perfect hell.... Well, one fine day the crash came. I had been away on a distant plantation and was riding slowly home in the evening, when my eye fell upon something all huddled together at the bottom of a steep nullah. I rode down to see what it was, and the cold struck through my heart when I found it was Dawson's wife, all cut into ribbons, and half eaten by jackals and native dogs.... I knew then that I could do my employer no good, but would only throw my own life away if I meddled in the matter. From where I stood, I could see hundreds of black fiends, with their red coats on their backs, dancing and howling round the burning house. Some of them pointed at me, and a couple of bullets sang past my head: so I broke away across the paddy fields, and found myself late at night safe within the walls at Agra. (145–46)

Although Small's narrative is only one of three in the novel, it is especially significant in that it discloses the novel's orientalist subtext. Given the subordination of these three partial narratives—Miss Morstan's narrative, Watson's narrative of the search for Small, and Small's narrative of his past—to Holmes's panoptic vision, the engagement of Miss Morstan and Dr. Watson also serves as a symbolic restoration of the horribly violated domesticity of the Dawsons by the spontaneously vicious natives during the mutiny. Their impending marriage symbolically restores order inasmuch as it reintegrates one outcast of English society, Miss Morstan, back into the stability of the disciplinary society through marriage, while another outcast, Jonathan Small, is integrated back into the disciplinary society of nineteenth-century imperial England via its most repressive institution—the prison. Ultimately, what allows for this conservative vision and what makes the form of *The Sign of Four* socially symbolic is its synthesis of ideologically charged conventions from adventure, detective, and sensational literature.

It is not going too far, then, to suggest that in Conan Doyle's fiction, political problems become decorations, part of a colorful background. The observation of class conflict, the representation of which for most Victorians constituted a necessary part of any general representation of society, becomes decorative, even quaint in Conan Doyle. Holmes's contact with the London underclass is similarly rhetorical: it is not so much represented as it is referred to.[9] The same is true of women, with the possible exception of Irene Adler in "A Scandal in Bohemia," the only woman in the world worthy of Holmes's admiration. Holmes observes women in great detail, and yet to him, as to Freud, they are a dark continent, as he readily admits in "The Illustrious Client": "Women's heart and mind are insoluble puzzles to the male. Murder might be condoned or explained, and yet some smaller offence might rankle" (*The Complete Sherlock Holmes*, 988).

Many of these strategies of exclusion are understandable in terms of imperialism and its related ideologies. Racism is one such ideology, and it has long served as an excuse for Western imperialism. In the nineteenth century, at the height of British expansionism, many took comfort in the rationalization that people of color were not fully human. This belief, so widely accepted that it often did not seem to be an opinion, had the advantage that it also functioned as a rationale for imperial domination. If a country had not independently achieved an advanced stage of industrialization and militarization, this signified a social and cultural backwardness, an inferiority on behalf of its people. According to this logic, it then became the duty of the developed nations to educate, civilize, and improve these primitive peoples. In this way, exploitation appeared as enlightenment.

As Arctic adventurer, Boer War field doctor, British propagandist, and writer of detective fiction, Conan Doyle ratified this imperial ideology of enlightenment. His adherence to it was the precondition, as it were, of the direction in which he took the adventure/detective genre: ever since *Robinson Crusoe,* one of the fundamental conventions of the adventure genre has been the diminished claim of affective ties on the heroic adventurer; we know more about Man Friday than we do about Crusoe's wife. Because the adventure genre stakes a claim to a type of experience completely different from that of the domestic novel or the novel of manners, little attention is given to social relationships—whether of love, marriage, family, or work. Instead what is stressed is action, the overcoming of challenge, and the hero's heroic virtues. Conan Doyle's incorporation of this convention and his acceptance of an ideology assuming female inferiority are responsible for the effacement of women from his narratives.

The argument that I have been making is not that Conan Doyle's fiction fails because it isn't progressive enough; rather, it is that his fiction is constrained by his narrow ideological outlook. Ultimately, these limitations on ways of seeing translate into severe formal constraints: if any English novelist in the 1880s and 1890s found it necessary to exclude the aspirations of women, the relations between the sexes, the tension between classes, and the experience of imperialism, and focused only on the exotic crimes that at most beset a narrow section of the professional middle class, then obviously there would be whole areas of social experience incapable of being represented and evaluated. Conan Doyle's work stands as one of the most extreme examples of the narrowed social vision of English writers in the late-Victorian period, a narrowness that, as Raymond Williams has argued, is attributable to the increasing cultural divide between an immensely strong and sophisticated bourgeois order and working-class culture.[10]

It would be misleading, however, to leave the impression that Conan Doyle's achievement is purely negative. Despite his extremely narrow social vision, Conan Doyle succeeded in bridging the gap between dominant (bourgeois) and subaltern (lower-middle and working class) cultures by bringing together in a single genre traditions that had previously been separate: although adventure literature and sensational literature were often read across class lines, this was not as true of detective fiction, as the example of Poe illustrates. Ultimately, Conan Doyle was not able to legitimize detective fiction as "serious": he could give it a new popularity, but he could not give it full literary respectability. Conan Doyle's hybrid genre was enormously successful in another respect, however. Through the figure of Sherlock Holmes, and through the empirical values he championed, Conan Doyle's fiction ratified the principles and ideologies of an imperial, patriarchal Britain. The conventions of sensation and adventure that Conan Doyle incorporated into his fiction enlivened and dramatized what would otherwise be static tales of ratiocination in the style of Poe. Although they give the stories excitement and suspense, these conventions are subordinated finally to the logical exigencies and the need for resolution typical of the detective-story genre. The strategy in Conan Doyle's detective fiction of marginalizing subjects capable of calling into question the narrow empirical ideology by which Holmes lives, of refusing to question Holmes's method and the causes of crime, and of avoiding any overt consideration of social questions regulates his vision, his characterization (or lack thereof) of women and non-Europeans, and the social base of his fiction, and finally creates the need for a vigorous and rich realistic style capable of offsetting these other deficiencies. In short, to an extent unusual in realist fiction, this radically conservative vision and the narrative absences that result from it determine almost every formal aspect of Conan Doyle's fiction.

Popularizing the Empire

Conan Doyle's detective fiction did not simply *reflect* a preformed, given, monolithic middle-class ideology; instead, his reworking of an ideology of empiricism in a popular form helped *produce* a comforting and reassuring image of society untroubled by sexual, economic, or social pressures. This image of late-Victorian society is itself ideological, and ultimately functions to produce consent to the existing socioeconomic order. Antonio Gramsci has argued that the production of consent among those governed in Western democracies is the most crucial element in maintaining and reproducing existing social relations. For Gramsci, the reproduction of social relations in capitalist society consists less in domination by force than in the struggle for what he terms "hegemony"—the struggle by different classes, blocs, and groups for moral, cultural, and ultimately political leadership over society. Hegemony, in other words, is not achieved in democracies by a mailed fist; instead it is acquired by getting the various groups and classes of society, especially the subordinate ones, to consent to the rule of the dominant classes. Within this theory of hegemony, popular culture is of the utmost importance inasmuch as it becomes the locus for the acceptance, rejection, resistance, incorporation, or hybridization of dominant values, beliefs, feelings, and ways of seeing.[11] To paraphrase Tony Bennett, popular culture is neither the site of a people's deformation (this was the emphasis of the Frankfurt school and some varieties of structural Marxism) nor of their own self-making (the culturalist emphasis of E. P. Thompson and others) but a field shaped by these conflicting pressures (*Popular Culture and Social Relations*, xiii).

The historical context of Conan Doyle's work is best understood in the light of this tension between human agency and ideological determination. His relations to the hegemonic values of late-Victorian England were complex; his detective fiction, however, did not simply affirm these values, but as a great popularizer of empiricism, it helped to produce them. His fiction, that is, helped to define the kinds of beliefs to which a reasonable, educated Victorian or Edwardian gentleman might subscribe. Through Sherlock Holmes, the image of science as cold, abstract, and impersonal changed, was given a human face. Conan Doyle showed that the scientific method could be interesting to the layman. He did not work this shift in perception singlehandedly—Victorian science fiction also contributed to this change—but his valorization of the efficacy of the scientific method was influential precisely because it was transmitted through a popular form.

At this point it is useful to recall Foucault's dictum "that there is no power relation without the correlative constitution of a field of knowledge, nor any knowledge that does not presuppose and constitute at the same time power relations" (*Discipline and Punish*, 27). As we have seen, the Victorian context confirms this correlation of knowledge and power: The values and methodologies of the Enlightenment provided the indispensable conceptual and material conditions for the organization of capitalism and, later, the British Empire; that knowledge created that form of power. Sherlock Holmes's knowledge, his ability to unravel the most intractable puzzles, gives him the power to penetrate the mysteries of London. The same form of knowledge that ultimately produced the empire also produced the figure of the empirical detective hero, Sherlock Holmes. Within the economy of power in late-Victorian England, the Sherlock Holmes myth produced consent to this economy by simplification and omission, processes that perform the naturalizing function of myth, as Roland Barthes has observed in *Mythologies:* "In passing from history to nature, myth acts economically: it abolishes the complexity of human acts, it gives them the simplicity of essences, it does away with all dialectics, with any going back beyond what is immediately visible, it organizes a world which is without contradictions because it is without depth, a world wide open and wallowing in the evident, it establishes a blissful clarity: things appear to mean something by themselves" (143). This is the world of Sherlock Holmes—a world in which crime is intriguing, individual, and eminently soluble, not an ugly social problem; a world in which urban squalor makes a quaint contrast to the elegance of London hansom cabs and gas street lamps; a world undisturbed by conflict, whether sexual or social. The myth of Sherlock Holmes is, therefore, a myth of England as well.

The myth lives on in books, films, and games. Recently I came across a large, illustrated omnibus edition of Conan Doyle's detective stories. It was a maroon, cloth-bound edition with gilded pages and a spine with raised horizontal lines—a bad imitation of the handsome Victorian novel. Yet it is remarkable that 100 years after Sherlock Holmes first made his appearance in *Beetons's Christmas Annual,* Conan Doyle's work still sells in popular editions published for the Christmas trade. The publishers of this particular edition were willing to further mar this impression of antiquity by including a foreword by Donald Friedman, warning the twentieth-century reader of Holmes's prejudices: "Our late nineteenth-century cavalier is not without his faults: the modern reader must ignore the sometimes jarring racism, distrust of foreigners, and condescension toward women with which Conan Doyle peppers his stories. If he does so, the reader will find himself engrossed in a fictional world most satisfying to enter" (Conan Doyle, *The Illustrated Sherlock Holmes,* viii). Despite the century's worth of social change reflected in such a caveat, the Holmes myth lives on, in more ways than one. The point is, Conan Doyle's work doesn't deserve to be disparaged or excused. It deserves instead to be understood—for all its complexity and for all its limitations.

Notes

1. For a more complete account of the origin of crime fiction, see Stephen Knight's *Form and Ideology in Crime Fiction,* especially chapter 1.

2. This is a recurring emphasis in Mikhail Bakhtin's work, especially in the essays collected under the title *The Dialogic Imagination.*

3. This formulation of the ideological structure of reason draws on the work of Max Horkheimer and Theodor Adorno in *Dialectic of Enlightenment,* and on Horkheimer's essay "The End of Reason" (collected in *The Essential Frankfurt School Reader*).

4. For more on the way in which the *form* of a literary text articulates and produces ideologies that may not be explicitly articulated, see Fredric Jameson's *Marxism and Form,* especially chapter 5. Also see Terry Eagleton's more program-

matic but instructive early work, *Criticism and Ideology,* especially chapters 2 and 3.

5. Although Moretti's comment is true of the formal English novel of detection (Christie, Sayers, and Allingham), it is not true of hard-boiled fiction, which tends to implicate society at large in criminal activity. I also take issue with Moretti's argument, contained in the chapter entitled "Clues," that as a genre crime fiction is "anti-literary" (148). Moretti's dismissal of crime fiction is part of a larger dismissal of mass culture in general: "Mass culture is, in this way, a full-fledged example of cultural fetishism" (152). As I argued in chapter 1, this unreconstructed Frankfurt-school approach to mass culture is highly problematic.

6. Paul M. Sweezy in *The Theory of Capitalist Development* offers a succinct characterization of this complex social and economic phenomenon: "Imperialism may be defined as a stage in the development of the world economy in which (a) several advanced capitalist countries stand on a competitive footing with respect to the world market for industrial products; (b) monopoly form of capital is the domi-nant form of capital; and (c) the contradictions of the accumulation process have reached such maturity that capital export is an outstanding feature of world eco-nomic relations. As a consequence of these basic economic conditions, we have two further characteristics: (d) severe rivalry in the world market leading to cutthroat competition and internal market combines; and (e) the territorial division of 'unoccupied' parts of the world among the major capitalist powers (and their satellites)" (307).

7. The argument that I am misreading Conan Doyle by projecting into the past purely contemporary concerns can, I think, be summarily dealt with. Many Victorians, both men and women, took as their subject precisely these issues. The Brontës, Eliot, Mill, and, later, James were deeply concerned about the plight of women. Hardy and Dickens, to mention only two among many, took the inequalities of class society as the subject of their fiction. H. G. Wells's *War of the Worlds* is an allegory of imperialism. And if few English novelists directly addressed racism, prejudice is a ubiquitous theme in Victorian literature.

8. This is consistent with Victorian representations of the Indian Mutiny in general. In *Rule of Darkness: British Literature and Imperialism, 1830–1914,* Patrick Brantlinger writes: "Victorian accounts of the mutiny display extreme forms of extropunitive projection, the racist pattern of blaming the victim expressed in terms of an absolute polarization of good and evil, innocence and guilt, justice and injustice, moral restraint and sexual depravity, civilization and barbarism. These categories are perceived as racially determined attributes in an imperialist allegory that calls for the total subjuga-tion of India and at times for the wholesale extermination of Indians.... After the Mutiny... India is portrayed as mired in changeless patterns of superstition and violence which can be dominated but not necessarily altered for the better" (200).

9. I am indebted to Stephen Knight for this point. See *Form and Ideology in Crime Fiction,* especially page 83.

10. In *Politics and Letters* Williams advances the following thesis: "Now in the same period [the last two decades of the nineteenth century], there had also been a very deep and successful reorganization of bourgeois cultural and educational institutions: the creation of the new public schools, the renovation of Oxford and

Cambridge, the development of a fully extended bourgeois press, the modernization of publishing. Together with these changes went an increasing centralization in London, which now functioned much more as an imperial cultural capital. The result was an integrated and confident set of bourgeois cultural institutions such as had never existed in any previous period of English history. The social basis of the writers themselves had a much more limited experience. The characteristic change is from a George Eliot to a Forster. Now Forster proclaims the same aims as George Eliot, but there are areas of social experience to which he is no longer open" (263).

11. For more on the importance of popular culture in the maintenance of social relations, see Antonio Gramsci's *Selections from Cultural Writings.*

Part II

Empire and Espionage: The "Great Game" Begins

The Heroic Spy Novel:
Kim and the Rhetoric of the
Great Game

4

> Orientalism is never far from what Denys Hay has called the idea of Europe, a collective notion identifying "us" Europeans against all "those" non-Europeans, and indeed it can be argued that the major component in European culture is precisely what made that culture hegemonic both in and outside Europe: the idea of European identity as a superior one in comparison with all the non-European peoples and cultures.
>
> —*Edward Said,* Orientalism

The Dominant Viewpoint

Many critics on both the left and right have observed that *Kim* is an imperialist novel. This almost self-evident proposition scarcely seems likely to provoke much argument. Yet it is interesting to note that any uncritical acceptance of this proposition obscures a somewhat less evident point: that *Kim* is not in any obvious way "about" the Indian experience of colonialism and indeed successfully excludes this traumatic national experience from the novel. As a formal and ideological "structure of experience," *Kim* is founded on this contradiction—it is an imperialist novel that at the same time denies the Indian experience of colonialism. This contradiction is common to many English colonial novels, but what is distinctive about *Kim* is the way in which this exclusion functions as part of the rationale of empire that, since Kipling, has become one major tradition in espionage fiction, the tradition of the heroic spy novel.

Kim, then, may fairly be taken as the most typical of the Englishman-in-India novels in that it embodies a way of seeing India that derives from what Edward Said, in his introduction to the novel, calls "the dominating viewpoint" of a nation that, with few exceptions, regarded English rule as natural, beneficial, even ordained. This way of seeing, this tacit acceptance of English supremacy and Eastern inferiority, profoundly affects the formal composition of the novel. *Kim* is a historical novel in the narrow sense that it embodies an ideology of ascendancy typical of English imperialism, but is ahistorical in the sense that Kipling's acceptance of this attitude in relation to India tends to transform his select observations of Indian life into timeless, universal truths. Because of his adherence to this attitude Kipling was unable to grasp the enormous changes in India produced by the imposition of colonial rule. In *Kim,* Kipling lovingly recreated an India populated by artisans, an India structured and regulated by ancient customs and traditions. Yet this India had already been radically transformed by the English "reformations" that eventually led to the Indian Mutiny of 1857. These "reformations" dispossessed or altered nearly every class: the new system of higher education based on the English model dispossessed the old religious elite; the egalitarian emphasis of the judicial system insulted the honor of the highest castes; the new economic system of free trade turned blacksmiths, weavers, shoemakers, and other urban artisans into beggars; and the wholesale imposition of capitalist agrarian methods on rural India, with the new profit-oriented disposition of land by individual ownership, fixed money rents, and the unrestricted sale of "encumbered estates," collectively destroyed the centuries-old pattern of rural life (Porter, *The Lion's Share,* 32–33).

It is ironic that Kipling—a writer renowned for his keen eye and genuine appreciation for artisanal labor—sees none of this. Indeed, *Kim* is distinctive in that feelings of social displacement, dispossession, or even mere disaffection are entirely absent. And yet Kipling's failure to grasp the consequences of the imperial ideology he publicly championed is not merely a local irony, detachable from history at large. Rather, this paradox is part of the paradox of imperialism in general. Historically speaking, English preeminence in the imperial arena began to wane in the last quarter of the nineteenth century, and, largely as a result, the major European nations engaged in an intense competition for raw materials, cheap labor, new markets, "new" territories, "new" countries. In South Africa this competition led to the Boer War; similar conflicts would culminate some years later in the Great War. For literary analysis, however, these common historical facts are less important than the ideologies that both supported and grew out of this phase of imperial domination. To Kipling, as to most Victorians and Edwardians, imperialism did not signify disruption, exploitation, or subjugation but economic development and moral enlightenment. The paradox of imperial ideologies is that they do not appear to be motivated by any but the highest moral values. Imperialism was not so much a narrow political subject discussed in Whitehall as an accepted way of life, a culture that permeated the aesthetic, moral, and social life of the nation. In *Propaganda and Empire* John Mackenzie notes that in Victorian England it was virtually impossible to buy a bar of soap or a tin of biscuits without being reminded of the glories of the British Empire. Picture postcards, cigarette cards, boys' journals, music-hall entertainment (especially of the upper- and middle-class variety), advertisements, sheet music, the cinema, novels, textbooks, and the self-named "imperial propaganda societies" all exalted the benefits and romance of the empire.[1] With the popularization of board games and jigsaw puzzles, the Great Game of the empire—the term used in British society to refer to the imperial experience and the intrigue that sustained it—quite literally became a game, but unlike the Great Game of espionage, it was played within the safe confines of the middle-class Victorian household.

The espionage novel emerged out of this culture of imperialism, for the general subject of all modern espionage novels, then as now, is the threat posed to a nation by a foreign power or conspiracy, whether external or internal. The modern spy novel, that is, takes imperialism, with its attendant systems of domination and political intrigue, as its necessary precondition. *Kim* is part of a body of literature that responded to the fear of a foreign conspiracy against Great Britain, a fear that was especially prevalent in the years leading up to the Great War. In *The Spy Story* John Cawelti and Bruce Rosenberg note that "in Britain, in addition to the growing fear of anarchism and later violence, an increasing anxiety about foreign invasion paved the way for the growing popularity of the espionage adventure" (38). One historical response to this anxiety was an extension and refinement between 1900 and 1915 of the techniques of surveillance on the domestic population and on external enemies, real or perceived.[2] To a considerable extent, then, the Great Game of imperialism turned, and still turns, on surveillance, the covert search for knowledge that allows one group or nation to preserve or thwart the designs of another group or nation.

In early espionage novels, the Great Game, the name for the covert activities performed by those in the secret service, is an important element in the imperial enterprise. The dramatic suspense and interest of these novels derives largely from the predicament of the protagonist, who typically is responsible for the destiny of a group or nation by searching for the knowledge that will allow him to protect the interests of the collective he represents. Within the espionage novel, knowledge-as-power takes on a new level of meaning, for in this genre knowledge determines the fate of nations. There is an obvious continuity here from the conventions of detective fiction, where detection, the search for knowledge, plays such a decisive role. But the difference between detective fiction and espionage fiction is that in the latter, the detective function takes on, to adopt Georg Lukács's phrase, a "world-historical" significance: it is no longer just the fates of individuals that are at risk, but, in the case of England, and English literature, the fate of a proud imperial nation; indeed, in many cases, what is at stake is the course of history itself.

In espionage fiction's valorization of exotic settings, the life of action, and the heroic individual—as well as in its denigration of domesticity, lack of interest in women, and rejection of the conventions of the psychological novel—it is possible, then, to see the continuation of the masculinist adventure tradition. In this sense, espionage fiction is a hybrid of adventure and detective fiction, transformed by the imperatives of an imperial age already in decay. In the remainder of this section, I will examine these ideological imperatives as they are contained within the rhetoric of the Great Game by focusing on two texts crucial to the development of the spy thriller, *Kim* and *The Secret Agent*. My general aim is to see how this rhetoric produces two different views of the Victorian culture of imperialism, and, formally speaking, two very different novels. These novels illustrate the two main paths that secret-agent adventure has taken in this century. Whereas *Kim* may be taken as the precursor to the romantic and heroic tradition of John Buchan, E. Phillips Oppenheim, and Ian Fleming, *The Secret Agent* may be seen as the forerunner of the critical or ironic tradition of Somerset Maugham, Graham Greene, Eric Ambler, and John Le Carré.

The Style of Empire

Kim is an espionage novel in the form of a bildungsroman. Briefly, the story concerns the fate of Kimball O'Hara, a young street boy in India orphaned by the death of his father, a former color sergeant in an Irish regiment. Because Kim's mother died giving birth, he is brought up by a half-caste Indian woman. Although Kim is European, his sunburnt complexion and facility with languages allow him to pass for a native. Kim lives by his wits and is never daunted by circumstance. One day a Tibetan lama comes to Lahore in search of the holy River of the Arrow that will cleanse him of all sin. Struck by the possibility of travel and adventure, Kim takes up with the lama and becomes his *chela* or disciple. The lama and Kim set about their search. On the road Kim meets an old friend, Mahbub Ali, a horse trader who is also a member of the British Secret Service. Kim delivers a coded message for him to a British officer in Umballa. The message indicates that thousands of troops are to be sent to the North to put down an uprising. Shortly thereafter, Kim and the lama stumble upon Kim's father's regiment. They discover Kim's identity and plan to send him away to school. Kim is separated from the lama, who nevertheless manages to pay for Kim's education at St. Xavier's, a Catholic school in Lucknow. But before Kim leaves for Lucknow, Mahbub Ali draws the attention of Colonel Creighton, the director of the British Secret Service, to Kim's many talents. Impressed by him,

Colonel Creighton hints that he might eventually become a valuable member of the secret service.

From this time on, Kim leads a double life as a student: during his school holidays, he works as a junior secret agent and *chela* to the lama. In his travels with the lama he meets many people on the road and involves himself in many intrigues. Much of the color and variety of India, for which *Kim* is famous, is depicted in the course of these exploits. Yet Kim's acceptance of the role of *chela* to the lama is not just a cover for his espionage activities, although it clearly has that purpose as well. What is interesting about the novel is that Kim really is devoted to the lama and his quest. To him, there is no contradiction between being a spy and being a spiritual disciple. For Kipling, espionage in the service of empire and the quest for spiritual harmony are complementary activities: at the end of the novel, the lama discovers the purifying holy River of the Arrow, and Kim, through his espionage, discovers his identity and earns for himself a role in the preservation of the empire as a member of the British Secret Service.

Throughout the novel Kim thinks of the business of espionage as a game. This is not simply an instance of naïveté or boyish ignorance. Kim quickly apprehends the dangers the game poses as well as the geopolitical stakes involved. But the association of espionage with games in *Kim* extends beyond the novel and indicates an immensely influential way of thinking about the British Secret Service in India that was widespread in Britain, indeed actively propagated in Victorian and Edwardian schools. In *Athleticism and the Victorian and Edwardian Public School* J. A. Mangan attributes the British belief in their colonial mission largely to the ideology of athleticism in public schools:

> It was the new imperialism of late Victorian Britain which produced the precarious fusion of Christian gentility and social Darwinism. Three sets of values became enmeshed: imperial Darwinism—the God-granted right of the white man to rule, civilise and baptise the inferior colored races; institutional Darwinism—the cultivation of physical and psychological stamina at school in preparation for the rigours of imperial duty; the gentleman's education—the nurture of leadership qualities for military conquest abroad and political dominance at home. In this amalgam Christianity came out second best. (136)

The practice of habitually thinking of the domination and exploitation of inferior races as a game effectively displaced questions of ethics and legitimacy to the realm of sportsmanship. At the same time, the habit of thinking of colonialism as a game offered the dominant country the consolation that there were rules that were being followed, that an ethic of sorts was being observed, and that the contemporary colonial situation was the result of fair play. Thus the public sporting world was explicitly connected to the ruling and maintaining of empire in a self-congratulatory and moralistic fashion.[3]

As a literary reworking of the experience of empire, *Kim* articulates with great verve its own version of these imperial beliefs. Nowhere in the novel is the British right to rule India challenged. On the contrary, Kipling creates a number of minor Indian characters whose specific function is to ratify the legitimacy of English rule. Kipling was not unique in this respect; most Victorian intellectuals either actively supported British imperialism or silently acquiesced to it. But this attitude of complicity does define a novelistic point of view that has formal consequences. Again, this can be clearly seen in the style of the novel. In the following passage, Kim, before falling asleep, muses to himself about his past and future as a participant in the Great Game:

> Well is the Game called great! I was four days a scullion at Quetta, waiting on the wife of the man whose book I stole. And that was part of the Great Game! From the South—God knows how far—came up the Mahratta, playing the Great Game in fear of his life. Now I shall go far and far into the North playing the Great Game. Truly, it runs like a shuttle throughout all Hind. And my share and my joy . . . I owe to the lama here. Also to Mahbub Ali—also to Creighton Sahib, but chiefly to the Holy One. He is right—a great and wonderful world— and I am Kim—Kim—Kim—alone—one person in the middle of it all. (273)

In this passage, Kipling makes use of the language of worship to emphasize the characteristics that the Great Game has enabled Kim to develop— spirituality, maturity, and identity. Rhetorically speaking, the passage's hesitancies, exclamations, and parenthetical statements exemplify Kipling's facility for recreating a sense of the rhythms of natural speech; at the same time, the piling up of these coordinate clauses suggests a sense of beneficence, of blessing added to blessing. This is appropriate, as the function of the passage within the novel is to glorify a world of almost limitless possibility, a world to which the lama and Colonel Creighton have given Kim access. This passage is an affirmation of self, of Kim's newly discovered identity and place within the world. But it is also a radical affirmation of the lama's conservative and rather innocent worldview. Two modes of perception are linked here: while Kim attains this new sense of self, he also arrives at a beatific vision of India, spiritually defined by the values of the lama and politically defined by the necessity of espionage as a way of keeping India within the British Empire.

But the passage also underscores how Kipling's "dominating viewpoint" affects the novel's style. The imposition of a poeticism such as "it [the Great Game] runs like a shuttle throughout all Hind" is clearly authorial, and is unlikely to occur to a sleepy boy, even one as resourceful as Kim: Kim's discourse, that is, is overridden by Kipling's. This is not particularly egregious, but in a small way it indicates a larger pattern of exclusion in *Kim*. For all its apparent breadth and appreciation of the variety of Indian races, customs, castes, cultures, and languages, the novel attempts to neutralize whatever oppositional elements exist within them. In a similar vein, Edward Said has noticed how Kipling's emotional and ideological investment in the values of empire translates at the level of character into a principle of selection. Speaking of the Great Mutiny of 1857, Said notes in his introduction to *Kim* that Kipling chose an old, loyalist Indian soldier as his spokesman:

> Moreover, when Kipling has the old soldier describe the British counter-revolt— with all its horrendous reprisals by white men bent on 'moral' action—as calling the Indian mutineers 'to most strict account,' we have left the world of history and entered the world of imperialist polemic, in which the native is naturally delinquent, the white man the stern but moral parent and judge. The point about this brief episode is not that it gives us the extreme British view on the Mutiny, but that Kipling puts it in the mouth of an Indian whose much more likely nationalist counterpart is never seen in the novel at all. (26)

In this sense, Kipling seeks to minimize the polyphonic structure of *Kim:* the novel offers almost no vantage point from which the reader can evaluate competing points of view, no belief system that calls into question the values and rationales that inform the novel's imperial vision of India. The diverse voices and languages within the novel are thus somewhat deceptive, for they do not so much signify an abundance of different beliefs, points of view, or ideologies as reveal the extent to which Kipling's imperialistic vision excludes them. Indeed, Kipling uses the multiplicity of languages and voices to suggest that the different cultures of India find stability and unity in their status as parts of the empire.

Contrary to the popular perception of the novel, *Kim* does not show us the clash of cultures within India, much less the clash between East and West. What Kipling offers instead is an almost completely harmonized vision of Indian society and one radically removed from historical actuality. Although this vision produces a unity of tone—a feeling of buoyancy, of possibility, of expansiveness, a sense that for Kim, anyway, the world is not capricious but benevolent—by virtue of its intensity and narrowness, the vision is incapable of entering into other ways of thinking, other ways of seeing. It would be unfair to say that the style of *Kim* is mere reportage, but it does share some of that genre's conventions: a detached and omniscient observer; a seemingly neutral stance toward "political" matters; a reliance on a "realistic" mode of representation; an attraction to "local color"; and the avoidance of narrative devices that call attention to the process of composition. In short, Kipling's dominating point of view means that there is little dialogic interaction between what Henry James referred to as different "centers of consciousness": because there is only one authorially ratified center of consciousness, there is only one style. That is to say, there is no interaction between different styles such that they call into question the ideological presuppositions of the dominant, pseudo-objective, descriptive style of the novel. Despite the Indian words and phrases incorporated into the novel, there is little attempt to grasp the cultures that those languages articulate, beyond the relatively superficial, quasi-cinematic appeal they hold as markers of the legendary variety of India. To a great extent, then, the homogeneous, descriptive style of *Kim* derives from the detached stance of the colonial observer.

Pax Anglo-Saxonica

As George Orwell noted in his celebrated essay "Rudyard Kipling," Kipling was not a fascist but a "prophet of imperialism in its expansionist phase" (*A Collection of Essays by George Orwell,* 118). In his biography *The Strange Ride of Rudyard Kipling,* Angus Wilson points out that Kipling despised progressivism, pacifism, socialism, trade unions, democracy, and all manner of liberal and left-wing politics, which he lumped together under the epithet "howling syndicalism." But he was also hostile to the "traditional, elitist country-house world" (233). To Kipling, the aristocracy was an effete formation that, through sheer ineptitude, had allowed the narrow-minded middle class to get the upper hand, thereby opening the way to the disintegration of the country into class hatred and apathy (238–46 *passim*). Kipling believed that Britain could create a Pax Anglo-Saxonica that would be the basis for social regeneration and revitalization (241). Wilson argues that Kipling's ideal society is one "organised along army lines, a classless society like a boy-scout jamboree" (243), and sees his affinity for hierarchies as a crucial element in his work. It is true that in *Kim* Kipling's affinity for hierarchies can be seen in his depiction of the British Secret Service as a more dangerous, but also more gratifying, version of the Boy Scouts. There is, however, nothing classless about the army, the Boy Scouts, or, for that matter, the British Secret Service. On the contrary, all of these organizations are essentially hierarchical, organized around a well-defined chain of command, and functioning on the basis of rank. And in Kipling's time, army officers' ranks were largely filled by members of the middle- and upper-middle classes.

The image of society that emerges from his work as a whole is not a classless one, but one specifically based on class or caste. Within this hierarchically organized society, each individual has an identity, but also a role and a function in the reproduction of the social order. The image of the ideal society that emerges in *Kim* is the result of this paternalistic, quasi-feudal imperial ideology. The careful description of different castes, the attention to different manners, the scrupulous detail given to religious differences, and the elimination of any internal social conflict from the novel all testify to Kipling's identification with this outlook. To Kipling, India's caste system represents the embodiment of his feudal ideal. Kipling delights in the cultural differences that stratify Indian society and give it an order imperceptible to most westerners:

> They [the lama and Kim] met a troop of long-haired, strong-scented Sansis with baskets of lizards and other unclean food on their backs, their lean dogs sniffing at their heels. These people kept their own side of the road, moving at a quick, furtive jog-trot, and all other castes gave them ample room; for the Sansi is deep pollution. Behind them, walking wide and stiffly across the strong shadows, the memory of his leg-irons still on him, strode one newly released from the jail; his full stomach and shiny skin to prove that the Government fed its prisoners better than most honest men could feed themselves. Kim knew that walk well, and made broad jest of it as they passed. Then an Akali, a wild-eyed, wild-haired Sikh devotee in the blue-checked clothes of his faith, with polished steel quoits glistening on the cone of his tall blue turban, stalked past, returning from a visit to one of the independent Sikh states, where he had been singing the ancient glories of the khalsa to college-trained princelings in top boots and white-cord breeches. Kim was careful not to irritate that man; for the Akali's temper is short and his arm quick. (109)

Kim, clearly, asserts that the many peoples within India exist in a delicate, intricate balance with one another. But this order is not, for Kipling, organic. It must be achieved. The hierarchy must be *managed;* most of all, it must have duty-minded, moral administrators dedicated to the maintenance of order and vigilant against outside threats.

For Kipling, significantly, social order and social justice are possible only if the rules of the Great Game are observed. As "legitimate" rulers, the British establish the rules and enjoy the authority their privileged position affords; this is even true of the sahib boy, Kim. Within the ideology of imperialism, as benevolent rulers at the top of the social scale, the British ensure an orderly, systematic mode of government. Below them the complex caste system obtains. Historically, these two tiers coexisted in varying degrees of tension, and sometimes outright conflict. But the paternalistic ideology of *Kim* does not permit the representation of any widespread popular conflict, for this would call into question the legitimacy of English rule, which forms the unspoken premise of the novel. The only dissent alluded to in *Kim* is the conspiracy hatched by the traitorous kings in the northern part of the country, and their action, significantly, appears not to have been motivated by ideological reasons but by greed.

In the interests of maintaining the empire, surveillance is of course required, but in *Kim* it is applied to the threat of a foreign or foreign-inspired conspiracy; within the ideology of the novel, the possibility of any internal, popular uprising seems remote. Kim himself undertakes various kinds of surveillance early in the novel and quickly grasps the power of this knowledge. Two relatively minor moments in the narrative are illustrative. In the first instance, Kim saves the life of Mahbub Ali by eavesdropping on the conversation of his would-be assassins. The second example occurs shortly afterwards. Kim's first act of commissioned espionage, we recall, was to transmit a secret message to a British officer in Umballa, with the result that thousands of troops were moved to the north to put down the uprising—a bit of knowledge that Kim later uses to good effect when attempting to convince the soldiers in the Maverick regiment that he possesses prophetic powers. But even before his formal education at St Xavier's, Kim demonstrates his knowledge of the rules of the Great Game. As he says to Colonel Creighton, "It is not good to sell knowledge for nothing" (167).

Indeed, the supreme example of the power of knowledge in the novel is Colonel Creighton. His encyclopedic grasp of the intricacies of Indian society and his appreciation of the uniqueness and diversity of Indian culture are rooted in his recognition that knowledge of India is paramount in controlling India. "There is," he says to Kim, "no sin so great as ignorance" (167). Creighton also exemplifies Kipling's profound respect for ordinary men of action, those unrecognized individuals responsible for the construction, maintenance, administration, and protection of the empire. Creighton, like Kipling, appreciates craftsmanship and devotion to work and its traditions; to both, work signifies discipline and, more particularly, submission to the class or caste limitations it imposes on the individual. For Kipling labor is never alienating. It is always projected as the fulfillment of the individual.

Kipling sees *types* of work with great discrimination, but he does not see the systematic appropriation of that labor or the economic and political system that enables it, as, for example, Conrad does. Despite his fascination with machinery and technology, Kipling possesses an idealistic, essentially artisanal conception of the social relations of labor. It is significant that the social formation founded on this mode of production was feudalism. Just as the juridical basis of feudalism was defined by the authority of the sovereign will, so in *The Jungle Book* is the observance of "the Law" sovereign. For Kipling the ideal society is the projection of "the Law" in social terms. In this respect, the ideal society imitates the law of the natural order, and, given that society's implicit affirmation of social Darwinism, it is almost inevitable that Kipling should see the structure of society idealistically, as a copy of the natural order in which hierarchies of power are determined by the survival of the fittest.

Morality and the Great Game

One result of this way of seeing is that there is no sense of history as process in Kipling's work. Consequently, the dominant image of society in *Kim* has a timeless quality. Clearly, for Kipling, society *is* eternal, representing an order mandated by nature and, for all of its complexity, existing in a timeless dimension, divorced from change, from continuity, ultimately from history. This is the price exacted for Kipling's dependence on a monologic style: unwilling to create a novel representing the contestation of cultures in all their stylistic and ideological specificity, Kipling produced a romantic, dehistoricized version of India, rather than the empathetic and unbiased novel of Indian life that *Kim* is so often taken to be.

Another indication of this monologic, romantic style is the discrepancy in the novel between physical and linguistic specificity: although Indians are scrupulously distinguished in terms of their appearance, they are scarcely ever distinguished linguistically; that is, they are not, as a rule, given the same linguistic individuality that Europeans in the novel have. By and large, they do not speak with the authority of the European characters; instead, they are spoken for. This, too, is the inevitable result of the position of the colonial observer that Kipling assumes throughout the novel.

Kipling's political vision is ultimately identified with moral sense. Since for him the social order is fated, power too is ordained: because the social order is moral, it cannot corrupt. For Kipling power is not intrinsically corrupting, but a discipline that cultivates the virtues. Power is ennobling. Creighton is political, but within Kipling's moral universe, he is also eminently virtuous. The same can be said of Kim. In the last chapter, both Kim and the lama experience an epiphanic moment of self-realization. At first glance Kim's seems to be a renewed awareness of the world and a keener sense of his place within it, while the lama's seems to be a metaphysical apprehension of a dimension beyond "the illusion of Time and Space and of Things" (337). Yet the two apprehensions are essentially complementary, not contradictory modes of understanding. The lama's epiphany gives him an understanding of his quest; Kim's gives him insight into his quest, too—his initiation into the arcane world of espionage. But more important, both epiphanies affirm the existing order of things. As the lama exclaims to Kim at the end of the novel: " 'Son of my Soul, I have wrenched my Soul back from the Threshold of Freedom to free thee from all sin—as I am free, and sinless! Just is the Wheel! Certain is our deliverance! Come!' He crossed his hands on his lap and smiled, as a man may who has won salvation for himself and his beloved" (338).

Odd as this ending may seem for a novel that helped to define the emergent spy-novel genre, in another sense it is not odd at all, for it provides a morality for the politics of the romantic, heroic tradition of spy novels, a morality that continues to assert the necessity of covert, essentially undemocratic activities in the name of state security. In various ways, that same morality is now used to sustain the politics of one tradition of spy novels, and one version of democracy.

Notes

1. For more on the differences between working-class culture and middle-class culture in Victorian England, see Gareth Stedman Jones's essay "Working-class Culture and Working-class Politics in London, 1870–1900: Notes on the Remaking of a Working Class," in *Languages of Class: Studies in English Working Class History, 1832–1982.*

2. See Michael Denning's *Cover Stories: Narrative and Ideology in the British Spy Thriller,* especially chapter 2, for a more detailed discussion of the effects of this spy fever on Edwardian spy fiction.

3. I am indebted to Robin Roberts for shaping my thinking on this point.

The Ironic Spy Novel:
Anarchy, Irony, and Empire
in *The Secret Agent*

5

> Civilization has to defend itself against the specter of a world which could be free. If society cannot use its growing productivity for reducing repression (because such usage would upset the hierarchy of the *status quo*), productivity must be turned *against* the individuals; it becomes itself an instrument of universal control.
>
> —*Herbert Marcuse,* Eros and Civilization

Destabilizing the Rhetoric of the Great Game

If Kipling's rhetoric of the Great Game in *Kim* sustains a morality justifying colonial rule, no such morality is possible in Conrad's *The Secret Agent* (1907). This novel reworks the fascination with the human consequences of imperial conquest present in Conrad's earlier work, but here it receives a new emphasis: whereas *Heart of Darkness* lays bare the moral corruption attendant upon European depredations in the Congo, and *Nostromo* depicts the extension of this corruption throughout the fictional country of Costaguana, *The Secret Agent* shows that the heart of darkness is not simply located in the undeveloped countries "peripheral" to Europe but in London, the administrative center of the British Empire. In *The Secret Agent* it is impossible to find a phrase like "Well is the Game called great" (*Kim,* 273): the Great Game of espionage in the service of empire still exists, but it is, plainly, no longer great. Conrad shows no faith in the morality that sustained Kipling's valorization of the game. There is no adventuring on behalf of a great and glorious empire, but instead only the grim and morally bankrupt business of bureaucratic infighting and pseudorevolutionary wrangling, both of which promote only individual interests within the sordid and diminished world of London.

In this respect, *The Secret Agent* is the antithesis of *Kim,* for in it Conrad deconstructs the self-serving rhetoric of the Great Game, in which, as one

historian has put it, "the middle classes were able to dress economic benefits in idealistic garb, substituting moral crusade for mercenary motive,
romance and adventure for political and military aggression" (John M.
Mackenzie, *Propaganda and Empire,* 258). In *The Secret Agent,* irony is the
dominant mode employed to destabilize this self-aggrandizing imperial
rhetoric. Conrad alludes to this function in the novel's preface: "Even the
purely artistic purpose, that of applying an ironic method to a subject of that
kind was formulated with deliberation and in the earnest belief that ironic
treatment alone would enable me to say all I felt I would have to say in scorn
as well as in pity" (41). One object of Conrad's irony is the politics of
administration, the function of which is to ensure the maintenance of the
status quo in what Conrad presciently sees as a decaying imperial society.
But administration in this sense extends beyond managing the ordinary
day-to-day bureaucracies that keep society going; it also includes the sordid
business of gathering intelligence on subversive groups or individuals, or
on groups or individuals suspected of subversion.[1] Interestingly, these
two forms of administration interlock, forming one process. Although there
are not separate bureaucracies for surveillance and counterespionage in *The
Secret Agent,* as there often are in subsequent spy fiction, this emphasis on
the necessity of surveillance against foreign-inspired intrigue has since
become a convention of the genre. Conrad, however, uses it to make the
point that these are not two separate processes but one, and one on which
the stability and security of a smoothly running civil society depend.

The Game of Pacification

For Conrad the game does not mean extending or preserving the empire,
but the much humbler aim of pacifying the middle classes. Now played
within the mother country itself, the game is anything but great; it is dirty,
exploitative, and petty, a power struggle in which no single group can lay
claim to moral ascendancy or contribute to a more enlightened social order.
For Kipling one plays the game of espionage by assuming an identity or
disguise that later is shed. For Conrad there is no possibility of this effortless
change of identities; indeed, being locked in the game of everyday surveillance,
in which there are no winners or losers, defines existence in an age of fading
imperial splendor. Sir Ethelred, the secretary of state, a man who wants "no
details but lucidity," is emblematic of the morally neutral, self-aggrandizing
bureaucrat. Yet he, along with the seamy world of revolutionary London, is
ruthlessly caricatured. Conrad's sweeping condemnation of anarchism in
the preface as a "brazen cheat" (39) is in fact directed at poseurs, pseudoanarchists and sham revolutionaries. Indeed, the only politically engaged

figure in the novel not caricatured is the Professor, a fanatic who carries an India-rubber detonator in his pocket capable of triggering an immense explosion. The Professor is the only revolutionary in the novel who lives according to his convictions. Paradoxically, then, the only character with integrity is a fanatical nihilist prepared to blow up himself and anyone else foolish enough to try to apprehend him.

By comparing other characters' values to the Professor's, Conrad is able to mount a sustained attack on all compromised individuals, institutions, and beliefs. Speaking to Ossipon, the Professor makes explicit the equivalence between law-abiding society and anarchism that had remained implicit up until their meeting: " 'You revolutionists,' the other continued with leisurely self-confidence, 'are the slaves of the social convention, which is afraid of you; slaves of it as much as of the very police that stand up in deference of that convention. Clearly you are since you want to revolutionize it. It governs your thought of course, and your action too, and thus neither your thought nor your action can ever be conclusive' " (93). Or again, later: " 'The terrorist and the policeman both come from the same basket. Revolution, legality—countermoves in the same game; forms of idleness at bottom identical. He plays his little game—so do you propagandists. But I don't play; I work fourteen hours a day and go hungry sometimes' " (94). Revolutionists and the staid bourgeoisie are both indicted for their lack of imagination, their narrowness, and their slavish adherence to "social convention," that is, to the existing social order. This is particularly ironic in that the theoretical agenda of anarchism calls for the dissolution of "social convention." But if the police and the upper and middle classes they protect are seen as philistines, to Conrad the anarchists are even worse, for they promote a political agenda they are unwilling to establish, and ultimately they are loathe to disturb existing social relations. For Conrad the object of the game played by the forces of revolution and legality is to conserve the existing social balance—not to force a checkmate, but to continually force a draw. In this game there can be no appeal to a higher morality, for both revolution, as represented by Verloc's circle of anarchists, and legality, as represented by Sir Ethelred, the Assistant Commissioner of the Special Crimes Department, and Chief Inspector Heat, are fraudulent. Indeed, the legal system is only a cover for the petty power struggles that take place within the various institutions and bureaucracies of London.

Typicality in Anarchy

Chief Inspector Heat, the putative guardian of the law, has perhaps less respect for it than the pseudoanarchists he makes it his business to watch.

He believes that his zeal sanctions the circumvention of inconvenient legal questions, as Conrad makes clear in an ironic statement: "But, in any case, Chief Inspector Heat, purveyor of prisons by trade, and man of legal instincts, did logically believe that incarceration was the proper fate for every declared enemy of the law" (126). The police not only possess a "vanity of power" (132), but they are also career-minded philistines who specialize in avoiding issues. The moral enervation of this existence is typified by the Assistant Commissioner's fondness for whist: he plays one game to forget his distaste for another game, the one that dominates his life; it is "as though the game [of whist] were a beneficial drug for allaying the pangs of moral discontent" (118). This moral exhaustion is not incidental or individual but systemic: the corruption of the police force stems from the fact that it is a bureaucracy, intensely regulated by the official administrators of what the Professor despairingly calls "social convention."

The anarchists, however, are also morally bankrupt: their anarchism is just a cover for other, no-less-immediate forms of exploitation. Verloc, the pornographer and double agent, as a spy for an unnamed foreign embassy cynically exploits his anarchist connections. He also exploits his wife, Winnie. For him she is a mere convenience. Ossipon too preys on women who support him, and eventually he too betrays Winnie's trust by robbing, then deserting her. Michaelis, the corpulent "ticket-of-leave apostle" (73) subsidized by a wealthy old lady, is able to proselytize freely about his dream of "a world like a beautiful and cheery hospital" (264). Yundt, the old "terrorist," makes a career of posturing on public platforms but "had never in his life raised personally as much as his little finger against the social edifice" (78). In his own way, each anarchist is an imposter, a poseur, an armchair revolutionary.

Seen collectively, both revolutionary and official characters are clearly intended to be "typical" characters in Georg Lukács's sense of the word, richly individualized figures that incarnate the transformative—or, in the case of *The Secret Agent,* the nontransformative—historical forces of a given time. However, although many of Conrad's caricatures have a Dickensian quality, the depictions of the anarchists in *The Secret Agent* do not have this same comic vitality. Not only are they all hypocrites—a dismissal rooted more in authorial feeling than in historical fact—but, more important, they lack specificity, the specificity that Conrad was able to give the revolutionaries in *Under Western Eyes.* The anarchists in *The Secret Agent* are not, as Lukács would have it, richly individualized; nor do they have compelling, psychologically complex characters. They are, in the literal sense of the word, mere "types," embodiments of a single emotion or idea.

One reason for this is that for Conrad they are both revolutionary and inauthentic. Within Conradian ideology, or at least the ideology of *The*

Secret Agent, all of them stand accused of being, to greater and lesser degrees, hypocrites; more important, they are also guilty of idealism, of indulging in hopes for impossible reforms. Within the ideology of the novel, every revolutionary movement is guilty of this double charge. This is also largely the reason why Conrad does not distinguish between radically different revolutionary philosophies. In *The Secret Agent,* therefore, a parodic version of crude Marxist rhetoric is put in the mouths of anarchists.

Conrad's lack of interest in distinguishing anarchism from other revolutionary philosophies produces a curious mixture of rhetoric. Doubtlessly, a parodic motive enters into this mix of discourses, but Conrad's lack of interest in discriminating reveals as much about his pessimism vis-à-vis social change as do the characters he lampoons. Michaelis, the "ticket-of-leave apostle" of anarchism, is perhaps the best example. Michaelis devoutly intones a doctrine of economic determinism, a doctrine associated with crude Marxist propaganda, although Conrad throws in a dash of anarchist rhetoric: " 'History is dominated and determined by the tool and the production—by the force of economic conditions. Capitalism has made socialism, and the laws made by the capitalist for the protection of property are responsible for anarchism' " (73). The rhetoric is as prefabricated and insubstantial as the speaker. Michaelis is insubstantial as a character not only because he represents a recognizable social type—a dreamy armchair revolutionary who is also an opportunist—but also because, like most of the other anarchists in the novel, he is not seen as implicated in affective relationships of work and love. Accordingly, the depiction of the anarchists in the novel lacks the force or clarity of Sir Ethelred's characterization, for example, or the psychological insight that distinguishes the depiction of Winnie Verloc. In short, because Conrad does not give his anarchistic characters a social basis beyond that of a stereotypical representation of a community of political exiles, any substantial engagement with historical reality, there is nothing to mediate between them and their status as self-parodies— which, it might be said, precisely suits Conrad's satirical purpose.

Irony of Naturalism

To fully understand the role Conrad's representation of anarchism plays in producing an ideology of equivalence between revolutionary movements and bourgeois society, and its persistence in subsequent espionage fiction (of Le Carré and Greene, for example), it is not sufficient to analyze the textual space that anarchists occupy in *The Secret Agent.* It is also necessary to examine, as Conrad does, their relation to bourgeois society. What is fascinating about *The Secret Agent*—and in this respect it is different from Le

Carré's fictions—is that in it anarchism is not posited as alien to bourgeois society but is instead seen as its basic principle. In this sense, the textual ideology of *The Secret Agent* is far more radical than any of the creeds espoused by the novel's characters, or, for that matter, by Conrad himself. In *The Secret Agent,* society is already anarchistic, although it still retains the trappings of bourgeois legality. Fundamentally, bourgeois legality, bourgeois morality, and bourgeois order aren't only a sham—the theme of *Madame Bovary* and countless other English and European novels of the time—but, far from being cohesive structures, however repressive, they are instead seen as disintegrating. This disintegration is figured most memorably in the basic unit of bourgeois society, the family. From the beginning, Verloc's family is a black satire on the morally upright, stable Victorian family: Verloc, after all, is a pornographer and spy; his relationship with his wife is one of convenience for them both; and his relationship with his idiot stepson Stevie is nonexistent until he hits upon Stevie's usefulness as the unwitting bomb carrier in Verloc's attempt on the Greenwich Observatory. Later, familial relations turn even more grotesque. Ultimately, of course, Verloc is instrumental in killing Stevie, a death Winnie avenges by murdering Verloc. Winnie's "anarchistic end of utter desolation madness and despair" (43) exists as a trope for the anarchy that has overtaken society in general.

The moral congruence posited in the novel between revolution and legality, the terrorist and the policeman, and the anarchist subculture and bourgeois society foregrounds the deeper, ultimately political principle of identification between these ostensibly opposite groups latent in the novel's subtext. The repressed signification within the political unconscious of *The Secret Agent* is the realization that society is already anarchistic. At least for Conrad, this repressed signification has the effect of neutralizing anarchism politically: if it already exists, for the anarchist there is nothing to change. Moreover, the novel's persistent emphasis on the moral and ethical bankruptcy of the legal and anarchistic organizations in London makes sense only by explicitly acknowledging that individuals and groups are guided not by socially shared legal or even ethical standards, but by self-aggrandizing motives. The absence of any effective government and the atomization of society into competing groups thus define the anarchistic social configuration of *The Secret Agent.* The much-remarked-upon nihilism of the novel is itself a response to this social chaos. Within the political economy of *The Secret Agent* anarchy is not creative but negative, the result of social disintegration. Neither the middle class nor the revolutionaries offer hope of regeneration.[2]

Irony, then, exists as a literary response to Conrad's apprehension of social collapse. Conrad's use of irony establishes an authorial distance in relation to the anarchistic representation of society he creates in the novel.

The negative capacity of irony is harnessed by Conrad to produce an ideology of nihilism toward the anarchy of London. As a literary device, irony is perhaps the only technique available to the nihilistic writer, for as a mode of literary representation it is incapable of simple affirmation; it works instead by negation, by affirming the opposite of what is said. Anarchy, and its literary correlative in *The Secret Agent,* irony, suggest the impossibility of community, for there can be no general community without a shared morality, a shared sense of social purpose, and an impartial and effective legal code.

Whereas Conan Doyle's London represented a "knowable community," a system of social relations and individuals made accessible by Holmes's keen intellect, there is no such "knowable community" in *The Secret Agent.* Individuals are known incompletely. Moreover, they don't have the vitality or dynamism of Conan Doyle's world: all of them are strangely static characters, with seemingly fixed, preordained personalities. Unlike Kipling's characters, Conrad's—with the exception of Winnie—undergo no development, no growth of awareness. And even Winnie's sudden consciousness of the world is negative. This static, stunted quality of Conrad's characters derives in part from their relation to an equally unreal, almost phantasmagoric landscape. Significantly, it is a landscape, and not a community. Conrad's London is far more unregenerate than T. S. Eliot's; it is a wasteland without redemption, as Winnie Verloc's death demonstrates. This lack of any sense of real hope or even order in London is eerily suggested in naturalistic descriptions such as the following:

> In front of the great doorway a dismal row of newspaper sellers standing clear of the pavement dealt with their wares from the gutter. It was a raw, gloomy day of the early spring; and the grimy sky, the mud of the street, the rags of the dirty men harmonized excellently with the eruption of the damp, rubbishy sheets of paper soiled with printer's ink. The posters, maculated with filth, garnished like tapestry the sweep of the kerbstone. The trade in afternoon papers was brisk, yet, in comparison with the swift, constant march of foot traffic, the effect was of indifference, of a disregarded distribution. (101)

Similar images of decay pervade the novel. Dirt, grime, and filth symbolize a more general social disorder, just as the inconsequential "march of foot traffic" suggests a state of normalized anarchy, an anarchy made routine by the exigencies of the working life of a generalized, nondescript population. It is, significantly, Conrad's naturalistic language that produces this image of routinized entropy, and it is this same use of language that is largely responsible for the nihilistic ideology of the novel.

Historically speaking, naturalism derived its emphasis on close and detailed observation from the application of developments in the natural sciences, particularly in geology and biology. This transference of technique from science to literature was typically carried out in order to give a new importance to the influence of environment on the individual or his actions. The tension within the naturalistic mode in *The Secret Agent* arises from Conrad's unwillingness to diagnose the reasons for the anarchy he sees around him. The tendency inherent in naturalism to analyze the individual in terms of determinative agency is thus thwarted. The naturalistic mode in *The Secret Agent,* that is, is inhibited by a nihilistic authorial ideology, with the result that finely detailed naturalistic description is possible, but naturalism as a dominant ideology is not.

The Secret Agent and the Ideology of Modernism

As I noted earlier, individuals in *The Secret Agent* appear unaffected by, separated from, their environment. The quasi-surrealistic texture of the novel derives from this separation: individuals respond to different pressures, but their personalities seem unaffected by these changes. The character of an individual in *The Secret Agent* typically does not expand or contract in relation to environmental pressures, but remains essentially the same. Yet, as the example of Winnie illustrates, environment *is* determinative; however, it is less a regulator of the boundaries of human possibility, as in the English realist novel, than simply an open space in which things happen. This apprehension of history as pointless, arbitrary, and fundamentally unknowable is, as Lukács notes in *The Meaning of Contemporary Realism,* a cardinal feature of modernism:

> This negation of history takes two different forms in modernist literature. First, the hero is strictly confined within the limits of his own experience. There is not for him—and apparently for his creator—any pre-existent reality beyond his own self acting upon him or being acted upon him. Secondly, the hero himself is without personal history. He is "thrown-into-the-world": meaninglessly, unfathomably. He does not develop through contact with the world; he neither forms nor is formed by it. The only "development" in this literature is the gradual revelation of the human condition. Man is now what he has always been and will always be. The narrator, the examining subject, is in motion; the examined reality is static. (21)

As Lukács suggests, the delineation of the protagonist and that of his environment are interrelated, generally determined by the author's attitude toward history. Although I do not agree with Lukács's dismissal of modernist literature, his theory of the interdependence of the "attenuation of reality" and the "dissolution of personality" (26) provides a theoretical framework for understanding the ideology of modernism at work in *The Secret Agent.*

As in the fictional environments of other high modernists—Joyce, Faulkner, Beckett—events in the environment of *The Secret Agent* happen almost arbitrarily rather than by necessity. This is not to say that there is no causality; plainly there is. The central event in the novel, the attempt by Verloc to blow up the Greenwich Observatory, is proof of this inasmuch as the botched attempt ultimately leads to the deaths of Stevie and Winnie, and even Verloc. But like many other modernist novels, *The Secret Agent* uses a sense of the pressures of social and human relationships to evaluate an experience of modernity that seems fragmented, arbitrary, and alienating.

The ironic accentuation Conrad gives to the rhetoric of the Great Game, then, indicates not only a nihilistic authorial ideology, but authorial investment in a general ideology, an ideology of modernism. Most heroic espionage thrillers differ from *The Secret Agent* in their tacit affirmation of the legitimacy of bourgeois institutions, or in their more overt patriotic celebration of these institutions and the Western way of life (as one finds in the works of Ian Fleming, for example), but both the heroic and antiheroic traditions of spy fiction have absorbed elements of modernist ideology, even while adhering to predominantly realist conventions and realist forms. Both George Smiley and James Bond, for example, are "without personal history"; they do not "develop through contact with the world" except to become more world-weary and wise in Smiley's case, and more adroit and sexually experienced in Bond's case. For both, significantly, "reality is static": the Cold War and the zero-sum game engaged in by the East and the West are constants, whatever else changes. There are, of course, many differences in the uses to which these two traditions put this ideology of modernism—but the ideology, however selectively used, has almost become a convention of contemporary spy thrillers.

In *The Secret Agent* the Professor is the quintessential alienated modernist. Within the vast and disintegrating metropolis of London, there are no rules in the game of survival: no generally legitimate government, no law, no morality. And no one understands this better than the Professor, as he makes clear in his taunting of Chief Inspector Heat after having accidentally met him on the street:

> "You'll never get me at so little cost to life and property, which you are paid to protect."
> "You don't know who you're speaking to," said Chief Inspector Heat, firmly.
> "If I were to lay my hands on you now I would be no better than yourself."
> "Ah! The game!"
> "You will be sure our side will win in the end. It may yet be necessary to make people believe that some of you ought to be shot at sight like mad dogs. Then that will be the game. But I'll be damned if I know what yours is. I don't believe that you know yourselves. You'll never get anything by it." (112)

But Chief Inspector Heat is wrong: the Professor knows exactly what the game is and why it is played. In fact, Heat unwittingly demonstrates that he has already lost the game, inasmuch as he is ignorant of the stakes. For the Professor, the game is not one of survival, of recognizing balances of power and accommodating himself to them. It isn't a matter of physically destroying society, of blowing up its major institutions. It is a matter of making society destroy itself. The chief reason the Professor carries around a bomb is not to use it, although he is glad of the protection it affords him, and is happy enough to distribute explosives to anyone who asks for them; rather, he carries it around in order to provoke the police into shooting him. This, he believes, will strip away the veneer of legality that bourgeois society clings to in order to justify itself, and will provoke a general realization of the anarchistic basis of society.

To the Professor, there is no generally accepted moral code, only the appearance of one disguising a hypocritical bourgeois order. Therefore, when he goads Inspector Heat into saying that "It may yet be necessary to make people believe that some of you ought to be shot at sight like mad dogs" (112), the Professor has already succeeded in persuading a representative of law and order to see the violation of the law as justifiable; and by forcing Heat to contemplate compromising the principles he supposedly stands for, the Professor has already won the game. In his absolute adherence to his principles, the Professor is, paradoxically, the novel's only genuine idealist. As such, he is the antithesis of the many self-seeking, hypocritical figures found in Conrad's anarchist underworld and in society proper.

In *The Meaning of Contemporary Realism,* Lukács points out that in modernist literature there is often a congruence between the subjective state of being of the alienated protagonist and his environment. This is true of *The Secret Agent.* The Professor's isolation relates to the more general social alienation within the novel, an alienation that is itself a function of the loss of a "knowable community" and in turn leads to a perception of the alienation of the individual within history. The recurrent imagery of the isolated individual illustrates this nihilism. But it is characteristic of the novel's anarchist subtext that it calls nihilism into question as an incontestable value, for in the novel even nihilism contains an idealistic kernel. The novel cannot, that is, even assert nihilism as an absolute value. At its deepest level, it reworks the agonized quietism that marked Conrad's own outlook toward philosophies of political reform into an affirmation of nihilism—but a notably impure form of nihilism, a nihilism contaminated by idealism. Skeptical of revolutionary change, cynical toward bourgeois values, Conrad tended toward a nostalgic affirmation of a quasi-aristocratic order, a way of life that, as *Nostromo* indicates, always exerted an attraction for him. Paradoxically, then, the only principle affirmed in *The Secret Agent* is this idealistic nihilism: within the novel's topsy-turvy world, the anarchists are really nothing more than poseurs, and the only idealist is really an anarchist.

Popular Fiction and *The Secret Agent*

Having considered *The Secret Agent*'s affiliations with naturalism and modernism, and having explored its political subtext, I would like to conclude by considering Conrad's contribution to the genre of espionage fiction. I have already argued that part of Conrad's legacy to espionage fiction consists of his deployment of a distinctly modernist ideology that can be seen in the static worldview inherent in many post–World War II spy novels that posit an alienated existence in which man is "unable to establish relationships with things or persons outside himself" and in which "it is impossible to determine theoretically the origin and goal of human existence" (Lukács, *The Meaning of Contemporary Realism,* 20–21). The world of the spy novel is, necessarily, always a vulnerable one, a world in which the satisfactory resolution of one conspiracy or threat does not ever finally establish the safety of the collective, whether it be a company, an intelligence agency, or a nation. For reasons relating largely to the genre's commitment to suspense as a conventional element, the world of the spy novel is always uncertain; nearly anything can happen. Unpredictability is valorized. The satisfactory resolution of one threat or one conspiracy is never sufficient. There is never any finality: there will always be another threat, another conspiracy, another crisis, as Bond readers and moviegoers well know.[3]

The Secret Agent, however, is distinctive in that it combines two modes of representation—naturalism and caricatural realism—rarely found together in subsequent espionage fiction. Detailed naturalistic description of the environment is combined with a caricatural realism reminiscent of Dickens to create a grotesque vision of Edwardian society. Like many moderns, Conrad is both repelled and fascinated by the grotesque. But Conrad uses these modes of representation to evaluate society, to accentuate the grotesqueness of ordinary existence and thereby condemn the official order that makes a pathology of everyday life. This condemnation also extends to the radicals who pretend to higher ideals but are as counterfeit as the class they want to replace.

The ironic representations of society, and the ironic inflections of the rhetoric of the Great Game produced by Conrad's combination of naturalism and realism, ultimately exist as a recognition of the end of the empire. This ironic attitude toward the empire—also found in the work of Joyce,

Lawrence, Forster, and Woolf—did not quash the tradition of adventure fiction; but by acknowledging that the old style of imperial adventure was breaking down, this new, critical attitude toward the empire figuratively attempted to undermine the worldview that sustained the genre of imperial adventure. By focusing on the social disintegration in London, the British Empire's administrative center, *The Secret Agent* suggests the entropy of the empire as a whole.

From this period forward, the elements that distinguish the genre of imperial adventure—its expansionist tone, its emphasis on action, its lack of interest in psychological nuance and in the morality of action—fracture and become subsumed into other popular genres. Elements of the genre of imperial adventure can be found in romance, science fiction (most obviously in novels of galactic imperialism), westerns, travel fiction, hard-boiled-detective fiction, crime thrillers, and espionage fiction, in which the Great Game of imperialism still continues, after a fashion, in the form of the contest between East and West (even if other countries now assume the role once played by the Soviet Union).

The importance of *The Secret Agent,* then, is that it marks the transformation of the tradition of imperial adventure into a new popular genre, the genre of espionage fiction. It is thus somewhat ironic that the ironic mode Conrad adopted in the novel, along with the book's modernist outlook and narrative structure, effectively prevented it from becoming a popular success. In *Conrad: The Critical Heritage,* Norman Sherry notes that

> Conrad was beginning to look for a larger audience, a more popular appeal, and he saw that in writing about anarchists in Soho he was at least treating a "widely discussed subject," but treating it on his own terms. Writing to his literary agent, J. B. Pinker, on 18 May 1907, while working on the final form of *The Secret Agent,* Conrad spoke of "an element of popularity in it . . . my mind runs much on popularity now. I would like to reach it not by sensationalism but by means of taking a widely discussed subject for the *text* of my novel," and further evidence of his desire to gain popularity appears in another letter written two and a half months later. There Conrad speaks of *The Secret Agent* as a book "to produce some sensation." (21)

Like *Nostromo* and *Under Western Eyes, The Secret Agent* was not a popular success. But within the history of popular fiction, it is that most unusual of literary artifacts: a failed popular novel that eventually became acclaimed as a "serious" novel. More than that, it helped to establish a tradition of its own, the ironic spy novel, a genre devoted to the questioning of the game of espionage and the political systems that engage in it.

Notes

1. For an interesting discussion of the structural relations between surveillance and realism in this same period, see Mark Seltzer's "Realism and the Fantasy of Surveillance" in *Henry James and the Art of Power,* 25–58. I ultimately disagree, however, with Seltzer's conclusion that realism invariably participates in and promotes social systems of constraint (50). Although this is often the case, the evaluative aspect of realism is also capable of powerfully conveying criticisms of those same systems of constraint.

2. In "Form, Ideology and *The Secret Agent*" Terry Eagleton makes a similar point: "The forms of the text, then, produce and are produced by an ideological contradiction embedded within it—a contradiction between its unswerving commitment to bourgeois 'normality' and its dissentient 'metaphysical' impulse to reject such 'false consciousness' for a deeper insight into the human condition" (25).

3. For a fascinating analysis of James Bond as a cultural phenomenon, see Tony Bennett and Janet Woollacott's *Bond and Beyond: The Political Career of a Popular Hero.*

Part III

Modernists and
Detectives

Modernism and the "Search for a Remoter Something" | **6**

No, it is impossible; it is impossible to convey the life-sensation of any given epoch of one's existence—that which makes its truth, its meaning—its subtle and penetrating essence. It is impossible. We live, as we dream—alone.

—Joseph Conrad, Heart of Darkness

When I set myself the task of bringing to light what human beings keep hidden within them, not by the compelling power of hypnosis, but by observing what they say and what they show, I thought the task was a harder one than it really is. He that has eyes to see and ears to hear may convince himself that no mortal can keep a secret. If his lips are silent, he chatters with his finger-tips; betrayal oozes out of him at every pore. And thus the task of making conscious the most hidden recesses of the mind is one which it is quite possible to accomplish.

—Sigmund Freud, Dora

Now, after our readers have seen the class struggle develop in colossal political forms in 1848, the time has come to deal more closely with the economic relations themselves on which the existence of the bourgeoisie and its class rule, as well as the slavery of workers are founded.

—Karl Marx, Wage Labour and Capital

Encoding Modernity

Whether fictional or philosophical, modernist writing is fascinated with uncovering, revealing, decoding, sleuthing. Within the modernist worldview, there is the assumption of a "remoter 'something' "—a hidden truth, a concealed clue to existence, a sense that experience is coded, and that "beneath" or "within" the code, there is an underlying pattern of meaning that is capable of resolving "the nightmare of history" into an understandable, stable, coherent narrative.[1] Thus a great deal of modernist writing is organized around the desire to translate the incoherent into the coherent, the inarticulate into the articulate, the unsaid into the said. Although most modernist literature also expresses severe doubts about the possibilities of successfully finding the concealed clue to existence and being able to then confer a hidden order upon it, this hermeneutic desire remains a fundamental dialectic within modernism.

Modernists, typically, pride themselves on being master sleuths, diagnosticians of this "remoter something." Modernist literature thus shares an analogous epistemological form with detective fiction: both are structured around the assumption that appearances disguise a deeper truth; both are organized around the attempt to decode and solve the mystery of existence. Much of William Faulkner's fiction, for example, reads like a labyrinthine detective novel in which the narrative circles around and around a dark secret (a secret that frequently operates as a trope for the repressed truths of a decaying social order), as seen in Quentin Compson's search for the truth about the Sutpen family in *Absalom, Absalom!* In Franz Kafka's *The Trial,* Joseph K. searches for the meaning to the charge that has condemned him, hoping that this discovery will convert his phantasmagoric existence back into a knowable, ordered one. Virginia Woolf's *To the Lighthouse* explores the desires of Mr. Ramsay, Mrs. Ramsay, and Lily Briscoe and their different attempts to penetrate the chaos of everyday event and locate some organizing truth. For Mrs. Ramsay, this organizing truth is represented by familial patterns of domesticity; for Mr. Ramsay, metaphysics performs this function; for Lily Briscoe, art holds out the possibility of framing reality and of arresting its ultimate essences. At the same time, *To the Lighthouse* suggests that these attempts at decoding the heterogeneity of existence are themselves illusory. In modernist fiction, this desire to recover a fuller sense of reality through a hermeneutic operation is often linked to a corresponding sense of the inherent impossibility of successfully doing so.

In this respect, Joseph Conrad's *Heart of Darkness* is a paradigmatic modernist novel. Marlow wants to reveal what is at the heart of darkness. He seeks to translate the mysterious, seemingly incomprehensible signs of the African jungle into a comprehensible narrative. Throughout Conrad's novella, Africa is figured as a mysterious landscape that nevertheless contains the clues to its own meaning (and holds the key to Marlow's self-knowledge). *Heart of Darkness* thus represents Africa as an encoded "other"—a rich and mysterious moral and geographical landscape that signifies, but in ways profound and unknowable to Europeans.[2] The heart of darkness speaks, but in a language incomprehensible to Marlow: "We penetrated deeper and deeper into the heart of darkness. It was very quiet there. At night sometimes the roll of drums behind the curtain of trees would run up the river and remain sustained faintly, as if hovering in the air high above our heads, till the first break of day. Whether it meant war, peace or prayer we could not tell" (58). Marlow cannot translate what seem to him the incoherent noises and sights of Africa into a stable, coherent Eurocentric narrative. By contrast, in Marlow's mind, Kurtz assumes the role of a master semiotician, a European adept who has penetrated Africa's linguistic and cultural barriers. From Marlow's early perspective, Kurtz has not only deciphered the strange languages of Africa, but in doing so has also achieved a state of supreme self-understanding. Of course, upon meeting Kurtz, Marlow is undeceived: far from having transcended the limitations of European culture, Kurtz has become the very embodiment of Western tyranny and despotism. Kurtz masters the natives and is able to communicate with them, but he can only relate to them by adopting a master/slave relationship with them.

The price Kurtz pays for the betrayal of his own earlier ideals is the full realization of his own degradation, acknowledged in his final cry, "The horror! The horror!" (118). The horror, however, is not simply Kurtz's own fall from grace, but that of the "civilization" that sanctioned the depredations witnessed by Marlow in the Congo. As Marlow says: "All Europe contributed to the making of Kurtz; and by and by I learned that, most appropriately, the International Society for the Suppression of Savage Customs had entrusted him with the making of a report, for its future guidance" (83). Although Kurtz glimpses the dark secret of Western civilization, Marlow's narrative suggests that no final understanding of Africa was achieved by Kurtz or himself. For Marlow, the Congo remains forbiddingly alien, ultimately mysterious. Its secrets remain untranslated and unknown. Indeed, Africa's alterity, its resistance to being colonized by Eurocentric epistemological and cultural ways of seeing, suggests the permanence of the "mind-forg'd manacles" William Blake sees constitutive of Western civilization. What Marlow sees as alien is alien because he cannot—or will not—concede the relativity of Western norms, Western ways of seeing. Because the Congo is not Western, it can only then be conceived as a mysterious, exotic "other." It is this, as much as Marlow's intermittent recognition of the pitiless savagery of imperialism, that creates the profound sense of alienation permeating *Heart of Darkness*. Marlow's attempt to apprehend the totality of events is thus stymied by his failure to challenge the Western values that distort and limit his understanding of Africa. And it is this same failure, as much as anything else, that accounts for Conrad's declaration that "it is impossible to convey the life-sensation of any given epoch of one's existence—that which makes its truth, its meaning—its subtle and penetrating essence. It is impossible. We live, as we dream—alone" (44).

Detection and Modernism

In "A Philosophical View of the Detective Novel" Ernst Bloch describes what he takes to be some of the characteristics of detective fiction. His analysis is equally applicable to modernist fiction:

> So we are now prepared for the style itself, knitting and knotting; for its *characteristics*, which are threefold, closely intertwined and full of intention. First comes the suspense associated with *guessing*, pointing itself, in detective-like manner, to the second characteristic, that of *unmasking* and *discovering*, with special emphasis on what is remote, often the most important source of information. And the act of discovery leads, in the third instance, to events that must first be wrested from their pre-narrative, unnarrated state. The third aspect is the most characteristic of the detective story, rendering it unmistakably independent of the detective figure. Before the first word of the first chapter something happened, but no one knows what, apparently not even the narrator. A dim focal point exists, as yet unrecognized, whither and thither the entire truckload of ensuing events is mobilized—a crime, usually murder, precedes the beginning. (*The Utopian Function of Art and Literature*, 249)

Even if modernist fiction does not feature murder as prominently as detective fiction, Bloch's analysis accurately describes a dominant modernist structure and style.

However, the narrative events identified by Bloch—"the suspense associated with guessing" what the secret consists of, the process of "unmasking," and the reconstruction of prenarrative events—are not all. There is also the tendency of detective fiction, like modernism, to read the incidental as *symptomatic:* "It is often the smallest, purely incidental signs from which the detective gleans the most salient information" (Bloch, 250). Just as detective fiction regards the incidental gesture, act, or comment as potentially significant, so too does much modernist literature. Partly because of this, modernist writing is devoted to what Bloch calls "the micrological perspective" (251). Because every detail is potentially significant, the minutiae of everyday life come under intense scrutiny. Since even minor details can signify the presence of a hidden truth, a submerged but determinate reality, they are incorporated without appearing to be censored. In this way, modernist writing projects the image of a narrative defined by a landscape (sometimes interior, sometimes exterior) that is expansive in its inclusiveness and use of detail; *Ulysses* is, perhaps, the classic example of the use of this "micrological perspective" in modern fiction.

But the similarities between modernism and detective fiction are not restricted to analogous conventions. Indeed, the two forms intersect at what is arguably the most defining feature of modernist writing—its interest in, even obsession with, alienation. This structure of feeling within crime fiction signifies the dominance of modernist ideology within the popular culture of the years between the two world wars (and in many instances, well beyond them), the period of time usually associated with high modernism: "If anything, alienation itself has increased, an alienation that holds people in opposition to themselves, their fellow humans, and the world they have created, and the concomitant insecurity of life . . . has added general *mistrust* to the duplicity. Anything can now be expected, consistent with the economy of exchange that now applies to faces as well and that, as in an Alfred Hitchcock horror film, does not even know the direction from which the blow will come" (Bloch, 253). The ubiquity of this alienation is not so much a sign of the aesthetic equality of popular culture (a red herring in any event) as it is a sign of the productivity of this structure of feeling within modern culture—and a sign that popular culture responds to the same social and cultural anxieties that produced high modernism. Indeed, it is possible to argue that one of the fundamental impulses of a modernist culture is the desire to uncover the sources of this alienation, to seek them out as a way of understanding them, as we shall see in the work of two enormously influential modernists, Sigmund Freud and Karl Marx.

Modernism, Detection, and Pathology

Freud's work, like the fiction of Conrad and other modernists, exhibits a fascination with revelation, with "unmasking" and discovery. Indeed, Freud's earliest work, *Studies in Hysteria* (1895), a collaborative effort with Josef Breuer, attempted to read the system of significations underlying and producing hysteria. In that book, Freud argued that hysterical symptoms were caused by, and represented, deeply disturbing, pathogenic, repressed memories. For Freud, such symptoms were the body's articulation of deeper mental secrets. The job of the psychoanalyst, then, was to unmask the unconscious memories signified by the physical symptoms. As Freud began to develop the theory and practice of psychoanalysis, he concentrated on interpreting "the smallest [seemingly] purely incidental signs from which the detective gleans the most salient information" (Bloch, 250). The psychoanalyst thus becomes a kind of psychiatric semiotician, but one who pieces together and interprets various texts—whether they are neurotic symptoms, dreams, parapraxes, or even cultural systems such as taboos—in order to reconstruct the larger wish-fulfillment of which they are only broken fragments. Thus Freudian psychoanalysis posits two realms of experience— the *manifest* level (the symptomatic level of experience expressed in dysfunctional physical manifestations) and the *latent* level (the larger determinate subtext of psychic tension). The primary function of the psychoanalyst, then, is to translate, or to have the analysand translate, the manifest content of symptoms into the more complete, but hidden, latent narrative. By integrating the two through the process of transference, the analysand "remembers" and, ideally, gains some measure of control by discovering his or her personal psychic narrative.

The hermeneutic aspect of the practice of psychoanalysis is perhaps illustrated most dramatically in *Dora: An Analysis of a Case of Hysteria* (1905), in which Freud works toward, as he says, "the discovery of the hidden and repressed parts of mental life" (135).[3] In *Dora,* Freud's first case history, the figure of the psychiatrist-as-detective becomes a drama in itself. Indeed, the Collier paperback edition exploits this sensational potential by luridly describing *Dora* as a "first-rate detective novel" on the blurb on the back cover:

> An appealing and intelligent eighteen-year-old girl to whom Freud gives the pseudonym "Dora" is the subject of a case history that has all the intrigue and unexpected twists of a first-rate detective novel. Freud pursues the secrets of Dora's psyche by using as clues her nervous mannerisms, her own reports on the peculiarities of her family, and the content of her dreams. The personalities involved in Dora's disturbed emotional life were, in many ways, as complex as she: an obsessive mother, an adulterous father, her father's mistress, Frau K., and Frau K.'s husband, who had made amorous advances to Dora. But through Freud's genius in unravelling Dora's motives and the tangled relationships that led to her confused inclinations toward men and women, the roots of Dora's problem are completely revealed to the reader.

Despite the blurb's paternalistic tone, simplifications, and deification of Freud, there is a sense in which Freud's narrative *does* read like a detective novel in its "knitting and knotting," in its drive toward "unmasking," and, perhaps most important, in its attempt to reconstruct a prenarrative of Dora's life that would account for her neurotic symptoms.

In "Freud and Dora: Story, Case, History" Steven Marcus has observed that *Dora* is also structured like a "modern experimental novel":

> The general form of what Freud has written bears certain suggestive resemblances to a modern experimental novel. Its narrative and expository course, for example, is neither linear nor rectilinear; instead its organization is plastic, involuted, and heterogeneous and follows spontaneously an inner logic that seems frequently to be at odds with itself: it loops back around itself and is multidimensional in its representation of both its material and itself. Its continuous innovations in formal structure seem unavoidably to be dictated by its substance, by the dangerous, audacious, disreputable, and problematic character of the experiences being represented and dealt with, and by the equally scandalous intentions of the author and the outrageous character of the role

he has the presumption to assume. (*In Dora's Case: Freud-Hysteria-Feminism,* 64)

Like *Heart of Darkness,* then, *Dora* is obsessed with the "search for a remoter something," which in this case consists of the search for the sources of Dora's psychic trauma. In other words, Freud wants to lay bare the psychic disturbances that produced Dora's hysteria. As Freud himself ruefully admits, his investigations end inconclusively, with only the fragments of his totalizing vision. Indeed, as Marcus notes, Freud continually calls attention to the fragmentary character of the case: the study's first section declares its incompletion in its title, "Fragment of an Analysis of a Case of Hysteria." Dora broke off her treatment before it could be concluded; hence, the conclusions reached failed to identify and treat the transference— i.e., Dora's identification of Freud with Herr K.—at work in the case. (This is to say nothing of Freud's countertransference, that is, his failure to confront and analyze the cultural and sexual biases that determine his analysis, a failure that leaves his own role unexamined and unaccounted for.)

Freud's case history thus becomes an analysis—and even a valorization—of fragmentariness, since Freud's own limitations and those of the psychoanalytic method effectively preclude any totalizing representation of all the determinants of hysteria and the treatment needed to assuage its painful symptoms. Despite these limitations, *Dora,* as Marcus notes, also becomes an occasion for Freud's reflections on narrative, and on the role narrative plays in constructing the individual:

> The history of any patient's illness is itself only a substory (or a subplot), although it is at the same time a vital part of a larger structure. Furthermore, in the course of psychoanalytic treatment, nothing less than "reality" itself is made, constructed, or reconstructed. A complete story—"intelligible, consistent, and unbroken"—is thus the theoretical, created end story. It is a story, or a fiction, not only because it has a narrative structure but also because the narrative account has been rendered in language, in conscious speech, and no longer exists in the deformed language of symptoms, the untranslated speech of the body. (*In Dora's Case,* 71)

Thus Freudian psychoanalysis, though it acknowledges the fragmentary nature of its own discourse, paradoxically holds out the hope of becoming a transformative narrative by constructing nothing less than reality itself.

Deciphering Symptoms of the Body Politic

If Freud attempts to translate the "deformed language of symptoms" into another language in order to write the narrative of reality itself, Marx attempts something similar: While Freudian analysis seeks to comprehend the body politic by investigating the psychodynamics of the family structure, Marxian analysis attempts to decipher the symptoms of the body politic by interrogating its socioeconomic structures. (This distinction between the psychic and the socioeconomic emphases of Freud and Marx should not be pushed too far, however, for both came to see the implications of the one dimension involved in the other.) In analyzing these socioeconomic structures, the Marxian project aims to write the true narrative of reality, a narrative that will disclose reality's hidden subtext: its organization, its social tensions, its determinants, and its motor forces. For Marx, as for Conrad and Freud, empirical reality is chaotic, at least partly illusory, and unreconstructed; it is nothing but the puzzle pieces or ciphers of a larger, as-yet-unwritten narrative of reality.

Hence Marx's insistence on interpreting, uncovering, revealing, and decoding: like other modernists, the dominant tendency of Marx's work is to uncover and recover the mystery of existence. Marx's work, that is, is always demystifying. In *The German Ideology* (1845–1846), he displays this hermeneutic drive by contending that life is not determined by consciousness, but consciousness is determined by life. Arguing against the various idealisms of Hegel and Feuerbach, in which reality is largely seen as mental or spiritual, or as the incarnation of consciousness, Marx seeks instead to develop a materialist view of history:

> This conception of history depends on our ability to expound the real process of production, starting out from the material production of life itself, and to compound the form of intercourse connected with this and created by this mode of production (i.e., civil society in its various stages), as the basis of all history; and to show it in its action as State, to explain all the different theoretical products and forms of consciousness, religion, philosophy, ethics, etc., and their origins and growth from that basis; by which means, of course, the whole thing can be depicted in its totality (and therefore, too, the reciprocal action of these various sides on one another). It has not, like the idealistic view of history, in every period to look for a category, but remains constantly on the real *ground* of history; it does not explain from the idea but explains the formation of ideas from material practice." (164)

As this famous passage indicates, the materialist view of society and history is represented as cutting through the disembodied concepts of idealist thinking in order to locate "beneath" them "the real ground of history." This view presents itself as decoding both the mystifications of earlier philosophical thinking and reality itself, which is seen as fully understandable only through a materialist hermeneutics. Unlike Conrad's or Freud's, however, Marx's narrative is unabashedly totalizing: *The German Ideology,* for example, sets out to explain nothing less than "civil society in its various stages" and all "forms of consciousness, religion, philosophy, ethics, etc." by dialectically relating them to "the real process of production."

Marx's totalizing hermeneutical inquiry uses what Bloch calls a "micrological perspective" to explain the undisclosed dynamism motivating capitalist societies. In *Capital,* Marx's micrological perspective draws on myriad sources in order to arrive at a macrological perspective. These sources include literary works, government reports, historical incidents, contemporary events, philosophical writings, mathematical texts, and economic treatises. Whatever the source, each is seen as symptomatic or expressive of the total socioeconomic interactions of capitalism. Partly because of their sense of a hidden but determinate subtext to reality, Marx and Engels resorted to a rhetoric of discovery to communicate the magnitude of their work, particularly when referring to Marx's discovery of the principle of surplus value, which for him underpinned and explained the behavior of the entire capitalist order. Engels invokes this same modernist rhetoric of discovery when summarizing Marx's life achievements in *Socialism: Utopian and Scientific:*

> But for this [the critique of capitalism] it was necessary—(1) to present the capitalist method of production in its historical connection and its inevitableness during a particular historical period, and therefore, also, to present its inevitable downfall; and (2) to lay bare its essential character, which was still a secret. This was done by the discovery of *surplus value.* It was shown that the appropriation of unpaid labour is the basis of the capitalist mode of production and of the exploitation of the worker that occurs under it; that even if the capitalist buys the labour power of his labourer at its full value as a commodity on the market, he yet extracts more value from it than he paid for; and that in the ultimate analysis this surplus value forms those sums of value from which are heaped up the constantly increasing masses of capital in the hands of the possessing classes. The genesis of capitalist production and the production of capital were both explained.
>
> These two great discoveries, the materialistic conception of history and the revelation of the secret of capitalistic production through surplus value, we owe to Marx. (700)

Engels may not be Marx's subtlest reader, but his rhetoric is illuminating. Here Engels explicitly presents Marx as the great diagnostician of the social text, the decoder of "the secret of capitalistic production," the visionary who discovers the motor forces of history. History's arbitrariness, contingency, and lack of direction are seen as only epiphenomena, "beneath" which Marx discerns an underlying pattern (historical materialism), an organization (class struggle), and a primary motor force (the structural compulsion to transform surplus value into capital). Within historical materialism, what appears to be historical accident is seen instead as the form of an underlying principle. Apparent incoherence is translated into narrative coherence.

With Freud, then, Marx shares a belief in the *liberating* possibilities of narrative. Just as Freud believes that the psychoanalytic narrative, via the process of transference, can effect the removal of neurotic symptoms and a return to normal unhappiness, so Marx believes that a materialist grasp of history, and the subject's understanding of his/her position within history, can ultimately lead to a transformation of history itself. Although neither Freud nor Marx pretends that history can be transcended, both argue that historical circumstances can be modified, even transformed. In this sense, Conrad emerges as more pessimistic than either of them: for him, historical events—such as the colonization of Africa—and individual moral failure—such as Marlow's discovery of the degraded Kurtz—are both fated. Freud and Marx are much more hopeful about the possibility of human agency, and about the function of narrative in recreating reality. Contrary to the popular views of Freud and Marx, they are not apostles of determinism; rather, their theories aim to emancipate individuals, even whole societies, from oppressive psychic or social circumstances.

Solutions?

One of the central conventions of detective fiction is the denouement in which the detective figure reconstructs the events leading up to the crime: in other words, there is the familiar "mystery" followed by the revelation of the "solution" (a misnomer, for often no solution is possible). Many different forms of crime fiction are structured around a reconstruction of events in which the power (or powerlessness) of knowledge is finally revealed. The desire for knowledge—the reader's as well as that expressed by certain characters—is realized or thwarted at the denouement, at which time a narrative of previously unnarrated events is given. The effect of the denouement in crime fiction is to reconstruct the assumed reality by restoring to it a lost subtext. What often emerges, then, is a more comprehensive narrative and a wider sense of the relations and motives between people and events—in short, a more extensive understanding of a represented reality, even if that knowledge is not liberating (as is frequently the case in hard-boiled fiction).

The conventional and experiential similarities between detective fiction and modernism discussed in this chapter—the search for a "remoter something" that will confer meaning on history; the deployment of a "micrological perspective" as a part of that search; the profound sense of alienation as the normative structure of feeling; the desire to apprehend the totality of experience through a narrative that simultaneously constructs reality—all suggest that modernism is a kind of detective fiction and that detective fiction is a kind of modernism. More important, in searching for the hidden but determinate subtext to existence, both detective fiction and modernism compel one final conclusion: that emancipation from "the nightmare of history" can only come through the imagined remaking of history enacted in narrative.

Notes

1. The phrase the "search for a remoter something" comes from Ernst Bloch's essay "A Philosophical View of the Detective Novel," in *The Utopian Function of Art and Literature: Selected Essays* (245). As subsequent pages show, Bloch's essay has been very useful in helping me to articulate my reading of modernism.

2. Within the vast body of writing on Conrad and imperialism, I would like to single out two essays in particular for stimulating my thinking on the European tendency to see Africa as "other" and on the ways in which this experience of alterity relates to colonialism: Chinua Achebe's "An Image of Africa: Racism in Conrad's *Heart of Darkness*" (in *Hopes and Impediments*) and Benita Parry's chapter on the novella in *Conrad and Imperialism*. Both are especially compelling and eloquent readings on this subject.

3. As Jacqueline Rose, Maria Ramas, Toril Moi, Jane Gallop, and others have noted, *Dora* also foregrounds the sexual politics involved in having a male psychiatrist speak for the bodily languages of a young woman. See Charles Bernheimer and Claire Kahane, eds., *In Dora's Case: Freud-Hysteria-Feminism*.

SECTION 1: AGATHA CHRISTIE'S CONSERVATIVE MODERNISM

> "It really is very dangerous to believe people. *I* never have for years."
>
> —*Miss Marple,* Sleeping Murder

Crime and the Pastoral Idyll

One of the most consistent features of Agatha Christie's half-century's worth of fiction is its conservative vision of modernity. Indeed, this aspect of her fiction is almost synonymous with the Christie name. Her first novel, *The Mysterious Affair at Styles,* was set in Styles Court, a sprawling country estate in Essex, far from the drawing rooms and warrens of Conan Doyle's London. *The Murder of Roger Ackroyd* was set in King's Abbott, a seemingly peaceful country village. Christie refined her portrait of the picture-postcard English country village of St. Mary Mead in *The Murder at the Vicarage.* All of these settings are variations on a pastoralism horribly violated but then restored by the mental acumen and moral agency of the detective figure—most often either by the indomitable Hercule Poirot or by the more modest but equally quick-witted Miss Marple. Of course not all of Christie's mysteries have this pastoral English setting. Many of them are set in very different locales, on trains, for example (*Murder on the Orient Express*), or in "exotic" locations (*Murder in Mesopotamia*). The more obvious pastoral settings express values implicit in all of Christie's fiction: a fondness for an orderly, circumscribed social world stratified by differences in manners. These gradations are always then seen to be class-based. The modern, post–World War I industrial world, the rising strength of the lower middle class, and the formation of a suburban mass society, with all of its billboards and garishness, are noticeably absent in Christie. One of the few times this world obtrudes into Christie's fiction comes in *Curtain,* which is in one sense a lament for the lost dignity and order of Edwardian England. Having come back to Styles, Hasting thinks to himself: "Styles St. Mary was altered out of all recognition. Petrol situations, a cinema, two more inns and rows of council houses" (6).

Whatever the location, the setting of the Christie novel is inevitably upright, proper, dignified, and English in an eternally Edwardian way. The Big House settings of her earlier fiction are simply the most obvious tropes for this ideology of England. Whether set in a country village or a country estate, Christie's characters are always middle-class or upper-middle-class persons who at the very least have a parlormaid. In *Sleeping Murder,* written during World War II but not published until 1976, Gwenda, the twenty-one-year-old protagonist, has to make do with a parlormaid and a part-time gardener; and everyone else visited either by her or by Miss Marple for tea has one, too. If one were to read the social history of England from Christie's novels, one would get a rather skewered view.

And yet in her conservatism and hostility to modernity (consistently reduced to petrol stations and sterile housing estates), Christie's nostalgia for upper-class Edwardianism is similar to English modernism in the interwar years—as seen in Evelyn Waugh's *Brideshead Revisited,* T.S. Eliot's "The Waste Land," and Ford Madox Ford's *The Good Soldier.* Although these canonical texts are generally more ambitious in terms of technique and social commentary than Christie's fiction, they display the same longing for a golden, preindustrial pastoral existence that characterizes Christie's work. None of these texts show an unambiguous desire for the Edwardian pastoral idyll, but all of them contain elements that explicitly or implicitly express some nostalgia for it. In this connection, Peter Miles and Malcolm Smith have shrewdly observed that "in Britain, pastoralism was articulated historically to the myth of the pre-industrial Golden Age, a time of supposed harmony and progress. Time and time again, the village community is represented as a microcosm of the national community. In the interwar years, much of pastoral England was in fact being eaten up by developing suburbia, yet the myth only grew stronger ideologically as the physical reality began to fade" (40). Paradoxically, the pastoral element implicit within Christie's fiction thus emerges as a distinctly modernist idealization of England, an England that exists in the popular imagination as a conflict-free, rural Arcadia sustaining the values and traditions that define "Englishness."

And yet Christie's fiction may be read as an implicit criticism of industrial modernism—in the name of a romantic conservatism, to be sure, but this reading cannot be ruled out, especially in light of the ubiquitous identification in English literature of the country with life-sustaining values and of the city with corruption and entropy. Dickens used this country/city opposition as an effective mode of social critique throughout his fiction (for example, the explicit contrast of the Maylies' bucolic country retreat with the dirt and vice of London in *Oliver Twist*). Christie's use of the pastoral tradition is much less politically oriented, and her criticisms of contemporary society are more incidental and implicit than Dickens's. Ultimately these factors delimit the extent to which her fiction can be read as mounting a sustained political analysis.

But there are other modes of criticism, and some of them are more directly related to the conventions of the formal English novel of detection. In *The Pursuit of Crime* Dennis Porter suggests that detective fiction, sui generis, projects the moral law that binds a given society together and simultaneously evaluates that society:

> Consequently, a crime implies the violation of a community code of conduct and demands a response in terms of the code. It always depends on a legal definition, and the law, as both Gramsci and Althusser make clear, is a key element of the superstructure in ensuring the reproduction of existing power relations in a society. As a result, in representing crime and its punishment, whether evoked or merely anticipated, detective novels invariably project the image of a given order and the implied value system that helps sustain it. By naming a place and by evoking, however glancingly, the socio-economic order that prevails within it, they confirm, in fact, that there can be no transgression without a code, no individual crime act without a community that condemns it. (120–21)

In *Sleeping Murder,* as in most of her fiction, Christie is less concerned with rendering a social order in all its class variations than with exploring its "implied value system" and the effects of the criminal transgression on the individuals involved. Before exploring these values and mores further, it is useful to briefly trace the plot of *Sleeping Murder.*

The novel is structured around the murder of Helen Kennedy Halliday, which occurred some eighteen years before the beginning of the novel. Gwenda Reed, the stepdaughter of Helen Halliday, was born in England, but because of the death of her parents, she was raised in New Zealand by relatives. At the age of twenty-one, Gwenda returns to England, married to Giles Reed. She settles in a small white Victorian villa in the seaside resort town of Dillmouth. As she sets about decorating and renovating the house, odd things begin to happen. She begins to "remember" things about the house, despite the fact that she has no recollection of ever having lived there. Eventually, these vague memories coalesce in the shocking recollection of a murder that she witnessed as a three-year-old child—the murder of her stepmother, Helen Halliday.

With the help of her husband and the inimitable Miss Marple, Gwenda sets about solving this murder in retrospect. She begins her search by soliciting the assistance of Dr. James Kennedy, the brother of the deceased. As she goes about her investigation, her search is complicated by the fact that she retains only a very partial image of the murder. Gwenda is the only witness, and she doubts her memory of the events in question. Gwenda and Giles Reed resolve that the best way of solving the mystery is to interview all of Helen Halliday's acquaintances. These consist mainly of rejected suitors—the staid solicitor, Walter Fane, and the flashy entrepreneur, Jacky Afflick—as well as the old parlormaid, Lily Abbott. The investigation takes on a new meaning for Gwenda when she learns from Dr. Kennedy that her father, Major Kelvin James Halliday, died in a mental asylum convinced that he himself had killed his wife. Events reach a climax when Lily Abbott, now Lily Abbott Kimble, is mysteriously murdered; shortly thereafter, an attempt is made on Gwenda's life. The murderer of Helen Kennedy Halliday, it turns out, was none other than her brother, Dr. James Kennedy, who was insanely jealous of his sister. In order to prevent Helen from moving away from Dillmouth, Dr. Kennedy killed her. To cover up his crime, he engineered the mental breakdown of his brother-in-law, Major Halliday. And in order to preserve his secret, he killed Lily, and attempted to kill Gwenda Reed, too.

As this précis suggests, Christie's crimes are the result of moral failure or individual pathology (Dr. Kennedy is clearly deranged, and this for Christie serves as an adequate explanation of his motives); unlike the American hard-boiled school of detection, there is in her fiction no sense of the environment as decisive, except in the matter of manners. Here class inevitably shows; here the implied value system of her fiction is most evident. A good deal of the specific detail in Christie's work consists of her narrator's narrow observation—and evaluation—of manners and behavior. The world of Christie's novels is always hierarchical, organized by a rigid adherence to middle-class values and mores.

This can be seen in chapter 16 of *Sleeping Murder,* in which Miss Marple tries to pump Mrs. Fane about her son's relationship with Helen Kennedy, who at that point is only suspected of being the victim of foul play. In this passage Mrs. Fane reminisces about Helen Kennedy:

> A *most* unsuitable girl—as seems always to be the way. Oh, I don't mean an *actress* or anything like that. The local doctor's sister—more like his daughter, really, years younger—and the poor man with no idea how to bring her up. Men are so helpless, aren't they? She ran quite wild, entangled herself first with a young man in the office—a mere clerk—and a very unsatisfactory character, too. They had to get rid of him. Repeated confidential information. Anyway, this girl, Helen Kennedy, was, I suppose, very pretty. *I* didn't think so. I always

thought her hair was touched up. But Walter, poor boy, fell very much in love with her. As I say, quite unsuitable, no money and no prospects, and not the kind of daughter one wanted as a daughter-in-law. Still, what can a mother do? (164)

There is much irony here, most of it directed at the prejudiced Mrs. Fane. In a more general sense, though, this passage is paradigmatic of Christie's use of evaluative realism. The object of Christie's irony is not so much Mrs. Fane's rather-mercenary material criteria for deciding on the suitability of her daughter-in-law; instead, it is her judgment, indeed her judgmental attitude toward Helen, that is treated ironically. As it turns out, Mrs. Fane's judgment is entirely inaccurate. The "poor" doctor turns out not to be so helpless after all: the reader subsequently learns that Dr. Kennedy murdered his sister out of jealousy. What Christie is undercutting, then, are Mrs. Fane's ill-founded moral judgments on Helen Kennedy's character, and not her entire worldview. As Miss Marple says at the end of the novel: "I think, myself, that she [Helen Kennedy] was a perfectly normal young girl who wanted to have fun and a good time and flirt a little and finally settle down with the man of her choice—no more than that" (285). At the heart of this passage, then, is a critical evaluation of a certain kind of gossipy moral condemnation.

Modernist Heresy: Ambiguous Language in Detective Fiction

Along with the evaluative realism of Christie's fiction there is another aspect of her style that relates to the literary mode of production most often identified with high modernism. I am referring to Christie's use of language. Although her language is less witty than Dorothy Sayers's, for instance, it is much more ambiguous, capable of bearing any number of different interpretations. Because of this, the reader can never be certain, at least not until the end of the novel, as to the signifieds of her signifiers. This is of course in keeping with the narrative structure of the genre, the function of which is to throw each character's motives into suspicion. Most of the time, this effect is achieved by ambiguous description. In chapter 22, for instance, Gwenda and Giles Reed are waiting for Lily, the Hallidays' former parlormaid, to keep an appointment at Dr. Kennedy's house. At this stage, neither Gwenda nor Giles suspects that Dr. Kennedy is the murderer, but they wait for Lily in the hope that she might shed some light on the mysterious disappearance of Helen Kennedy Halliday. So, although readers might suspect that the doctor is the villain of the piece, they have no way of knowing that Dr. Kennedy has just killed Lily Abbott Kimble in order to prevent the disclosure of what he thinks is damning evidence. As time goes by, the Reeds and Dr. Kennedy (for different reasons) grow increasingly restive. It is within this context that Christie describes Dr. Kennedy's behavior: "He walked restlessly up and down the room. His face was lined and haggard" (235). It is natural enough that he should be restless—as far as the reader and the Reeds know, he has been made anxious by the tardiness of his guest. The first sentence may portend some skulduggery, but again there are other seemingly neutral descriptions within the novel that could be read in an equally sinister light. The second sentence of the description, however, does seem to suggest something sinister. Why should Dr. Kennedy's face be "lined and haggard" unless he has been involved in something untoward? And yet it is also possible that the strain visible in his face is due merely to the stress related to the mysterious disappearance of his sister nearly two decades ago.

Very often, the language of Christie's novels appears to be transparent, but in actuality it is quite opaque. The reader never knows for certain what is being signified. This linguistic ambiguity—which is often taken to be one of the definitive characteristics of modernism—arises out of the fact that meaning in fiction is contextual; in Christie's fiction the reader never knows the full context. As Volosinov and Bakhtin contend, to understand a verbal utterance it is necessary to know its extraverbal context. They argue that essentially three factors constitute the extraverbal context of the utterance: 1) the common spatial purview (an understanding of the physical setting); 2) the interlocutors' common knowledge and understanding of the situation (what is jointly known); 3) their common evaluation of that situation (their shared attitude toward the situation) (*Freudianism,* 98–99). The ambiguity of Christie's language, then, stems from the reader's uncertainty in relation to the last two factors mentioned by Volosinov and Bakhtin—not only does the reader not know what is jointly known and felt by the characters in a detective novel, but, as the example of Dr. Kennedy indicates, frequently the reader doesn't even know what a *single* interlocutor or character truly knows and feels about a given situation. This is not necessarily "bad"; this uncertainty adds to the suspense of the novel, and thus may be regarded as an indispensable element of detective fiction. Indeed the structure of the genre is largely determined by the detective figure's reconstruction of the "extraverbal" situation. Once this is known, the meaning of the key utterance or utterances is understood, and the crime, then, typically becomes susceptible to resolution. In *Sleeping Murder,* the key enigmatic utterance is Mrs. Halliday's statement, overheard by Lily, "I'm afraid of you" (152). Once Miss Marple figures out to whom Helen Halliday was speaking—in other words, her "interlocutor"—she is able to understand the utterance, and is able then to effectively solve the crime.

Although language may seem referential and clear in the formal English novel of detection, this surface is deceptive. Cut off from its extraverbal situation, every signifier is capable of having an almost infinite number of signifieds, and it is only when the detective figure is able to reconstruct the extraverbal situation of a specific utterance that meaning can be conferred upon it. The process of interpretation is thus a convention of detective fiction. In "The Hippocratic Smile: John Le Carré and the Traditions of the Detective Novel," Glenn W. Most proposes a taxonomy of the English and American traditions of detective fiction based on the difference he sees between the attitude toward interpretation in the formal English novel of detection and that in the American hard-boiled school. Whereas the Americans "are caught up in the uncertainties of the activity of the interpretation itself, for which a final and valid result may be imagined but can never be confidently predicted," the English "presuppose the certainty of a correct reading," with the result that their fiction is fixated on the "joy of result" (*Poetics of Murder,* 350). Although Most's argument is persuasive, it leaves out any consideration of the reader's role in interpreting the text. Most is right in insisting on the English tradition's ultimate assurance in the interpretive process, but this assurance is complicated by the deceptive simplicity of the language in this genre, and by the interpretations it gives rise to in the reading process itself. Ambiguity in language and in interpretation thus have a much greater role than Most suggests.

It may be said that all this puts the reader of the formal English detective novel at a distinct disadvantage, which of course it does. But the more important point is that the act of reading this particular subgenre is more complex and ambiguous than has previously been thought. In one sense, the reading of this subgenre may be regarded as paradigmatic of reading fiction in general inasmuch as it requires an act of participation—a sifting and winnowing of motives, character, and circumstance—typical of the activity engaged in by all readers of fiction. Ultimately, too, readers engage in analysis and evaluation of these fictitious circumstances. No doubt the reader's evaluation of the narrator's evaluation of contemporary manners and mores constitutes one of the main pleasures involved in reading this brand of domestic fiction.

The tradition of domestic fiction, from which the formal English novel of detection descended, was made internationally famous by Samuel Richardson in the eighteenth century, and to this day attracts a predominantly, though not exclusively, female readership. Christie's fiction not only taps into the conventions of domestic fiction—most notably in its interest in domestic life and evaluation of manners—but it has also managed to capture its latter-day readership. In *Reading by Numbers* Ken Worpole situates the type of fiction produced by Christie in the years after World War I in terms of this changed but still recognizable readership:

After the First World War a new formula within the genre of detective fiction emerged—the country house murder. This is clearly to do with the way in which the reading public was changing from a magazine or yellow-jacket *buying* public into a public or commercial library *borrowing* public. The 1919 Public Libraries Act created the Country Library system which brought library facilities to a much wider proportion of the British people than before—particularly those living in country districts. During this period, however, the *private* library systems, such as Boot's libraries and others, were still growing—and were often sited in small places with a largely female clientele. . . . It is not surprising, therefore, if a detective story form emerged which had a rural and domestic setting, was more genteel and set amongst a better class of people. The country house murder was also a novel of manners, etiquette, fashion, and occasionally sexual passion, all subjects which were at the time thought the customary province of women readers. (48–49)

This readership expanded dramatically with the production and distribution of popular fiction in the post–World War I era. In the 1930s Allen Lane began the paperback revolution by launching the first series of Penguins, carried by the Woolworth chain. This series included both popular writers, such as Christie and Sayers, and more highbrow authors. The cheaper prices of the Penguins helped to widen the social range of the reading public, and thus added other formations to this readership. Part of Christie's phenomenal success, then, seems to consist in her combination of ratiocination and Jane Austen–like sensitivity to class and manners. Another part seems to consist in her attempt to project an idealized England, an England of bucolic country villages and country houses disturbed by nothing more vexing than the occasional ungentlemanly murder. Part of the success of this attempt, in turn, appears to be due to her ambiguous use of language, which in the detective novel has the effect of intensifying the reader's involvement in the interpretation of the narrative.

Unstable Identities

Most of the elements I've discussed so far in relation to Christie's fiction could be taken to be strategic means for the reinforcing of an essentially conservative textual ideology. And indeed Christie's valorization of middle- and upper-middle-class society and mores, her resolute individualism, her nostalgia for an Edwardian type of domesticity, and her remarkable exclusion of social conflict from her fiction (in Christie's world, all working-class people are happy domestics and all women are happy homemakers) would seem to substantiate this view. And yet there is another aspect to her fiction that forces us to call into question an equivalence between her fiction and a purely conservative ideology: her fiction is obsessed by the question of identity. Indeed, part of Christie's skill consists of her incorporation and adaptation of this interest to the requirements of the "whodunit" subgenre. The most basic conventional requirement of this type of fiction is that it call into question the identity of every individual within the circumscribed boundaries of the community in which the crime takes place. Although the legitimacy of the law may not be in question—as it often is in the hard-boiled tradition—or even the possibility of a final, and accurate, interpretation of the events leading up to the crime, the identity of the murderer is always in question since it could plausibly be just about anyone. Thus the formal English novel of detection operates on the premise that the individual's claim to a certain identity is false. The appearance of the well-spoken, urbane, law-abiding bourgeois subject often turns out to be a mask, disguising a more sinister identity. In using highly conventional settings and characters, Christie and other practitioners of this subgenre show—however fleetingly—the conventional nature of identity itself. Although on one level they reaffirm the identity of the subject, on another they show that appearances are not necessarily commensurate with reality, that in fact identity is neither as stable nor as natural as it seems to be. In this, the formal English novel of detection reveals a congenital similarity to one of the cardinal tenets of radical modernism, namely, the rejection of the bourgeois claim to a stable ego, consistent with its perception of itself.

Taking different lines of attack, Marx, Freud, and Nietzsche all sought to demonstrate that the ego's sense of self-identity was essentially constructed and, if not illusory, then ideological. Marx's attempt to develop a theory of ideology, Freud's development of the theory of a divided ego and forms of treatment for some of its most painful afflictions, and Nietzsche's deconstruction of all forms of system based on assumptions of identity stand as landmarks in any geography of modernism. In one form or another, many of these tenets became accepted facts of experimental modernism, and it is one measure of their ubiquity that the questioning of identity should become a convention in a popular genre such as the formal English novel of detection. This is not to say that Christie's view of the subject can be wholly equated with the view of the divided subject articulated in different ways by Marx, Freud, and Nietzsche: for them, identity is a highly problematic notion, whereas Christie assumes the existence of an essential identity. Nevertheless, there is in Christie's fiction a fascination with split identities that replicates an important characteristic of the modernist worldview.

It may be objected that although identity is problematized for a time in this type of fiction, it is problematized only to be confirmed more powerfully at the end of the novel: the identification of the murderer ultimately serves to confirm the identity and efficacy of the detective hero.[1] There is some truth to this argument, but conventionally, ideologically, and dramatically, this subgenre works by simultaneously questioning and affirming identity. Only by dramatically questioning the suspects' claims as to their identities can the detective figure resolve the crime and lift the cloud of suspicion that has fallen on the innocent—and yet the questions about motives and character that have arisen in the course of the inquiry always serve to throw into question the claims of the innocent about who they are. Within this subgenre, then, there is always an unresolved tension, a tension necessary to the generation of suspense concerning the identity of characters within the novel.

As a novel that shows a fascination with the formation of identity, *Sleeping Murder* dramatizes this point well. The problem of identity is compounded in this book because the "sleeping murder," or the killing that Gwenda thinks she witnessed as a child some eighteen years previous, causes her to question the integrity of her identity. When Gwenda hears the fateful lines from the *Duchess of Malfi,* "Cover her face; mine eyes dazzle: she died young," she becomes terrorized because for some unknown reason they recall the vision of a strangled woman. As she says to Miss Marple: "I was back there—on the stairs, looking down on the hall through the banisters, and I saw her lying there. Sprawled out—dead. Her hair all golden and her face all—all *blue!* She was dead, strangled, and someone was saying those words in that same horrible, gloating way—and I saw his hands—grey, wrinkled—not hands—monkey's paws . . . it was horrible, I tell you. She was dead" (33–34). Wondering if she actually did witness this bizarre death or if it is merely the product of her deranged mind, Gwenda begins to question her own sanity. Thus in *Sleeping Murder* the solution to the mystery involves more than the classical exoneration of the innocent; for Gwenda it becomes also the key to understanding her psyche, understanding whether she is sane or insane. *Sleeping Murder* is unusual in the extent to which it is concerned with the possibility of insanity, but it is an interesting—and little-remarked-upon—aspect of the formal English novel of detection that insanity nearly always figures as part of its atmosphere or mental landscape. Gwenda's fear of insanity stems from her dread that her father, Major Halliday, may have killed her stepmother and that murdering is somehow genetic within her family.

Solving the mystery of Helen Halliday's disappearance and Gwenda's violent childhood recollection thus become part of a single process of reconstruction. In *Sleeping Murder* this process is structurally identical to the classical psychoanalytic method in which the patient must return to the source of the blockage in childhood before she or he can hope to achieve any relief from the neurotic symptom. Significantly, chapter 10 of the novel is entitled "A Case History," and though it ostensibly details the peculiar circumstances surrounding Major Halliday's strange delusion and death, it is also Gwenda's case history. For until she can uncover a satisfactory explanation for her father's behavior toward her stepmother and for the circumstances that gave rise to her macabre childhood recollection, her claim to her identity, and even her sanity, is in question and doubted by no one more than herself. Indeed Christie's language and narrative resemble nothing so much as a dream, or, in Freudian terms, the manifest content of a dream. At this level, motive, event, and character exist for both the reader and the detective figure as a kind of text, as ciphers or representations of a latent content whose unknown logic the detective must decipher. As Miss Marple says: "It really is very dangerous to believe people. *I* never have for years" (291). The job of the detective is thus roughly analogous to that of the psychoanalyst: to read a phenomenon in terms of a hidden pathology that, once brought to light, confronted and articulated, ultimately helps to resolve the aberrant symptom.

In the case of the formal English novel of detection, the detective figure's identification of the murderer has the ideological effect of extirpating the diseased agent (the murderer) and thereby confirming the body politic in its sense of its own collective moral and political decency. This is because Christie's murderers either are actuated by moral failure (greed, lust, avarice, etc., sins that are the result of consciously made decisions), or else commit their crimes because of mental or emotional derangement. In any case, none of these causes call into question the justice of the current social and economic arrangements characteristic of her settings. Christie is interested in moral and behavioral evaluation. Thus the politics of her fiction are contradictory: on the one hand, she is critical of the modern democratic welfare state, but on the other hand she is reluctant to question the economic and class structures that determine the form that the body politic takes.

Although the whole structure of the formal English novel builds up to and climaxes with the detective figure's revelation of the murderer, this closure is never ideologically complete in its assertion of the integrity of identity and the ideality of the human community. In constructing a credible whodunit, the detective writer is of necessity required to dramatize the deceptiveness of identity, the fact that the human personality can never be assumed to be identical with outward appearance. This hermeneutic of suspicion is never completely eradicated by the triumphant disclosure of the villain; the casting of suspicion has already compromised the identities of many "innocent" characters, as well as the notion that the quasi-Edwardian society of the writer's fictional world can conduct itself harmoniously. Thus if Christie's fiction is fixated on order and stability, it is also obsessed by disorder and instability, both psychic and social. Even as it affirms the legitimacy and, indeed, the superiority of modern bourgeois existence and the stability of the bourgeois subject—like most experimental, "radical" examples of literary modernism—the formal English detective novel is fascinated by disorder, by the cracks in the facade.

Similarly, even as it employs commonsense, empirical methods to find the murderer, this subgenre asserts the inadequacy of empiricism as a guide to human behavior. The tacit message of this subgenre—that all is not what it seems—contradicts other ideologically charged messages, conveyed in the imagery of idyllic country villages and orderly country estates, that all is what it seems, that indeed all is well. Writing of the detective fiction of a somewhat earlier time, Walter Benjamin sees this tension as a foregrounding of a contradiction always implicit in modern bourgeois existence:

> The bourgeois interior of the 1860's and 1870's, with its gigantic sideboards distended with carvings, the sunless corners where palms stand, the balcony embattled behind its balustrade, and long corridors with their singing gas flames, fittingly houses only the corpse. "On this sofa the aunt cannot but be murdered." The soulless luxuriance of the furnishings becomes true comfort only in the presence of a dead body. Far more interesting than the oriental landscapes in detective novels is that rank Orient inhabiting their interiors: the Persian carpet and the ottoman, the hanging lamp and the genuine Caucasian dagger. Behind the heavy, gathered Khilim tapestries the master of the house has orgies with his share certificates, feels himself the Eastern merchant, the indolent pasha in the caravanserai of otiose enchantment, until that dagger in its silver sling above the divan puts an end, one fine afternoon, to his siesta and himself. This character of the bourgeois apartment, tremulously awaiting the nameless murderer like a lascivious old lady her gallant, has been penetrated by a number of authors who, as writers of "detective stories"—and perhaps also because in their works part of the bourgeois pandemonium is exhibited—have been denied the reputation they deserve. (*Reflections*, 65)

If we allow for a less exotic taste in furnishings, much of what Benjamin claims is applicable to Christie's fiction. Although her settings are not as consistently oriental as the description above would suggest, and the tension in her fiction rarely approximates "bourgeois pandemonium," *Sleeping Murder*, in its quiet, English, understated way, suddenly, if only briefly, suggests as much. Thus, in the drama with which the formal English novel of detection suggests the instability of identity and human community, and in the intensity with which it affirms both in its denouement, this subgenre resembles nothing so much as the canonized English conservative modernism produced in the interwar years.

SECTION 2: DASHIELL HAMMETT'S
HARD-BOILED MODERNISM

The division between the personal and the class individual, the accidental
nature of the conditions of life for the individual, appears only with the emergence of the class, which itself is the product of the bourgeoisie. This accidental
character is only engendered and developed by competition and the struggle of
individuals among themselves. Thus, in imagination, individuals seem freer
under the dominance of the bourgeoisie than before, because their conditions of
life seem accidental; in reality, of course, they are less free, because they are
more subjected to the violence of things.

—*Karl Marx*, The German Ideology

Cities of Blood

Dashiell Hammett's fiction has always occupied an uncertain position within
the literary canon. Although his work has generally been relegated to a kind
of second-tier status thought to be appropriate to "genre" fiction, because of
its stylistic sophistication and existential atmosphere it has also attracted its
share of literary admirers. Critics often praise Hammett's spare, chiseled
prose for its stylistic similarity to Hemingway's minimalist fiction. It would
be misleading, however, to read Hammett's fiction as a pale reflection of
high modernism. Hammett's modernism, and the modernism of the hard-
boiled school, is based not on a repudiation of mass culture, but instead on
an embracing of its possibilities. The distinctiveness of Hammett's fiction
consists of its recuperation of modernist themes and techniques in a
predominantly realist form that Hammett made contemporary through his
command of American English. In the process Hammett virtually produced
the distinctively American hard-boiled detective genre.

Hammett's modernism is thus different from the European modernism
rooted in the avant-garde, but, as Ken Worpole notes, it is a modernism
rooted in similar responses to the modern urban world of the early twentieth century: "The jungle of the cities which Brecht wanted to portray to
European theatre audiences, Hammett had already fictionalized for his
dime magazine readers" (*Dockers and Detectives*, 43). But unlike many
avant-garde movements in Europe, Hammett did not reject the artistic forms
of the past; instead, he transformed a seemingly exhausted form into a
distinctively new genre, a genre with its own distinctive language and
worldview. As Raymond Chandler testified in his famous essay "The Simple
Art of Murder," Hammett "gave murder back to the kind of people that
commit it for reasons, not just to provide a corpse; and with the means at

hand, not with hand-wrought dueling pistols, curare, and tropical fish. He put these people down on paper as they are, and he made them talk and think in the language they customarily used for those purposes" (Howard Haycraft, ed., *The Art of the Mystery Story*, 234). Though Chandler plays down Hammett's stylization of ordinary language, his comments do suggest the transformations Hammett made in the detective-story genre. It is thus ironic that although Hammett's fiction was not regarded as serious in his own time, it succeeded in reaching the mass audience that the European avant-garde coveted but could never reach.[2]

Although Hammett was a modernist in his response to the post-world-war society he observed and criticized, he was, characteristically, a modernist on his own terms, albeit an unorthodox modernist writing for pulp magazines. In what follows, I will explore the ways in which the combination of a number of ideological elements—Hammett's individualism, his skepticism toward bourgeois law and order, his philosophical and ideological relativism, the contradictory sexual politics of his fiction, and his rejection of rationality—produced the hard-boiled modernism found in *The Glass Key* and Hammett's other fiction.

If crime fiction partly exists as a response to the anxieties produced by modern, industrialized, urban environments, it attempts, and not always successfully, to mediate that anxiety by producing consoling versions of society. As I noted in chapter 2, Poe sought to resolve his distaste for a democratic, industrialized America by creating a detective figure whose independence, superiority, and omniscience ensure his freedom from the demands of any kind of affective community. Dupin is thus outside society, but capable of resolving its most perplexing mysteries. Sherlock Holmes represents another version of the empowered detective figure, but one whose function resides in affirming, not rejecting, the industrial society for which the labyrinthine complexity of London is the most obvious symbol. Christie's work, like Poe's, expresses a desire to eliminate the modern landscape, but unlike Poe's, her protagonists are not alienated from society but are its staunch members, guardians almost of its order and propriety. Hammett's protagonists—the Continental Op, Sam Spade, Ned Beaumont et al.—generally exist on the margins of society, and although they are for the most part isolated and estranged from it, and its values and political systems, their interest as characters derives from their connection, antagonistic as it may be, with bourgeois society. Unlike Poe, Conan Doyle, and Christie, Hammett tends to offer critical, rather than consoling, images of society. Thus the principle of equivalence between the underworld and bourgeois society proper that produces an essentially anarchistic vision of society in *The Secret Agent* finds resonances in the violent, mayhem-filled cities described in Hammett's fiction. Indeed, for Hammett, as for Marx, the "violence of things" is due to class and the kinds of conflicts it engenders.

Hammett's fiction thus is part of the tradition of crime fiction that grew out of and responded to the urban, industrial moment of modern history. Part of a general culture of modernism that has its most recognized representatives in the work of high modernism, Hammett's detective fiction similarly explores what it means to be modern. Unlike many high-modernist novelists, however, Hammett does not try to convey the meaning of this experience by accentuating subjective consciousness, but instead evaluates the social and political forms modernity took in the early decades of the twentieth century. In *Red Harvest* he analyzes the gangland violence that consumes the industrial town of Personville, otherwise known as "Poisonville," a town that, as its name suggests, is supposed to be representative of any middle-American town. The urban blight of Personville objectifies the diseased social relations of the town: "The city wasn't pretty. Most of its builders had gone in for gaudiness. Maybe they hadn't been successful at first. Since then the smelters whose brick stacks stuck up tall against a gloomy mountain had yellow-smoked everything into uniform dinginess. The result was an ugly city of forty thousand people, set in an ugly notch between two ugly mountains that had been dirtied up by mining. Spread over this was a grimy sky that looked as if it had come out of the smelters' stacks" (3). The rest of the novel is essentially an elaboration of the political corruption that led to the disfigured landscape of Poisonville. This sense of political decay pervades Hammett's fiction: In *The Maltese Falcon* deceit and mistrust erode all social relations, even relatively nonpolitical ones like the one between Sam Spade and Brigid O'Shaughnessy, come under intense scrutiny.

Similarly, in *The Glass Key* official politics have become indistinguishable from the actions of gangsters; Senator Henry, it transpires, is responsible for the murder of his own son. As Steven Marcus has noted, Hammett's fiction calls into question some of the most fundamental distinctions by which bourgeois society operates: "The respectability of respectable America is as much a fiction and a fraud as the phony respectable society fabricated by the criminals. Indeed, he unwaveringly represents the world of crime as a reproduction in both structure and detail of modern capitalist society that it depends on, preys off, and is part of" (*The Continental Op,* xxiv). After Hammett, this skepticism toward the self-representations of the powerful, and toward their claim to respectability, becomes a convention of the hard-boiled poetic found in Raymond Chandler, James M. Cain, Ross Macdonald, and more recent practitioners of the genre, such as Chester Himes and Sarah Paretsky.

Thus, although in one sense Hammett's protagonists are as alienated from modern urban "civilization" as are D. H. Lawrence's, in another sense they are deeply identified—and identify themselves—with it. It is almost impossible to imagine Sam Spade or the Continental Op working outside the city. For the Continental Op the city is the locus of corruption and vice, just as it is for Sam Spade and Ned Beaumont. And while all of these protagonists feel they have a duty to rectify these ills, all of them, to a man, feel the attraction of the criminal life, not merely because of the lifestyle that the dirty money supports, but because they have grasped, as Marcus notes, that the facade of respectability that legitimate society puts up is also essentially a fiction. This is why all of these detectives adhere so tightly to their own personal codes of behavior. In a world in which order and integrity inevitably give way to disorder and corruption, it becomes all the more necessary to have a stable personal code by which to operate. As the Continental Op confesses to Dinah Brand in *Red Harvest:*

> This damned burg is getting me. If I don't get away soon I'll be going blood simple like the natives. . . . I've arranged a killing or two in my time, when they were necessary. But this is the first time I've ever got the fever. It's this damned burg. You can't go straight here. I got myself tangled at the beginning. When old Elihu ran out on me there was nothing I could do but try to set the boys against each other. I had to swing the job the best way I could. How could I help it that the best way was bound to lead to a lot of killing? (102)

For Hammett, unlike Poe, the possibility of mastering the city by means of a superior intelligence no longer exists; the city has now become dominant, and threatens to crush the detective.

At first glance, the dominance-of-the-city motif seems to signal the similarity of Hammett's fiction to naturalism. Ultimately, however, Hammett's detective fiction cannot itself be considered naturalistic inasmuch as a certain degree of human agency must be accorded to the detective figure in order for him to perform his job. The hard-boiled detective can never be entirely defeated by his environment, for that would result in his abdication of his role as problem solver; moreover, one of the most basic conventions of the hard-boiled genre is an active, physically vigorous protagonist who can give a punch as well as take one. Hammett's "naturalism" is tempered by a full-blooded individualism; more specifically, there is an unreconciled tension in his fiction between two ideologies, one stressing the efficacy of human effort, the other asserting its ultimate futility. This ambiguity concerning the effectiveness of human agency, this uncertainty about the potency of human effort in the face of what appears to be an increasingly dominant and determinative social reality—a determinacy represented in modern literature by its obsession with the metropolis as the preeminent locus of modern life in which everything is in a constant state of becoming and flux, propelled forward by the dynamic energies of capitalism—is but another sign of the modernism of Hammett's fiction.

Codes and Questions: The Style of Hard-Boiled Fiction

The detective figure's personal code, therefore, is as much a means of survival as it is an alternate mode of behavior, often almost indistinguishable from the less savory forms of behavior that the detective investigates. Ultimately the Continental Op and Sam Spade owe their highest allegiance to a workmanlike devotion to a sense of doing a job well; Ned Beaumont's allegiance, on the other hand, is based solely on his sense of personal loyalty to friends, particularly to Paul Madvig, one of the city's big political bosses. In this sense, the personal codes that structure the behavior of Hammett's detectives are as much a sign of the entropy that has overtaken the urban landscape of his novels as are the corruption and deceit that they are paid to undo, for the circumscribed, violent, almost emotionless lives these protagonists lead assert the ascendancy of the city over the individual. The Continental Op can work effectively in the war-torn city of Personville, but he cannot afford to have any kind of affective life, for this would leave him too vulnerable to danger. This is why he resists the blandishments of Dinah Brand, and partially why Sam Spade resists the pleas of Brigid O'Shaughnessy at the end of *The Maltese Falcon*. For the Continental Op, as for so many other heroes of American literature, the only solution—even it is unsatisfactory—is for him is to flee the civilization represented by Personville.

In his essay on Hammett, Steven Marcus calls attention to another modernist trait in Hammett's work, "the ethical irrationality of existence, the ethical unintelligibility of the world" (xvii). It could be argued that Hammett made this an intrinsic aspect of hard-boiled fiction in that he created a genre that registers this sense of irrationality and unintelligibility in details that emphasize the disordered, contingent, almost hallucinatory quality of reality—a mode of writing most famously associated with Kafka and Joyce. This sense of irrationality and unintelligibility is also conveyed by Hammett's creation of narratives that are committed to the posing of questions. Like many high modernist heroes (and antiheroes), Hammett's detective figures are obsessed with questions, ones that have to do with the fundamental contradictions of modernity. *The Glass Key* is thus a representative text for any case focusing on a popular form of modernism inasmuch as it is evaluative, committed to exploring institutionalized corruption as social and political forces in American society. Hammett's exploration of the role of the individual in this society is enabled by his choice of protagonist. Ned

Beaumont is the lieutenant of the political boss, Paul Madvig. As such, he participates in the manipulation of big-city politics that the Continental Op, for example, attempts to end in *Red Harvest.*

Indeed, like *Red Harvest, The Glass Key* foregrounds the connection between the novel of big-city politics and hard-boiled fiction. Undergirding a number of seeming unrelated subplots in the novel is the political career of Senator Henry, who at the start of the novel is running for reelection. Paul Madvig supports the candidacy of Senator Henry; in return, Madvig hopes to marry the senator's daughter, Janet Henry. Madvig's power and ascendancy are due in large part to the political acumen of his right-hand man, Ned Beaumont. When Senator Henry's son, Taylor Henry, is murdered, political tensions in the city escalate. While the senator's opponents see in the murder an opportunity to discredit the incumbent, some of Madvig's henchmen begin to betray their leader because they think that Madvig is the murderer. Madvig's troubles are compounded further when a rival gangster (and ward boss) makes a bid to challenge Madvig's ascendancy. Beaumont is made special investigator by the district attorney's office to get to the bottom of Taylor Henry's murder. In the end, surprisingly, Madvig admits to the murder but Ned doesn't believe him. Deducing that Madvig is only protecting someone else, Ned then accuses the senator of murdering his son. After trying to shift the blame to Madvig, Senator Henry admits that he killed his son accidentally, in a fit of rage. The novel ends with the departure of Ned Beaumont and Janet Henry, and the poignant acceptance of this relationship by Madvig, who remains loyal to Beaumont despite the fact that Beaumont is leaving with the woman Madvig loves.

Within hard-boiled detective fiction Beaumont is thus a not-unusual protagonist—an amateur detective who sanctions political corruption at the same time that he uncovers more virulent forms than his own morality allows him to condone. In creating an obviously flawed detective figure in Beaumont, and in placing him in a situation that calls attention to a compromised social and political order, Hammett is able to question some of the most basic conceptions of morality while at the same time destabilizing some basic conventions of detective fiction. Hammett's fiction doesn't offer any answers to the questions it raises, but in one sense that doesn't matter: as Sinda Gregory notes, "Hammett's plots, then, and the overall structure of his novels satisfy genre conventions by answering the questions that must, by definition of the form, be raised (who is the murderer? how was it done? how was the solution found?) while at the same time they nullify through irony and paradox the validity of those answers" (*Private Investigations,* 14). It is partly this open-ended quality of his fiction, its refusal to yield to pat answers and easy solutions, that marks its affiliation with one ideology of modernism. Hammett brought detective fiction into the modern world, not merely by seeming to be more realistic, as Chandler believed, but also by introducing this ideology into the genre. In part, he achieved this by undermining some of the oppositions typical of detective fiction. Hammett not only brought detective fiction to a new level of technical and artistic achievement, he also inaugurated the antidetective novel by dissipating the binary oppositions of detective/villain, good/evil, and order/disorder that characterized the rational moralism of the formal English novel of detection.[3] The textual ideology of much of Hammett's fiction is relativistic inasmuch as it does not subscribe to any absolute worldview (except its own, another characteristic of modernism), but it is not relative in regard to the social reality it evaluates. In this matter, hard-boiled detective fiction as a genre is critical of civilization, of bourgeois law and property, and ultimately of the ideologies that assert an absolute distinction between the criminal and the law-abiding citizen. Much of critical edge of this fiction is due to its incorporation of representations of the "lower classes," whether they are the working classes or simply the disenfranchised and criminal classes. In any event, this incorporation of disenfranchised experience, and its worldview, throws into question assumptions of justice, orderliness, and naturalness by which predominantly bourgeois societies typically justify and legitimate their existence.

Like any other fiction, hard-boiled fiction mediates this evaluation through language; like the classic English novel of detection, it lays claim to being referential. Yet both are fictions of crime, regulated by the demands of their subgenres; both are conventional (although they adhere to different conventions); both represent stylized versions of ordinary speech. Hammett's fiction purports to use more ordinary English—and indeed one finds registers of English in his works that one doesn't find sympathetically represented in Christie's novels—but these registers have been reworked and tailored into a stylized version of lower-class speech. The tough-guy speech in hard-boiled fiction, like the genteel diction of the classic English detective story, is thus a literary representation of a speech type, but there is nothing natural about it. Take, for example, the famous first line of *Red Harvest:* "I first heard Personville called Poisonville by a red-haired mucker named Hickey Dewey in the Big Ship in Butte" (3). Few tough guys, or, for that matter, novelists, have the sense of pace, slang, alliteration, and syntactic control displayed in Hammett's style. Hammett was responsible for refining a style that was to become famous in modernist and postmodernist fiction. As Ken Worpole observes in *Dockers and Detectives:*

> The narrative styles of Hemingway and Hammett are clear examples of this renunciation of all detail other than the action, the dialogue and the minimal description of the setting. No characters ever have their thoughts articu-

lated; what we know about their inner lives has to be inferred from their speech and their behavior. The omnipotent, all-seeing narrator of conventional narrative discourse has been dispensed with, and one can argue that the "dime novel" arrived at this position several decades ahead of the "nouveau roman" (40)

Although Hammett's style gives his fiction the spareness characteristic of this kind of experimental writing, his style is also oriented "outward," toward an assessment or evaluation of society.[4] It is this role of language in his fiction that I now want to examine more closely.

Evaluative Modernism

Unlike the nineteenth-century classic realist novel, Hammett's fiction contains very little description of external reality. Most of his fiction consists of dialogue, and it is through dialogue that Hammett establishes the worldview of his protagonists and, ultimately, the novel itself. The element of social evaluation in his fiction is thus mediated through the language of his protagonists. The judgments are never direct; they remain implicit, typically made in terms of the individual. Hammett's fiction exists as a literary response to the moment of modernity in the twentieth century defined by the Depression-era, labor-capital conflicts of urban capitalism; and though it is ideologically modernist, by availing itself of the negative capability of evaluative realism, his fiction is able to critique the dislocations of modernity. Hammett's fiction remains intellectually and emotionally compelling, however, because that critique is made "in terms of the qualities of persons" (Raymond Williams, *The Long Revolution,* 278) and is not imposed as an abstract, tendentious schema on the narrative; on the contrary, the critique arises out of the tensions within the narrative. As an example, then, of what might be called Hammett's evaluative modernism, consider the following passage from *The Glass Key,* a heated exchange between Janet Henry and Ned Beaumont near the end of the novel:

> She asked: "Why don't you like Father?"
> "Because," he said hotly, "I don't like pimps."
> Her face became red, her eyes abashed. She asked in a dry constricted voice: "and you don't like me because—?"
> He did not say anything.
> She bit her lip and cried: "Answer me!"
> "You're all right," he said, "only you're not all right for Paul, not the way you've been playing him. Neither of you were anything but poison for him. I tried to tell him that. I tried to tell him you both considered him a lower form of animal life and fair game for any kind of treatment. I tried to tell him your

father was a man all his life used to winning without much trouble and that in
a hole he'd either lose his head or turn wolf. Well, he was in love with you, so—"
He snapped his teeth together and walked over to the piano.

"You despise me," she said in a low hard voice. "You think I'm a whore."

"I don't despise you," he said irritably, not turning to face her. "Whatever
you've done you've paid for and been paid for and that goes for all of us." (585)

This passage represents both the emotional climax of the novel and the
culmination of its social evaluation. Most obviously, the scene discloses the
rising sexual tension between Ned Beaumont and Janet Henry. This disclosure,
interestingly, occurs at the same time that the reader learns the full extent of
the corruption of city politics and its morally debilitating effects on the
citizens, particularly Senator Henry. The senator, the civic leader of the
community, turns out to be the most ethically base, for not only is he
responsible for the murder of his own son, but he was also willing to kill
Paul Madvig in order to protect his secret and his career. Thus the emotional denouement and the moment of sharpest social criticism coincide in
The Glass Key and are dependent on one another. Without the social
criticism implicit in Beaumont's comments, the sexual confrontation would
not be so charged, insofar as the criticism lends the scene an emotional
energy, one rooted in Janet Henry's realization of the various forms of
betrayal in her life: Senator Henry has betrayed his son by killing him; he
has also betrayed his daughter by using her as bait for Madvig; conversely,
Janet has betrayed Madvig and her own integrity by colluding in her
father's plans. Janet's anger and frustration reach their peak when she
realizes the cost of these betrayals in terms of her own lost integrity and that
of her father. Similarly, without the emotional impact of the confrontation
between Ned and Janet, the political critique would be arid and abstract.

Sexual Politics of Hard-Boiled Fiction

The encounter between Janet Henry and Ned Beaumont also foregrounds
the sexual politics of *The Glass Key* and illustrates those of hard-boiled
fiction in general. One crucial difference between the English gentleman-
detective and the American hard-boiled detective is that the latter's presence usually marks the recognition of the crime; indeed, frequently he
himself is deeply implicated in the crime. By contrast, the gentleman-
detective—Hercule Poirot or Peter Wimsey, for example—usually arrives at
the scene of the crime long after the crime has been committed and sets to
work solving it, secure in the knowledge that ultimately intellect will triumph
over evil (typically, evil is seen in moral rather than social terms). Rarely
does his mere presence initiate a murder or set in motion a chain of effects

resulting in the crime that the novel will untangle. Even rarer is the gentleman-detective's sexual involvement with another character. Yet casual liaisons of this sort are quite common in hard-boiled detective fiction—although Sam Spade may not think it is good business practice to let Brigid O'Shaughnessy off the hook, he is not above sleeping with her. This might lead one to conclude that the sexual politics of the hard-boiled school diverge radically from those of the classic English detective story, and in many senses this is true. But there are, however, startling similarities. One of the most striking of these is the empowered position of men in detective fiction.

With the exception of Nora Charles in *The Thin Man,* all of Hammett's detectives are men. They are all astute, physically able, and tough (as well as sentimental). Some of them, like Ned Beaumont and Sam Spade, are both intellectually and sexually vigorous. Their superiority does not arise primarily from mere strength or cleverness, although they are that, too; rather, it arises from the fact that they have grasped fundamental truths about society that few other people understand. Other people often know at least as much about this or that murder as the detective, but he alone sees the corpse as the signifying presence of institutionalized social corruption. He sees the crime not as a localized incident, but as a social phenomenon, implicating and involving every level of society. In short, hard-boiled detectives see ideology as myth.

However, in hard-boiled fiction, when women are not sultry seductresses, they are supplicants, most often supplicants after knowledge. Hammett thus most frequently figures women as intellectually inferior—and this has become a common topos in hard-boiled fiction. As Hélène Cixous has noted, this kind of superior/inferior opposition is an all-too-common way of representing women: "Organization by hierarchy makes all conceptual organization subject to man. Male privilege, shown in the opposition between *activity* and *passivity,* which he uses to sustain himself. Traditionally, the question of sexual difference is treated by coupling it with the opposition: activity/passivity" (*The Newly Born Woman,* 64).[5] As the supplicant after knowledge, Janet Henry is represented as intellectually passive, as intellectually inferior to Ned Beaumont. Beaumont tells her the identity of the murderer, but more important than that is the fact that Janet seeks a more comprehensive knowledge of her situation and her relations with others. Significantly, it is to Beaumont that she turns. At one level, then, this ending to the novel reaffirms a cultural stereotype—that men are sexually and intellectually superior to women. In terms of its sexual politics, then, Hammett's fiction may be read as conservative, even reactionary. Although his fiction is radically antibourgeois in that it affirms the corruption at the heart of bourgeois society, and society's complicity in producing that corruption, the sexual politics of his fiction undercut this radicalism by maintaining the essential superiority of men. Indeed, the sexual politics of much of the hard-boiled genre in general undermine the genre's political radicalism by affirming the hierarchies and relations between the sexes sanctioned by bourgeois society. ‾

At the same time, though, Ned Beaumont rejects the easy suggestion that Janet Henry is a whore, and to this rather limited extent he rejects the virgin/whore opposition that informs much hard-boiled fiction (and much fiction in general). Although this is hardly emancipatory, it does suggest a movement away from some of the distorting stereotypes of women that *The Glass Key* otherwise uncritically accepts. Janet may be culpable, but in this society, everyone else is, too. Nor does Beaumont presume to judge Janet; he rejects the ubiquitous cultural assumption that a man has a right and a duty to pass judgment on the moral character of women. The sexual politics of the novel are thus contradictory, containing elements that range from the culturally stereotypical to the atypical. If the ending of *The Glass Key* is a reprise of the famous ending of *The Maltese Falcon,* it is clear that in the later novel Hammett has not entirely rejected his earlier stereotypical representations of women as treacherous seductresses; nor has his fiction initiated a radically different exploration of the relationships between women and men (or indeed between women and society). However, the sexual politics of *The Glass Key* suggest the contradiction involved in embodying a radical critique of society while implicitly affirming some of that society's most reactionary and repressive relations. To this extent, ironically, the hard-boiled detective supports the status quo about which he is so scathing. Something of the inverse situation obtains in the formal English novel of detection, which often features a conservative ideology and female detective figures. Here too the sexual politics of the novel often contest the textual ideology by suggesting the capability of the female detective, a capability that is often at odds with the restrictive gender roles sanctioned by a hierarchical, patriarchal society. In both subgenres, then, sexual politics call into question some of the novel's dominant ideological assumptions.[6]

Class Politics, or the Fiction of Crime

The exchange between Janet Henry and Ned Beaumont also effectively demonstrates that Hammett achieves his evaluation of the "quality of a whole way of life" (Williams, *The Long Revolution,* 278) by suggesting in fictional terms the way in which the political has perverted the personal. Part of this evaluation consists of a criticism of class relations, relations that during the Depression assumed a more prominent character as divergences in wealth and class became more pronounced. Much of Beaumont's criticism of the Henrys is rooted in his belief that they assumed an attitude of class superiority to Paul Madvig because he came from a lower class. As he says bitterly to Janet: "I tried to tell him you both considered him a lower form of animal life and fair game for any kind of treatment" (585). It is significant that part of the criticism of city politics and urban life in general in *The Glass Key* is made against the pretensions that are enabled by, and thrive in, a class-based society. This is significant because the criticism is made by a character who has wittingly participated in the manipulation of the political system, and who therefore cannot claim moral ascendancy over anyone. In this sense, crime as such is not criticized. For Hammett, crime is in one sense democratic and entrepreneurial: it has the potential of making those excluded by class society financially and politically as powerful as those who have benefited by class division. Moreover, Hammett's antibourgeois social vision also grants criminals a kind of integrity: they may be criminals, but they don't pretend to adhere to ethical standards they can't maintain. They thus lack the hypocrisy found in legitimate society, which condemns criminals and yet sanctions and participates in illegal activities ranging from the relatively minor (bootlegging) to the very serious—the manipulation of the political system by the business community, the underworld, the politicians, and the police. As Ken Worpole notes: "In Hammett's hands, especially, the detective novel became an important vehicle for radical social criticism, without reading like a polemical text. The assumption which informs all Hammett's work is that the police, politicians and big business combine together to run the city administration in their own interests, even though this often involves murder, gang-slayings, bribery and perjury" (*Dockers and Detectives,* 43).

Hard-boiled fiction represents America as an empire, but it is an empire in decline, built on the legality of a class system and the illegality of corruption. By Hammett's standards, class society is both hypocritical and covertly criminal; however, unlike the underworld, it is not susceptible to change by the criminal-entrepreneur but maintains its identity and power by seeing itself as morally superior, even while it punctiliously supports an inherently biased social order. Senator Henry thus stands as the most egregious example of this middle-class hypocrisy. In *The Glass Key,* as in Hammett's other fiction, the detective figure navigates in this seedy, morally skewed environment. In hard-boiled fiction, the decaying urban landscape articulates a set of moral equivalences that are the inverse of normative bourgeois values: the city may be the locus of crime, and may be run-down and shabby, but it is no more or less corrupt than the well-kept houses of the well-to-do, as the famous opening description of the Sternwood mansion in Raymond Chandler's *The Big Sleep* attests. Hard-boiled fiction starts from the assumption that everyone's point of view is a fiction or an ideology, and the genre is particularly suspicious of bourgeois claims to represent a morally transparent order that the reader can take straight without having to read it as a fiction.

Hard-boiled fiction, that is, revels in its negative capacity, in its ability to evaluate the post–World War I urban American experience of modernity. Although it does not have any pretensions toward documentary truth, it is oriented toward an evaluation of this reality, and this suggests that Hammett's fiction does not see itself as a self-reflexive, autonomous work of art, detached from the time and place of its production, but instead sees itself as engaged with contemporary society, as a part of it. By incorporating slang, wisecracks, and more colloquial, vernacular registers of English, Hammett not only enlarges the creative possibilities of detective fiction, but also explores the possibilities for writing in a modernist mode using the language of the streets. In so doing, the language of Hammett's fiction asserts the dialogic nature of his fiction, its relations to society. Far from being independent of society, Hammett's hard-boiled fiction indicates the linguistic resources available in colloquial speech. Even the colloquial language in Ned Beaumont's speech—for example, "I don't like pimps" and "only you're not all right for Paul, not the way you've been playing with him"—asserts a kind of connection with ordinary life. Indeed, this connection with lower- and working-class life, as well as with the criminal underworld, expressed in a stylized version of those discourses, is used to make a political point. Tough-guy speech shows irreverence for authority and establishes the hero's disdain for bourgeois norms. So when Ned labels Janet's father a "pimp," Hammett is establishing, among other things, Ned's perception of his individualism: he sees himself as both uninhibited and independent in relation to authority. Hammett's use of language thus contains a class element that is used to criticize class society. Hammett uses the language of the hard-boiled world's lower-class criminals to impugn the pretensions of legitimacy, morality, and ethical behavior that characterize middle-class characters in his novels. Thus, the colloquial language within Hammett's fiction exists as a marker between "less hypocritical" crooks—the class defined as criminal by bourgeois law— and "dishonest" crooks, which for Hammett include virtually all of the middle classes.[7]

Unlike Poe's, however, Hammett's language does not affirm a positive vision of knowledge. There is for him no master epistemology such as rationalism that will allow him to solve the dilemmas he is presented with, partly because the problems he engages are not limited to the solving of a whodunit: a crime in hard-boiled fiction always signifies the presence of a wider social or political malaise of which the corpse is merely the signifier. Ultimately, there can be no solution to a crime, because crime is not extrinsic to the system but intrinsic, part of it. Even if the detective discovers the identity of the murderer, the implications of the crime extend far beyond the matter of a mere corpse and are so endemic that they are, finally, intractable. If in the formal English novel of detection the resolution of the crime seeks—unsuccessfully, I would argue—to exonerate society, the ending in a hard-boiled novel almost invariably suggests the wholesale corruption of society. Individuals may be exempt, but the social order stands condemned. In *The Glass Key,* as in most hard-boiled fiction, society itself is essentially unknowable. Nothing is what it seems (in this narrow sense the formal English novel of detection and the hard-boiled novel are alike); everyone and everything is tainted in some way; every institution is compromised. Ned Beaumont's statement that "whatever you've done you've paid for and been paid for and that goes for all of us" (585) is the acknowledgment of this ineluctable fact of life in hard-boiled fiction. This is why the endings of Hammett's fiction often describe the departure of the detective figure from the city he has investigated. The only thing the hard-boiled dick knows for sure is that you can run but you can't hide.

Notes

An altered version of parts of this chapter appeared in my essay "Realisms and Modernisms: Raymond Williams and Popular Fiction," in *Views beyond the Border Country: Raymond Williams and Cultural Politics,* ed. Dennis L. Dworkin and Leslie G. Roman (London: Routledge, 1993).

1. The best elaboration of this argument is David I. Grossvogel's "Agatha Christie: Containment of the Unknown," excerpted in *The Poetics of Murder,* 252–65.

2. For more on the failure of the European avant-garde to achieve any connection with a genuinely mass audience, see Andreas Huyssen's *After the Great Divide: Modernism, Mass Culture, Postmodernism.*

3. I am paraphrasing Sinda Gregory's argument that Hammett is the inaugurator of the antidetective novel. This argument is elaborated in greater detail in *Private Investigations: The Novels of Dashiell Hammett,* especially page 13.

4. See, for example, Dennis Porter's *The Pursuit of Crime: Art and Ideology in Detective Fiction,* especially chapter 7.

5. For more on the ways in which the feminine is inscribed, or significantly absent, in twentieth-century literature and theory, see Alice Jardine's impressive study *Gynesis: Configurations of Woman and Modernity.*

6. It should be noted that this neat mirroring of the disruptive effects of sexual politics in each form of detective fiction is disturbed by the emergence of a relatively new subgenre, the feminist hard-boiled detective novel, which brings together the critical ideology of hard-boiled fiction and the intellectual capability of the female detective figures of the formal English novel of detection, although many of them are more active physically than their Edwardian antecedents.

7. On the subject of Hammett's use of colloquial speech I am indebted to LeRoy L. Panek's essay "The Naked Truth: The Origins of the Hard-Boiled School," in *The Armchair Detective.*

Part IV

Postmodern Crime Fiction

Agents and Human Agency in the Postmodern World | **8**

> Simulation is no longer that of a territory, a referential being or a substance. It is the generation by models of a real without origin or reality: a hyperreal. The territory no longer precedes the map, nor survives it. Henceforth, it is the map that precedes the territory—PRECESSION OF SIMULACRA—it is the map that engenders the territory and if we were to revive the fable [of Borges's] today, it would be the territory whose shreds are slowly rotting across the map. It is the real, and not the map, whose vestiges subsist here and there, in the deserts which are no longer those of the Empire, but of our own: *The desert of the real itself.*
>
> —*Jean Baudrillard, "The Precession of Simulacra"*

Maps and Territories

For Jean Baudrillard, the real is a palimpsest continually rewritten by simulacra. As such, it becomes indistinguishable from its infinite simulations. Indeed, with the notion of "the desert of the real" Baudrillard writes the death of history, for history likewise has entered the circuit of the hyperreal, in which the boundaries between the true and the false, the real and the imaginary, and the present and the past combine and recombine in a dance of signs, reducing all oppositions to an algebra of equivalence. Ironically, Baudrillard's version of postmodernism is thus a totalizing one, but one that erases not only history, but the *subject* of history as well: "No more subject, focal point, center, or periphery: but pure flexion or circular inflection. No more violence or surveillance: only 'information,' secret virulence, chain reaction, slow implosion, and simulacra of spaces where the real-effect again comes into play" ("The Precession of Simulacra," *Simulations,* 53–54). In this respect, Baudrillard's theory is very different from Marxian totalizing systems, which have as their object the delineation of history.

Of all the so-called popular genres, espionage fiction is probably the most concerned with the constellation of issues raised by Baudrillard, and by much other postmodern theory. Often regarded as paranoic in structure, espionage fiction is directly concerned with whether the real is knowable.[1] The antiheroic, ironic tradition of this genre, the tradition that I will concern myself with here, poses questions such as the following: Can the real be differentiated from the models or simulacra that others have produced of it? In the covert world of espionage, what is truth and what is not? Is there such a thing as truth? Is there such a thing as external reality? If there is such a thing as truth, is it put in the service of the ethical? Can the real be signified "objectively," outside the codes that are the stock in trade of espionage? And most important, what are the limitations of, and possibilities for, constitutive human action within this postmodern, seemingly totalitarian world? Taking John Le Carré's *The Spy Who Came in from the Cold* (1963) as my representative text, I shall explore the responses to these questions provided by espionage fiction.[2] Given that *The Spy Who Came in from the Cold* and the birth of postmodern theory are roughly contemporaneous, it is not surprising that they should be concerned with similar issues. I shall offer a "map" of postmodernism, but it is not one devised by simply imposing Baudrillard's theory onto the territory of the spy thriller; rather, what I hope to do is to articulate a theoretical understanding of postmodernism alongside a "fictional" understanding—indeed, we may want to refer to both as fictional *and* theoretical—in order to generate a reading of *The Spy Who Came in from the Cold* as a postmodernist text. At the same time, I hope to use this reading as a basis for a critique of some of the assumptions now dominant in postmodern discourse. This "map" will necessarily be incomplete and partial, necessarily fragmentary—but, *contra* Baudrillard, this seems to me to be the nature of maps.

Vestiges of Empire

Unlike the modern espionage novel, the postmodern espionage novel is concerned not with the threat posed to a nation by a foreign power or conspiracy, whether internal or external, but with the threat posed to individual freedom and action by an increasingly determinative system of social relations and institutions. These systems of incorporation have as their emblem the ubiquitous image of secret intelligence agencies, huge covert bureaucracies with vast powers. Postmodern spy fiction thus differs substantially from the modern spy fiction of Rudyard Kipling and his successors. In *Kim,* for example, Kipling projects a vision of society defined by "the Law," his version of a quasi-feudal empire society held together by social Darwinism. One of the distinguishing features of the modern spy thriller is that it upholds this type of ideal principle; by contrast, the postmodern thriller tends to avoid subscribing to the jingoistic ideals of a Kipling.[3] This is not to say that this type of fiction is morally and political neutral: that would be impossible. Instead, it adopts a critical attitude toward the bureaucracies, whether public or covert, that dominate late-twentieth-century life.

The plot of *The Spy Who Came in from the Cold* exemplifies this. Alec Leamas, the spy in the title, accepts the offer extended by British intelligence, otherwise known as the "Circus," to participate in an intricate plot to topple one of East Germany's most effective spy masters, Mundt. Leamas is especially interested in helping to dispose of Mundt, since Mundt destroyed the Circus's spy networks in Berlin run by Leamas. As presented to Leamas, the plan is to discredit Mundt by fabricating evidence that will make it appear to the East German intelligence organization (Abteilung) that Mundt has worked for the Circus for years, betraying secrets to the British. The hope is to convince Mundt's already-suspicious subordinate, Fiedler, that Mundt is a traitor. As deputy head of security in the Abteilung, Fiedler would have the power to convene a tribunal with the authority to depose Mundt. Leamas's role in this elaborate plot is to pretend to be a burnt-out, embittered, pensionless British agent who is prematurely put out to pasture and who, as a result, becomes an alcoholic wreck. The idea is to use Leamas as bait: the GDR's spies in England will notice Leamas's decline, and as a former spy-runner, Leamas will possess many details about British intelligence operations in the GDR of interest to East German intelligence. Leamas's task, therefore, is to pretend to be a down-and-out who, out of necessity, becomes a traitor. The most important part of Alec Leamas's mission is to let slip certain details that will confirm Fiedler's suspicions about Mundt, and that will corroborate the frame-up of Mundt that the Circus already has in place.

Everything appears to go according to plan. Alec goes into a decline, and alienates his colleagues at the Circus. Very soon afterwards he is reduced to odd jobs. In one of them, he meets Liz Gold, a somewhat muddled but warm-hearted idealist. Despite Alec's knowledge of the dangers of the relationship, and his knowledge that Liz is a member of the British Communist Party, they become lovers. After a short time, Alec makes it known that he cannot continue the relationship and breaks it off. Liz does not know about Alec's involvement in espionage, but resigns herself to waiting in the hope that he will return. Shortly thereafter, he is accosted by a representative of the GDR, is propositioned, and is eventually brought to a remote farmhouse in East Germany to be interrogated by Fiedler. Fiedler takes the bait, and uses the information provided by Alec to put together a case against Mundt. In the course of the trial before a tribunal of the Abteilung, Mundt turns the tables against his accuser, and by bringing in Liz Gold as a surprise witness, is able to establish that Fiedler's charges are part of an elaborate scheme fabricated by British intelligence in order to discredit him. After the trial, in a flash of illumination, Alec realizes that all along he has been double-crossed by the Circus, used by them to *protect* Mundt, who, it turns out, is a highly valuable English double agent. The whole point of the scheme, it transpires, is not to destroy the former Nazi Mundt, but to strengthen his position by doing away with his suspicious deputy, Fiedler. Fiedler is arrested, and after the trial Alec and Liz are surreptitiously brought back to a supposedly safe part of the Berlin Wall in order to escape to the West. As Alec and Liz are scaling the Berlin Wall, though, Liz is shot dead and falls back on the eastern side of the wall. Alec has a chance to throw himself over the wall to safety on the western side, but instead he drops down to join Liz, thereby forcing the East German guards to kill him as well. Thus Alec has been double-crossed by both the East and the West.

As this outline suggests, by the time of the postmodern thriller, very little idealism persists; the ideals that sustained the British Empire have been pretty thoroughly discredited. Alec was betrayed not only by Control—and possibly by Smiley—but also by Mundt, who apparently lured Alec and Liz to the wall with a promise of safe passage. Given Mundt's unsavory personality, this is not very surprising; what is surprising is that the morally "superior" English should willingly sacrifice the only characters with integrity—Alec Leamas, Liz Gold, and Fiedler—to save the murderer and former Nazi Mundt. Or, more precisely, it is intriguing that an English novelist, and a former intelligence officer at that, at the height of the Cold War should suggest that the techniques and subterfuge of the British are not any more pristine than those of their communist counterparts. As the narrator remarks at the beginning of the novel: "Intelligence has only one moral law—it is justified by results" (9). Much of the irony in the novel stems from its sense that the sacrifices made on behalf of the ruins of empire are simply not worth the human cost. This awareness of the disparity between the high-flown rhetoric of empire and the cost, in human terms, of maintaining the empire goes back to Conrad, and extends with force into Le Carré's fiction. In the post–Suez Canal era of Le Carré, the British Empire has collapsed in everything but name, and indeed has largely been subsumed into the American alliance. But to Le Carré, the British have lost even more than an empire; they have lost their ideals as a nation, hypocritical and self-aggrandizing though they may have been. The end of the novel thus forces the reader to read in a very ironic light Control's claim that the English behave on the world stage defensively. As Control says to Leamas early on in the novel:

> "Thus we do disagreeable things, but we are *defensive*. That, I think, is still fair. We do disagreeable things so that ordinary people here and elsewhere can sleep safely in their beds at night. Is that too romantic? Of course, we occasion-

ally do very wicked things.... I would say that since the war, our methods—ours, and those of the opposition—have become much the same. I mean you can't be less ruthless than the opposition simply because your government's *policy* is benevolent, can you now?" He laughed quietly to himself. "That would *never* do," he said. (14)

What is registered in Le Carré's novel is not only the end of the empire, but also the end of any belief in the moral ascendancy of the empire. As the quotation above suggests, the cynicism bred by the Cold War gives an ironic inflection to the ideals that sustained the empire.

This loss of the sense of the moral ascendancy of empire has its origin in the "disagreeable things" that the government does with more abandon in the post–World War II era to both foreigners and English citizens. Whereas Conrad characterized society as anarchistic, lacking any sense of a shared social purpose or identity, and dominated by governmental and extragovernmental alliances, in *The Spy Who Came in from the Cold* this anarchy is no longer possible. In the postmodern world, that anarchistic energy has been subdued, channeled, and contained. Real power has been consolidated, in this world, into two power blocs, two institutions—the Circus and the Abteilung. Interestingly, this representation of world power does not correspond to the historical division of power in the post–World War II era, in which the U.S. and the U.S.S.R. are the dominant powers; rather, the Cold War is cast in terms of the antagonism between Great Britain and East Germany, the chief allies, respectively, of the superpowers. Or more accurately, the historical conflict between the East and the West is cast in terms of the secret wars between the Circus and the Abteilung. Le Carré's dramatization of the Cold War suggests that power is indeed monolithic and corporate inasmuch as the superpowers are able to incorporate smaller, weaker countries into larger economic, cultural, and political alliances. Yet, by centering his representation of the Cold War on the minor principalities of Great Britain and East Germany, Le Carré succeeds in conveying a sense of the life and political destinies of these two countries that also suggests that there is another dimension to the Cold War struggle, and other players in it besides the superpowers. It is partly this sense of the international complexity of the Cold War that gives Le Carré's novel its sense of authenticity.

In the case of both the Circus and the Abteilung, there is the facade of a government for the people—in the case of Great Britain, this facade takes the form of a liberal democracy; in the case of the GDR, centralized, authoritarian communism—but for Le Carré, both political systems exist as window dressing for the secret intelligence agencies. For Le Carré, governmental politics are a fiction written by the intelligence world for the consumption of that country's population.

In *The Secret Agent* Conrad projected a vision of a fractured society riven by competing interests, a corrupt government, and a divided community. Indeed, for Conrad there is no genuine community. In *The Spy Who Came in from the Cold* just the opposite situation obtains. Le Carré's novel projects a grotesque version of the "knowable community," for the community is incorporated, secretly monitored, and regulated to a large extent by intelligence agencies of the state. Not quite Orwellian in the degree to which the state determines the actions of its citizens, Le Carré's community nevertheless is all *too* knowable. Surveillance gives the state access to the most intimate areas of human life—as the Circus's cynical use of Leamas's liaison with Liz Gold suggests. Within this monitored environment, the individual thus exists either in a state of tension and alienation from the claustrophobic, managed community around him, or else in a state of ignorance. In either case, the options for individual or collective action are limited. This is as true in the West as it is in the East. Indeed, in the postmodern espionage novel, the community is no longer defined by the borders of the city, or even those of the metropolis: the community is now international. In this sense espionage fiction can be understood as an evaluation of the experience of modernity in its putatively postmodern phase. The ceaseless change and transformation of social life found in espionage fiction gesture toward the international dimension of contemporary experience.[4] Indeed, one might even say that the breathless pace of the genre captures something of the speed and hyperactivity of the lives of urban dwellers in the age of information. At the same time, *The Spy Who Came in from the Cold* is able to comment on the capacity of the large corporate structures of the postmodern world to channel and absorb, or to seem to channel and absorb, the dynamic energies of modernity in order to maintain stability. For what any corporate body—for example, the intelligence bureaucracy—values above all is stability. Instability, not ideology, is the most dangerous character trait in the postmodern spy thriller. A Mundt can be renovated; an Alec Leamas, a Liz Gold, or a Fiedler cannot.

It is mistaken, therefore, to regard the postmodern spy novel as paranoic, for its suspiciousness about the motivation of behavior is not so much the result of an internal conflict that is symbolically resolved by projecting it outside, onto external reality (the classical Freudian definition of paranoia), as it is in some sense a justifiable response to a postmodern environment in which Foucault's panopticon seems to be everywhere, an environment in which surveillance and monitoring are commonplace.[5] Betrayal, too, assumes the dimensions of a complex moral problem: betrayal cannot be equated with treachery (as it was for, say, Kipling), for what is betrayed? If one political system is as ruthless as another, and if every political system regularly betrays the trust of its citizens by spying on them, betrayal then can be read as a moral act, insofar as it is a repudiation of a violated social contract between the individual and the government.

But the difficulty with this view of betrayal as a moral act, as Le Carré shows, is that the traitor inevitably delivers his or her secrets to a power that is as morally bankrupt as the one betrayed. Thus the possibilities for moral action via betrayal are represented as also extremely problematic. As an author, Le Carré's solution to this dilemma is to symbolically "betray" Great Britain in his fiction by exposing the ways in which the state produces cover stories for its own amoral or immoral actions. He does not, of course, divulge state secrets, but by generating fictional models of the ways in which secret intelligence agencies operate, by exploring the tension between individual conscience and social duty, Le Carré is able to make the same point as the conscientious traitor—but without having to alter his political allegiances. Le Carré uses the critical capacity of evaluative realism in his spy fiction to comment on the political structures in the postmodern era that circumscribe individual action. That any form of realism should find its way into a postmodern text seems on the face of things to be anomalous at best, anachronistic at worst. But as Fredric Jameson has suggested in *Postmodernism, or the Logic of Late Capitalism,* one of the characteristic features of postmodern art is its "aesthetic populism" (2). Eschewing the stigmatization of popular culture, postmodern literature takes whatever literary techniques and modes of representation it finds most suitable from literary history, regardless of conventional periodization or traditional valuation. Thus, along with more canonical literary traditions, the realm of popular culture is opened up for "aesthetic colonization" (19). In this sense, Le Carré's opportunistic use of realism to evaluate a postimperial but neocolonial reality (as the division of the world into monolithic blocs suggests) is itself a quintessentially postmodern act.

Simulacra

Simulacra are models or discursive formations (political institutions, television, film, advertising, media, even human discourse) that produce and reproduce the real. For Baudrillard, once the production of the real is under way, it not only becomes indistinguishable from the model or production of it, but quite literally becomes the real: "truth, reference, and objective causes have ceased to exist" (255). In *The Spy Who Came in from the Cold,* nations no longer seem morally differentiated. No nation is politically superior to another. The model of the West that the Circus constructs initially seems different from that of the East, but this does not turn out to be the case, as Alec confesses to Liz at the end of the novel: " 'Oh Liz,' he said desperately, 'for God's sake believe me. I hate it, I hate it all, I'm tired. But it's the world, it's mankind that's gone mad. We're a tiny price to pay ... but everywhere's the same, people cheated and misled, whole lives thrown away, people shot and in prison, whole groups and classes of men written off for nothing. And you, your Party—God knows it was built on the bodies of ordinary people. You've never seen men die as I have, Liz'" (166). The Circus is, as Alec learns, ultimately no different from the Abteilung; at least politically, the West is no different from the East. Each political system is regulated and overseen by massive intelligence conglomerates, and because these conglomerates are identical in method, aim, and structure, the political systems are also, for Le Carré, homologous. The West is more affluent, and its people enjoy more freedom than people do in the East, but within the ideology of the novel, these obvious differences are not as decisive as the hidden structural similarities between the East and the West. Truth, reference, and objective cause are no longer absolute values in the postmodern thriller—as they are for Ian Fleming—but are instead strategic values, easily disposed of or changed. In the postmodern espionage novel, truth and objective cause are not impossible to ascertain, but they are often obscured, if not obliterated, by simulacra. Truth is always part of systemic simulation, part of systems of information and systems of disinformation. Alec Leamas, for example, ultimately figures out the real reason for his mission, but only after having already committed himself to it; his original decision was based on the disinformation provided by high-ranking members of the Circus.

Much of the narrative complexity of the postmodern espionage novel stems from the difficulties the protagonist encounters in attempting to distinguish an event from the simulations made of that event, typically by intelligence agencies with a vested interest in concealing or transforming particular historical facts. The real, as Baudrillard claims, becomes one simulation among others; the logical extreme of this position is that the real is reduced to an effect of simulacra. This situation is doubly ironic in *The Spy Who Came in from the Cold* inasmuch as Alec Leamas, for most of the novel, takes the attitude that the East and the West are not fundamentally the same, only to find out that in some very basic ways they are. Indeed, the "fact" upon which his whole involvement in the Circus's elaborate plot depends—that he is going after Mundt in order to avenge old scores—turns out to be a simulation of the truth, a generated truth, as it were, designed to protect Mundt. "Everything," Baudrillard says, "is metamorphosed into its inverse in order to be perpetuated in purged form" ("The Precession of Simulacra," *Simulations,* 37).

At the same time, the postmodern spy novel arrogates to itself a demystifying function. In this, it departs from those postmodern theories that collapse history into, say, spectacle or simulacra. One of the conventions of this genre is that history is being made elsewhere, away from the public proclamations of politicians and the public laws and findings of governments and their committees. Thus the postmodern espionage thriller differs from postmodern theory in several important respects. First of all, it upholds the notion of history as a narrative of determination *and* exertion against determination. Second, history is not seen as eternal and changeless, but rather as the outcome of human choice and action. However improbably, this genre presents history as man-made, and hence susceptible to change. Third, history is seen as made outside the public sphere, outside the realm of spectacle and simulacra.[6] I will return to these points in more detail shortly, but for the moment I want to note that crime fiction is in this sense part of a larger formation of popular culture that purports to give the reader or viewer a rare and uncensored glimpse into the way history is really made—for example, supermarket scandal sheets, historical fiction, investigative reporting, television "docudramas," biographies, and political memoirs.

In the case of the postmodern espionage novel, events in the public sphere are regarded either as wholly fictitious or as staged manifestations of covert, nonpublic plans implemented by intelligence agencies. The postmodern espionage novel thus exists as an attempt to locate and meditate on "real" history, and not simulacra. On the other hand, it acknowledges the difficulties of this effort in a world dominated by simulacra. In this world, the individual no longer knows his or her place; social, political, and personal relations seem fixed, but in fact are mercurial, fluid, and subject to sudden reversals. Although these reversals are experienced as changes, they are instead manifestations of a deeper principle of social organization that, once revealed, demonstrates that the "reversal" is not a reversal at all but merely the logical result of a hitherto-unknown principle. The postmodern espionage thriller thus typically depicts the transformation of the protagonist from a modernist into a postmodernist: Alec Leamas assumes that his relations to others are known and stable, and his actions proceed from this premise. His recognition is not incidental, but an observation on the nature of the determinant indeterminacy that typifies the postmodern world he occupies. He discovers, of course, that his assumptions are incorrect, that he has been set up by the Circus in order to save a more valuable operator. It may be objected that Leamas suspected that everything was not aboveboard in the first place. But he never suspected the scale of the deception. He never suspected, nor could he have, that the social, political, and personal relations upon which he depended either were a sham or were implicated in a vast scheme of plans over which he had no control. Leamas does, in the end, understand his position in relation to the forces around him, but his realization is not an epiphany that illuminates and affirms his place in the world, like the one that Kim experiences in Rudyard Kipling's novel; rather, his epiphanic moment is ironic. He realizes that his sense of his relations with others (with the exception of Liz) has been managed and illusory. His recognition that he has no place in the world becomes quite literal in his death at the end of the novel.

One of the most frequently remarked-upon features of postmodernism is its affinity for surfaces rather than depth. In this sense Le Carré's "Quest for Karla" trilogy (*Tinker, Tailor, Soldier, Spy, The Honourable Schoolboy,* and *Smiley's People*) is the paradigmatic example of the depthlessness of postmodern fiction, in which the labyrinthine complexity of events is emphasized over the development of character. Interest in internal consciousness is not absent; indeed, it is a significant part of the interest of this genre. But usually the state of mind of the protagonist has to be deduced from his behavior.

In one respect, as I have argued, this depthlessness is not true of the postmodern spy thriller: it attempts to assert the instability of appearances in favor of a hermeneutic of suspicion, a skepticism toward accepted truths, especially widely accepted political truths. But the mode in which postmodern spy thrillers perform this analysis rejects modernist notions concerned with developing "centers of consciousness," and rejects the valorization of internal consciousness in general that one finds in such high-modernist works as *Ulysses.* It is, instead, a mode sensitized to an analysis of external behavior, to characterizing the possibilities for action in a world in which action is planned, routed, and organized.

The Desert of the Real

What does Baudrillard mean by "the desert of the real"? Not the space formerly occupied by the real, and not the absence of the real—for both of these notions imply the presence of the real. Rather, what Baudrillard has in mind is the *loss* of the real by the technologies of hypersimulation: "Illusion is no longer possible because the real is no longer possible" ("The Precession of Simulacra," *Simulations,* 38). Reality—and illusion—have been superseded by simulacra. In this account, as I have already noted, history too dissolves into simulation: diachrony endlessly recirculating within synchronic reality-effect machines. What exists is not an illusion, a pale reflection of a full-blooded existence somewhere else; what exists, rather, is a world of simulacra. There is no going beyond it, for inside and outside have likewise collapsed, and have been co-opted into the surface world of simulacra. The real becomes for Baudrillard an antiquity, part of the montage of images that define the world of simulacra.

Reality is thus a "model of planned infallibility" (63), and socialization is "the process in which nothing will be left to chance" (63). Although Baudrillard would not use the same vocabulary, the process he describes—the complete organization of social life by monopoly capitalism—corresponds very closely to Marxian theories of fascism, such as those put forward by the Frankfurt school. Postmodern "reality" expresses the fulfillment of fascist tendencies that are always latent within capitalism, but that are now dominant. Within this dystopian vision, there is no possibility for "explosion" (revolution), only "implosion": "a generalized deterrence of every chance, of every accident, of every transversality, of every finality, of every contradiction, rupture, or complexity in a sociality illuminated by the norm and doomed to the transparency of detail radiated by data-collecting mechanisms" (64). Indeed, this vision of contemporary existence negates any possibility for human agency—individuals are not only objects of simulacra, they are themselves simulacra. Resistance, or even negotiation, is impossible within this monolithic view of postmodern existence. Individual or collective action against these regimented, totalitarian conditions cannot be taken inasmuch as there is nothing, for Baudrillard, to react *against.* The interpellation of the subject by the technologies and discourses of simulacra is so complete that seeing beyond simulacra is impossible. Again, it is interesting to note the similarity of structure and emphasis between Baudrillardian postmodernism and the theories of the "administered society" advanced by members of the Frankfurt school. Like Baudrillard, they allow little space for tranformative change.

The postmodern spy novel, similarly, is fascinated by the monolithic organizations, institutions, and systems that regulate contemporary existence—but unlike Baudrillardian postmodernism, it asserts the possibility of human agency. This possibility is not to be confused with the romantic individualism that typifies James Bond stories and films, in which the empowered individual meets and overcomes fantastic difficulties with effortless panache. The ideology of the heroic tradition of espionage fiction insists on the final triumph of the individual over the forces arrayed against him, even though for purposes of suspense it is necessary that the protagonist be endangered. In this sense, the modern heroic tradition of the espionage novel differs markedly from the vision of the individual presented by the type of postmodern theory I have been examining: While the heroic tradition insists on the individual's Promethean power, postmodern theory tends to find only powerlessness.

The postmodern spy novel, on the other hand, does not deny the determinative capability of the agencies and forces that Baudrillard describes; what it does deny is that these multinational agencies totally determine every aspect of human existence. Although choices are narrowed and determined, they do exist in a way not allowed by Baudrillard. In *A Perfect Spy* (1986), Le Carré attempts to trace the full range of influences that lead a British spy to betrayal. As in *The Spy Who Came in from the Cold,* social, political, and personal factors are determinative, but they do not eradicate human choice and action. Indeed, in *A Perfect Spy,* Le Carré is interested in delineating the subtle chain of choices, beginning in childhood, made by Magnus Pym that ultimately lead to his betrayal. Alec Leamas's life is determined and regulated in ways he is unaware of—ironically enough by a putatively liberal democratic form of government—but his life story is not only the story of co-option and regulation and determination. He is indeed co-opted, but he also participates in his own destiny. Leamas makes two crucial decisions. First of all, he elects to involve himself in the Circus's plan. Granted, he is unaware of its real purpose and is deceived about his own role. But he is not without choice; he is not coerced in the fascistic sense that Baudrillard claims is typical of postmodern life. The second decision is equally fateful. At the end of the novel, while scaling the Berlin wall, he decides not to throw himself over onto the western side; this choice results in his death. Despite all the manipulation and deception on the part of the Circus, Leamas probably could have survived. In the postmodern spy novel, then, contingency and choice have not been entirely eliminated from the postmodern world. Indeed, as Graham Greene suggests in *The Human Factor* (1978), in the overdetermined, hyperregulated postmodern world—now the "natural" domain of espionage rather than the exotic setting favored by so many early espionage novelists—it is the human factor that is decisive: all the other variables are known, and quantifiable.

It is thus possible to conceive of the postmodern espionage novel as one that posits a dialectical exploration of determination and human agency: the individual is depicted as determined by the corporate structures of postmodernism, but he or she is also depicted as capable of resisting these seemingly all-powerful agencies. This is not done without cost, as evinced by the fates of Alec Leamas and Maurice Castle, the traitor in *The Human Factor* who ironically gains a freedom in Moscow unavailable in South Africa and England, but at the cost of losing his family. Nevertheless, the individual is not seen as a stamped reproduction of state will. Unlike the vision of postmodern existence projected by Baudrillard, the individual retains some degree of autonomy. Because this tradition within the spy genre tends to focus on the friction between the individual and the government, and on the cost of this conflict in human terms, the outcome for the protagonist is usually bleak. Although the characteristic tone of this tradition of espionage fiction is tragic (or melodramatic), the eulogy is not merely for the individual but also for the social order, which in one way or another has betrayed the democratic contract between the individual and his government.

In the postmodern espionage novel, Baudrillardian simulacra have as their corresponding formulation the sense of "a wilderness of mirrors" in which the real is obscured by the reflections or simulations made of it by different interests or agencies, simulations that, for the protagonist, are almost impossible to differentiate from reality. Yet, in the drama of distinguishing the simulation from the real object in question, the postmodern spy novel sustains both the concept of an objective, determinative reality and that of a determined but still active human agency. In the conflict between the two, the postmodern espionage novel also sustains a notion of history. In showing the construction of history in fictional terms, the postmodern espionage novel attempts to show that history *is* a fiction: fictional in the sense of being radically selective, but also in the sense that it is a man-made, constructed narrative with its own kind of truth. The desert of the real for this kind of novel is its acknowledgment of the necessarily problematic attempt to find a way out the wilderness of mirrors; however, in making the attempt, the postmodern spy novel also affirms the notion of history, and the possibility of locating its political truths.

Territories and Maps

Positioning the contemporary ironic spy novel in debates about the nature of postmodern existence is necessarily problematic for a number of reasons, but its formulations are ultimately no more problematic than the theoretical ones that dominate the debate. It is true that as fiction its formulations have to be interpreted and recontextualized in theoretical terms that tend to give little place to the formal properties of the genre. But this process of interpretation and recontextualization is also an inevitable part of engaging in the debate, if only because the debate is always in process, always changing, and never contained by any of the interventions that contribute to it. The debate about the nature of postmodernism is changing not only because the nature of postmodern reality is evolving, but also because the many developing perspectives on it to a greater or lesser extent shift the terms in which the debate is understood and thus conducted. It is in this sense that I claim that postmodern theories are also fictions of postmodernity. This is not to say that they are untrue because they are fictions; rather, I am saying that the process of theorization relies, like the process of producing fiction, on selection and perspective. The process of theorization therefore is also a compositional one: the signs of "inner consciousness" have to be translated into conventionalized, semiotic systems or identifiable genres (understood in the widest sense of the word).[7] The terms of translation in theory tend to be more discursive than most fiction (but not all), and there tends to be less translation in terms of characterization, setting, and the exploration of the conflict between the two, but there is a sense in which much postmodern fiction reads like much postmodern theory and vice versa, as anyone who has read Barthes and Borges can attest.

My aim here is not to identify all the points of convergence or divergence between postmodern theory and fiction, but simply to note that the processes of interpretation and composition are intrinsic to both. I would now like to read the fiction of postmodernism produced by Baudrillard in light of the fiction of postmodernism produced by Le Carré. My assumption in doing so is that the postmodern espionage novel not only offers another perspective on the nature of postmodernism as a social phenomenon, but also provides a basis for criticizing some current notions about postmodernism.

Although I believe it is useful to approach Baudrillard's work from the point of view of fiction, his work claims a very different status, that of objective analysis. Despite its lyricism, "The Precession of Simulacra" presents itself as an analysis of the structure and experience of postmodern life. Baudrillard's work seems most problematic in terms of its elision of perspective. Baudrillard claims that the precession of simulacra has effectively destroyed perspective: "We are witnessing the end of perspective and panoptic space" (54). If this is true, from what position does Baudrillard himself write? The implied answer here would seem to be that he writes from the position of an already-interpellated subject position defined by simulacra. If this is the case, then it is clear that what Baudrillard presents in his theory is not so much analysis (for that genre of writing takes perspective and distance as its precondition) as an unmediated reproduction of the postmodern world— what might be called an unreconstructed version of it. In effect, Baudrillard offers a reflection of the world of simulacra, a report on what it *looks* like. This, I believe, is the reason for his fetishization of capital, his tendency to see capitalistic relations as fixed and eternal. Baudrillard's is a futurological world in the present dominated by commodified images and simulacra, a world in which the economic system is beyond human management. For Baudrillard, because the logic of capital is beyond human control, society is, too: individuals are subject to systems that dictate their lives. Individuals are seen as the objectified human residue of simulacra: nowhere is there any suggestion that we can gain control of capital, or that we can manage the simulacraic systems that dominate our world. Baudrillard's fetishization of monopoly capitalism ultimately leads him to call into question reality itself: "It is now impossible to isolate the process of the real or to prove the real" (41).

This in turn leads to a contradictory way of conceptualizing power. Power is at once anthropomorphized and denied. In a characteristic sentence, Baudrillard writes that "power, too, for some time now produces nothing but signs of its resemblance" (45). This is, of course, a personification of power, but a necessary one if Baudrillard's system is to be animated in any way. The problem with this theory of power is that it is really a theory of non-power—it is said to exist, it is sporadically endowed with agency and action, yet its motives are systematically unknowable, as are its beneficiaries. His notion of power is, therefore, as fetishistic as his conceptualization of social relations. Indeed, one implies the other: a notion of power as unknowable and mysterious is the inevitable corollary of any theory positing the impossibility of human management of economic and social systems. There is, quite literally, no social differentiation within Baudrillardian postmodernism; there are no classes, no power blocs, no alliances—just atomized monads existing, after a fashion, in a simulated environment. The question of who benefits from power is not merely elided; it is denied. Since power has no discernible motive, there are no structural beneficiaries of it. After this theory of postmodernism has denied the existence of reality, history, the individual, human agency, and human-inspired change in social systems, its logical conclusion is the negation of the notion of power. Ultimately, this is what Baudrillard claims: "Power is no longer present except to conceal that there is none" (46). Like everything else, power is dissolved into the metareality of simulacra.

In the last analysis, I believe that Baudrillard's conclusions follow from his rejection of perspective. Paradoxically, and most damagingly, this leads to a negation of everything except his own perspective. Baudrillard's theory, in other words, founders on its own absolutism, its own quasi-totalitarian vision, and its own tacit privileging of the position of the intellectual observer. If the precession of simulacra is as determinative and all-encompassing as Baudrillard suggests, how can Baudrillard stand outside it, analyze it, and make the discriminations he does? The logical conclusion to Baudrillard's theory is the complete penetration of human consciousness by simulacra. If this were the case, Baudrillard would be unable to achieve any distance in describing and analyzing this condition.

Baudrillard's epistemological position, as exemplified by this valorization of the intellectual observer, is a rationalistic one: although his theory posits the complete subjugation of human consciousness by the social system, or its decentered remains, the theory confers upon the mind of the authorial observer a special status, an exemption from the domination of simulation that obtains everywhere else. Reasoning, and not historically based modes of analysis, is regarded as the source of all knowledge. Some of these features—the death of the subject, history, and reality; the tendency to eschew historical detail and social analysis in favor of abstract reasoning; the fetishization of capitalistic relations and the contradictory affirmation and denial of power—are motifs of postmodernist theory in general. Although Foucault's work, for example, is broadly "historical," and has a quite different emphasis from Baudrillard's, many of these features can be found in his analyses of the totalizing systems (e.g., prisons, mental asylums, indeed sexuality itself) that he argues have determined Western civilization since the eighteenth century.

These postmodern theories have led to a problematizing of notions often assumed to be true in other theoretical discourses, and have stimulated rethinking on virtually every level of theory. French postmodernist theory in particular has succeeded in revolutionizing contemporary notions of space and time. It is also sensitive, as few other intellectual formations are, to the pleasures, and the pleasure systems, produced by postmodern society, as the work of Barthes, Debord, and Deleuze and Guattari attests. But, although these conceptual transformations have been invaluable, the rejection of certain concepts, such as history, seems to me to be debilitating insofar as it leads to a loss of perspective: whether by simulacra, by spectacle or by the panopticon, the subject is dominated by contemporaneity, quite literally lost in it. What is sacrificed is the analytical equipment by which contemporaneous experience can be placed in a historical context, analyzed, and then, at least partly, understood. The death-of-history strain of postmodernism has to a very large extent internalized the totalizing, imperial ideologies of late-twentieth-century monopoly capital, which subliminally, and sometimes overtly, suggest that resistance and opposition are impossible. At least one current in postmodern theory, therefore, concurs with the world of monopoly capital in that incorporation into this rationalized world system is the only available option.

The postmodern espionage novel, as we have seen, takes a very different position. Its opportunistic use of perspective—both the narrator's perspective on reality created in fiction and, more generally, the historical perspective on postmodern reality afforded by this mass-cultural form—allows it to make discriminations and evaluations that, as we have seen, some postmodernist theories, ironically enough, deny themselves from the outset. In its dramatization of the conflict between determination and human agency, the postmodern espionage novel suggests the primacy of history in human experience, and by dramatizing the *making* of this history, the genre does not so much offer a way of escaping from reality as a way of returning to it through the heightened possibilities of narrative.

Notes

1. In *Thrillers: Genesis and Structure of a Popular Culture,* Jerry Palmer, for example, argues that as a genre the thriller is paranoic inasmuch as it offers a paranoid representation of the world. See especially chapter 3.

2. Other examples of the antiheroic postmodern espionage novel include Anthony Burgess's *Tremor of Intent,* Graham Greene's *The Human Factor,* Raymond Williams's *The Volunteers,* and Chris Mullins's *A Very British Coup.* As this list suggests, the major practitioners of this genre are British. This critical brand of espionage fiction is not dominant; most recent espionage fiction displays an affinity for right-wing politics.

3. In his elegant essay "The Hippocratic Smile: John Le Carré and the Traditions of the Detective Novel," published in *The Poetics of Murder* (341–65), Glenn W. Most argues convincingly that the true antecedent to Le Carré's fiction is not the English tradition but the hard-boiled, socially critical American tradition of Hammett, Chandler, and Macdonald. The same case could be made for what I have termed the postmodern spy novel.

4. In *Cover Stories: Narrative and Ideology in the British Spy Thriller,* Michael Denning makes a similar point: "Rather the intelligence community serves as a shadowy figure for the social world of late capitalism where the opacities that surround human agency are cut through by projecting an essentially magic figure, the secret agent" (29). Although I disagree with Denning's claim that the spy novel contains only a "feigned realism" (29), his book is the most theoretically sophisticated, consistently intriguing study of British spy thrillers available.

5. For more on Freud's theory of paranoia, see "On the Mechanism of Paranoia" in his collection of essays entitled *General Psychological Theory.* Also see his *Introductory Lectures on Psychoanalysis,* especially pages 423–29. For an interesting discussion of paranoia in another genre usually identified as "popular," see Carl Freedman's "Towards a Theory of Paranoia: The Science Fiction of Philip K. Dick," in *Science-Fiction Studies* 11 (1984).

6. For more on the unifying aspect of the spectacle, see Guy Debord's *The Society of Spectacle.*

7. For more on the way in which consciousness is constituted by signs, see V. N. Volosinov's *Marxism and the Philosophy of Language,* especially chapter 3 in part I.

Conclusion:
Postmodern Fictions of Crime

> Things then did not delay in turning curious.
> —*Thomas Pynchon,* The Crying of Lot 49

Postmodern Crime Fiction and the Real

I would like to conclude by exploring what it means to assimilate the concept of postmodernism that I have been developing into the vast literary territory occupied by crime fiction. What follows is, inevitably, an abbreviated answer to that question. My contention is that Thomas Pynchon's *The Crying of Lot 49* offers a paradigm for understanding postmodern crime fiction, a field that might also be said to include, among many other works, Ishmael Reed's *Mumbo Jumbo,* Gabriel García Márquez's *Chronicle of a Death Foretold,* and Don DeLillo's *Libra.* Three initial questions seem central: What does it mean to refer to a body of writing as "postmodern crime fiction"? How does postmodern crime fiction treat the power-knowledge connection that has been such a dominant feature of detective and espionage fiction from Poe to Le Carré? And what is postmodern crime fiction's posture toward the real (or external reality)?

In one sense *The Crying of Lot 49* is a problematic text to use as an example of a postmodernism, for its difficulty and density of language would seem to identify it with high modernism. As with most of Pynchon's fiction, the reader is continuously compelled to backtrack in order to decipher Pynchon's long, abstract, often strangely lyrical sentences. Yet the novel is unmistakably postmodernist insofar as it violates some of the most widely accepted tenets of high-modernist aesthetics. If, for the moment, we return to the most privileged of these—namely, the notion of the superiority of high culture over low (or mass) culture—then *The Crying of Lot 49,* with its absorption of the hard-boiled California detective novel of Dashiell Hammett and Raymond Chandler, at the level of form transgresses this hierarchy. Another tenet of modernist aesthetics, or at least one version of it—that art and life are fundamentally opposed, and that art exists as a refined retreat from the banalities and crassness of modern existence (recall Wallace Stevens's famous dictum that "reality is a cliché from which we escape by metaphor")—is also abandoned in Pynchon's work. Some of the most lyrical passages in *The Crying of Lot 49* are poignant reflections on the refuse and waste of contemporary American culture, the rusted cars and thrown-away mattresses that for Pynchon preserve the imprint of human use, and a whole way of life. For Pynchon, then, the refuse of contemporary culture is not so much a sign of spiritual sterility (as it is for T. S. Eliot) as it is socially symbolic: Pynchon, that is, looks at refuse as a semiotician of culture, and not as a moral and aesthetic critic.

Where, then, does this leave Pynchon's novel? Is it "modernist" or "postmodernist"? Although the distinction between Pynchon and Eliot might suggest an absolute difference, this question is best understood in the light of the argument elaborated in earlier chapters, in which postmodernism is seen as an emergent formation that is continuous with modernist practices and ideologies. In any event, putting the question in an either/or fashion seems to create a false dilemma—a dilemma that artificially forces the reader to choose between one set of formal characteristics and another, whereas in fact they coexist within the same text. The point I am reiterating here is that literary modernism is not a single literary formation with a single, universally agreed-upon tradition, but a field of writing (and reading) practices that contains residual, dominant, and emergent elements. An example here might better illustrate my meaning. Nowadays, many contemporary crime novelists write not so much "whodunits" as "whydunits," the focus of attention being less on identifying the criminal than on the reasons why he or she committed the crime. Typically, this leads to an exploration of the disturbed consciousness of the criminal. Now the techniques used here are "modernist" in that they are devoted to an exploration of a "center of consciousness"; the mode of representation often used is classic realism; but the form of a novel such as Ruth Rendell's *The Lake of Darkness* is a "whydunit," a transformation of the popular-culture "whodunit" formula.

This combination of high- and low-cultural elements (realism from low culture and the high-modernist preoccupation with consciousness) is typical of postmodernism. But in postmodernism, high and low culture are frequently mixed in such a way as to distinguish this combination from the use of popular culture in modernism. Astradur Eysteinsson suggests that "modernist works, through the 'thickness' of their referential texture, establish a radical distance between themselves and such products of popular culture that we perceive in the background. Postmodernism, on the other hand, self-consciously working with the desires involved in the production and consumption of such products, seeks to seduce its audience into compliance with the work before setting about to reveal the sources of its illusion" (121). Postmodernism is distinctive, therefore, not only in its use of popular culture, but in the *way* in which it uses it. Indeed, these self-conscious, ironic, demystifying elements are also typical of much crime fiction, particularly hard-boiled detective fiction; and if this is the case, then the work of Hammett and Chandler can likewise be regarded as a kind of emergent postmodernism. Indeed, the conventions of crime fiction lend themselves to this ironic postmodern worldview.

Andreas Huyssen's reading of postmodernism likewise stresses its heterodox nature:

> My argument, however, is that this [modernist] project has run its course and is being replaced by a new paradigm, the paradigm of the postmodern, which is itself as diverse and multifaceted as modernism had once been before it ossified into dogma. By "new paradigm" I do not mean to suggest that there is a total break or rupture between modernism and postmodernism, but rather that modernism, avantgarde, and mass culture have entered into a new set of mutual relations and discursive configurations which we call "postmodern" and which is clearly distinct from the paradigm of "high modernism." As the word "postmodernism" already indicates, what is at stake is a constant, even obsessive negotiation with the terms of the modern itself. (ix–x)

Most crime fiction is in this limited sense postmodern—that is, in seizing upon the possibilities of a mass-culture genre, much contemporary crime fiction finds itself allied with the destabilization of the dichotomies that typify high modernism. And there are a smaller but recognizable number of contemporary crime fiction novelists who self-consciously combine elements from modernism, the avant-garde, and mass culture in such a way as "to reveal the sources of [the work's] illusion" (although sometimes it is unable to find the sources of illusion or even to determine if the illusion really is an illusion). While different in other ways, Le Carré's espionage novels and Pynchon's *The Crying of Lot 49* can thus be understood as emergent forms of postmodernism, but forms that necessarily contain elements of modernism.[1]

When this vocabulary is used, however, there is an unfortunate sense in which the terms of analysis distort or even betray the phenomenon they are meant to engage. "Postmodernism" as a compound term explicitly asserts the supersession of the experience of modernism, when what is really at stake is modernism's persistence within a larger cultural field in which mass culture and related technologies of representing the real lead to new perspectives and new forms. Baudrillard's sense of simulacra and his theorization of the role of exchange value, Debord's exploration of the society of spectacle, and Foucault's archaeologies and microsystems are valuable ways of coming to terms with this new space, especially when recast as allowing for subjectivity, as well as for resistance and transformation.

The social experience referred to in postmodernist literature is not, then, a superannuated modernity, but an intensified version of it. I am not saying that the modernity referred to, and evaluated, in high-modernist literature is identical to that in postmodernist literature.[2] Rather, I use the term "postmodernism" to signify the presence of a transformative modernity, a modernity that creates postmodern phenomena such as spectacle and simulacra.[3] At the same time, postmodernism retains the combination of disintegration and renewal that for Marx and other modernists characterizes the perplexing experience of modernity.[4]

This sense of living in contradiction informs *The Crying of Lot 49.* For Oedipa Maas, the clues might be clues, or they might not be; she might be a detective, or she might just be a victim of a plot, or of her own wild imagination; the Tristero system might be an underground rebellion against the centralized postal system, or it might just be a hallucination, or even a practical joke played on her by her dead ex-lover Pierce Inverarity. It is impossible for her—and for us—to know for sure. If it is true, as I have maintained in earlier chapters, that the conventions of crime fiction give novelists a particular way of exploring social relations (and social manners), the meaning of social laws (and what it means to violate them), and the ways in which these interactions affect human identity and the making of history, then it is fair to suggest that postmodern crime fiction also attempts to make these kinds of connections, but it emphasizes the difficulty of doing so in an environment in which reality is seen as determined in complex and surreptitious ways. One characteristic of the more experimental current in postmodern crime fiction is, as I mentioned earlier, this extreme state of indeterminacy. In *The Crying of Lot 49,* it is impossible to tell if there is a crime, who the criminal is (if there is one), what the clues are (if they even exist), or even what kind of rationality, or even irrationality, might be applied to the situation in order to resolve the protagonist's state of doubt. As the narrator says, things do not delay in turning curious. The uncertainty suffered by Philip Marlowe or Sam Spade has intensified; indeed, has become the human condition: "Oedipa wondered whether, at the end of this (if it were supposed to end), she too might not be left with compiled memories of clues, announcements, intimations, but never the central truth itself, which must somehow each time be too bright for her memory to hold; which must always blaze out, destroying her own message irreversibly, leaving an overexposed blank when the ordinary world came back" (69). Here Oedipa figures in some sense as an Everyman (or Everywoman) in this postmodern world—the individual who is uncertain about how to read the signs given, and unsure of what they might mean.

Whereas for Poe and Conan Doyle knowledge is empowering, for Pynchon's characters it often leads to confusion and paralysis. For Poe, rationalism is a means for the solitary genius to assert his superiority over the mass of men; ultimately, it is a means of liberation from affective ties and from society itself. For Conan Doyle, empiricism is used to valorize imperial values and society's existing class structure. Despite these differences, for both authors knowledge confers upon the detective figure a certain amount of power.

In Conrad, and then in the hard-boiled school of fiction, this knowledge-power connection becomes more attenuated. Sam Spade and the Continental Op do come to understand the mysterious circumstances that involve them in their cases in the first place, but this knowledge is not liberating. Indeed, more often than not it reveals the corruption in civil society, and the effects and limitations this corruption places on the individual, including the detective figure. Unlike Dupin, Holmes, or Poirot, hard-boiled detectives are not immune to the forces, social or sexual, that entrap their clients. They too are caught up in the networks of intrigue in which their clients have become entangled. They can understand their situation, but this knowledge does not enable them to dominate it. Although hard-boiled detectives pride themselves on their wit and independence, this knowledge is tempered by an awareness of the limitations within which they must operate. Ned Beaumont in *The Glass Key* and the Continental Op in *Red Harvest* choose in the end to leave the city; Sam Spade at the end of *The Maltese Falcon* elects to stay in San Francisco, but with a cynical awareness of the price he has to pay in doing so. In the dawn of monopoly capitalism—a reality represented by the Personville Mining Corporation in *Red Harvest*—this fiction represents choices as whittled down to leaving or resignation to a status quo defined by favoritism and graft.[5]

For Pynchon, the value of knowledge is even less certain, since its reliability is always in question. Knowledge is always contingent, always incomplete. Power exists, but the machinations of power (figuratively represented here in the well-entrenched and insidious power of the Yoyodyne Corporation) are more difficult to identify and resist. Nevertheless, the results of that power are everywhere evident. The landscape of *The Crying of Lot 49* is a world of highways, motels, and the commercial bric-a-brac and waste of consumer capitalism,[6] which is "less an identifiable city than a grouping of concepts—census tracts, special purpose bond-issue districts, shopping nuclei, all overlaid with access roads to its own freeway" (12).

Pynchon's world is a world dominated by the determinacy of indeterminacy, a world in which "all that is solid melts into air."

This brings us to the last question: What is the posture of postmodern crime fiction toward the real? Although Pynchon represents the end of the spectrum, the attitude expressed in *The Crying of Lot 49* approximates that of most postmodern crime fiction. The real exists, but Oedipa Maas's difficulty lies in understanding and interpreting it. Indeed, in Pynchon's novel reality has a strange clarity. It is a fantastic, almost surreal environment, bereft of the traditional markers that organize space in modern cities. Thus it exists, but as a cipher:

> She drove into San Narciso on a Sunday, in a rented Impala. Nothing was happening. She looked down a slope, needing to squint for the sunlight, onto a vast sprawl of houses which had grown up all together, like a well-tended crop, from the dull brown earth; and she thought of the time she'd opened a transistor radio to replace a battery and seen her first printed circuit. The ordered swirl of houses and streets, from this high angle, sprang at her now with the same, unexpected astonishing clarity as the circuit card had. Though she knew even less about radios than about Southern Californians, there were to both outward patterns a hieroglyphic sense of concealed meaning, of an intent to communicate. There'd seemed no limit to what the printed circuit could have told her (if she had tried to find out); so in her first minute of San Narciso, a revelation also trembled just past the threshold of her understanding (13).

Oedipa spends the rest of the novel searching for the "hieroglyphic sense of concealed meaning" to the "outward patterns" that she sees. In the process Pynchon commits the reader to the same search. The sheer indeterminacy of the clues and the ambiguity of Pynchon's language effectively force the reader to become, alongside Oedipa Maas, a detective as well. Although neither Oedipa nor the reader learns the "central truth" (69) about the Tristero system, both learn a good deal about contemporary America. Pynchon's version of the antidetective novel ultimately suggests that there is no final truth, no crucial clue that will tie together all the threads of Oedipa's life. The reality of the postmodern world *is* its mixture of kitsch and sophistication, sadness and excitement, uncertainties and ambiguities that have no final resolution but that are expressed in a novel that offers the reader a self-guided tour through the weird landscape of postmodern America.

Like all crime fiction, then, *The Crying of Lot 49* takes as its subject the perplexing experience of modernity, an experience that finds one of its most resonant and mysterious moments at the end of the novel in Passerine's oddly affirming gesture, "a gesture that seemed to belong to the priesthood of some remote culture; perhaps to a descending angel" (138). As a conclusion, Passerine's gesture is deliberately mysterious, deliberately vague—and yet it is an affirming gesture. In this sense, Passerine's gesture exists as a trope for the novel's exploration of postmodernity: just as the gesture is ambiguous yet somehow affirmative, so too does the novel deny "a central truth" without denying *all* truth; indeed the novel's dominant tropes consistently point to the logic of late capitalism as implicated in the production of the bizarre landscape in which Oedipa is compelled to navigate.

Verifying the Real, or Narrative and History

What Pynchon suggests, then, in *The Crying of Lot 49* is not that reality is nonexistent, but that the postmodern condition is characterized by the absence of an epistemology of praxis (of the type developed by Freud and Marx) that will allow Oedipa to relate and understand the felt discontinuities of her existence. She lives without the narratological resources that would permit her to at least partly transform herself and her world. Instead, within the power-knowledge relations of the novel, Oedipa is more a passive object than an active agent. Passerine's final gesture is not so much the expression of what Jean-François Lyotard calls "the nostalgia for the unattainable; that which searches for new presentations, not in order to enjoy them but in order to impart a stronger sense of the unpresentable" (81) as it is a poignant, fictional configuration of the hallucinatory power of the real.

This is to say that Pynchon is a good deal less pessimistic than Lyotard about "new presentations" and their power "to impart a stronger sense of the unpresentable." Indeed, *The Crying of Lot 49* represents the narrator's success in achieving what Oedipa could not: namely, a sense that the "unpresentable"—the discontinuities and idiosyncrasies and mysteries of America—is representable. Although it does not purport to explain or resolve them, the novel, by representing them in all their complexity, does offer a vision and a kind of knowledge about the contradictions of contemporary American society. Pynchon thus moves beyond the position that post-modernity represents the final negation of contemporary reality (it is absent, it is under erasure, it is pure effect, it is unpresentable), a position that currently dominates much postmodern theory. He does this by at once acknowledging the overdetermined nature of postmodernity (significantly, for Oedipa, as for Freud, effects are produced by "networks" of multiple causes) and by affirming the bizarre historicity of contemporary America in all of its TV and motel culture, its commercial vulgarity, and its unabashed mix of innocence and crassness.

Although *The Crying of Lot 49* registers all this, it also self-consciously acknowledges the complexity of representation. For Pynchon the novel form itself is an example of "the G-strings of historical figuration" (36) inasmuch as it both reveals and hides history. Pynchon's eroticized metaphor suggests that fiction embodies history while tantalizing the reader by not revealing aspects of it. Perhaps more important, Pynchon's phrase suggests that fiction makes of history—both of what it shows and doesn't show—a spectacle or performance that is ultimately seductive.

Far from evolving into a radical skepticism of the real, *The Crying of Lot 49* affirms the tantalizing, bewildering experience of the real and the power of fiction to convey this experience. Though the novel refuses "the central truth," it nevertheless suggests a critical attitude toward (as well as a subliminal attraction for) the hypercapitalism that lends the novel its exoticism and excitement, its pathos and terror. It should not be surprising, then, that the primary trope for postmodernity in the novel is the labyrinth. Oedipa's search for a way out, for an answer to "the central truth," accordingly yields no pat answers, solutions, or easy exits. It is this keenly developed sense of the contradictions and limitations of contemporary life that characterizes Pynchon's postmodernism.

Despite this, for Pynchon, as for other postmodern writers of crime fiction, detection does not become an impossibility so much as it becomes a primary interest in itself: the desire to locate and identify the real, and the forces that have led to its formation, becomes a dominant convention. This desire is all the more urgent in an era in which the technologies of reproducing the real have proliferated to such an extent that the status of what is reality—the representation of reality or its referent—assumes a new primacy, especially in developed, Western nations. Indeed, as we have seen with *The Crying of Lot 49,* much postmodern fiction appropriates the conventions of detective fiction in order to explore the nature of postmodernity itself. Rather than focusing on identifying the murderer or perpetrator of a violent crime, or on its own representation of events, this strain of postmodern fiction reworks many of the conventions of detective fiction—conventions of investigation, pursuit, scrutiny, inquiry, analysis, and final inference—in order to evaluate the values, norms, and socioeconomic arrangements that produce postmodernity. In this fiction, the characteristic movement is thus an expansion of the social base of the novel outward from a highly localized murder (or similar mystery), until the movement of the novel encompasses the evaluation of a whole culture or society.

The Crying of Lot 49 achieves this inasmuch as it explores what it means to live in a hypercommodified, existentially labyrinthine America. Ishmael Reed's *Mumbo Jumbo* (1972) adopts many of conventions of the "whodunit" in order to suggest that the real crime under investigation is nothing less than the criminal foundations of Western civilization, which, Reed suggests, in its racism, ethnocentrism, imperialism, militarism, and history of cultural theft is barbaric, not civilized. In *Chronicle of a Death Foretold* (1982),

Gabriel García Márquez appropriates the form of a crime novel in order to explore the relationships between illicit love, machismo, and the hypertrophic honor and collective guilt in a backwater town, to lay bare the social and moral ironies of Latin American culture. Similarly, Ngugi wa Thiong'o's *Petals of Blood* uses the conventions of the murder mystery in order to evaluate Kenya's transition from a colonized country to a decolonized one.

Each of these novels uses conventions drawn from crime fiction in order to critically evaluate contemporaneous life. Far from questioning the reality of reality, these novels interrogate the values, structures, and relations of dominance that are responsible for the reproduction of inequitable societies. In this sense, reality is seen as fundamentally *political;* all these novels are concerned with authority and power and their effects on what is consistently seen as a social organization.[7] Whether the novelists are non-Western (Ngugi wa Thiong'o), or from marginalized cultures (Reed), or simply from the developed world and critical of it (Pynchon), they exploit the critical possibilities of crime fiction, particularly those of hard-boiled fiction, and have seized upon the conventions of this "first world" form in order to critically examine the failures and corruption of political life. Ultimately, the question of whether the perspective embodied in this fiction originates in a marginalized experience or whether it is simply that of a mainstream writer from a developed country is less important than the shared recognition that it is precisely those relations of dominance—whether they are effected through state force or decentralized forms of intimidation or terror, or simply mediated by ideologically charged discourses—that make reality *common,* that make seemingly discontinuous social experiences necessarily shared ones. In other words, the narrative critique of contemporaneity arises because the coercion applied excludes, but cannot wholly suppress, divergent or even dissident versions of reality.[8] Thus, in this fiction there is a move away from the solipsistic perception of the isolated, atomized individual. Alienation exists, but it is often recognized as a shared experience.

The message in much contemporary crime fiction, postmodern or otherwise, is that reality exists, and exists with a vengeance. The etymology of "history" suggests that "history" and "story" were used interchangeably in early English to refer to imaginary and supposedly true events. In *Keywords* Raymond Williams notes that

> in its earliest uses *history* was a narrative account of events. The word came into English from fw *histoire,* F, *historia,* L, from rw *istoria,* Gk, which had the early sense of inquiry and a developed sense of the results of inquiry and then an *account* of knowledge. In all these words the sense has ranged from a *story* of events to a narrative of past events, but the sense of inquiry has also often been present.... In early English use, *history* and *story* (the alternate English form derived ultimately from the same root) were both applied to an account

either of imaginary events or of events supposed to be true. But from C15 history moved towards an account of past real events and *story* towards a range which includes less formal accounts of past events and accounts of imaginary events.

This etymological connection between "history" and "story" suggests the importance of creativity in both activities. There is a sense in which these postmodern narratives or stories are also histories of a kind inasmuch as they represent inquiries into how society developed the way it did, although they do so in fictional form. These narratives use a number of strategies—among which the creation of suspense and/or anxiety is primary—to encourage reader identification with the represented reality. Fiction is thus employed to affirm the sheer weight and force of history.[9]

If it is true that postmodernism is characterized by the tension between a hyperreality, produced by the continual social and cultural transformations of capitalism, and an attendant epistemological obsession as to how to make sense of this hyperreality, then one crucial question for crime fiction is, how is crime verified? Or to put this question in larger terms, how can we know history?

At issue here is the notion of verification. In crime fiction, as in Western judicial systems in general, verification is arrived at through the amassing of micronarratives (affidavits, institutional reports, personal accounts, eyewitness accounts, interviews, memoirs, histories, and so on) by an individual (a detective figure) or an institution (most often some part of the legal system for which the courtroom is the dominant literary trope). Typically, these micronarratives and existing pieces of physical evidence are ultimately translated into a larger, constructed narrative that purports to convey knowledge of the circumstances surrounding the alleged crime. Through these and other micronarratives a point of critical mass is achieved: even if they lack the certainty of formal logic, conclusions can be achieved. Even if the circumstances surrounding the alleged crime remain mysterious, indeed even if it is impossible to create a completely totalizing metanarrative, the potential exists for the alleged crime to be seen within a larger pattern of relationships. Although this narrative of events may not lead to absolute knowledge, much less justice being served, at the very least the narrative form offers the possibility of communicating a contingent form of knowledge. Very often, the only alternative is to deny an agreed-upon, or consensual, reality.

The situation of postmodern crime fiction is different in a number of ways, most obviously in the improbability of its ever resulting in the establishment of a judicial verdict, one way or the other. Nevertheless, postmodern crime fiction tends also to be evaluative; that is, it tends to critically represent culture as in a state of crisis, whether politically, socially, or legally (or in combination). The underlying assumption of this fiction is that conclusions are arrived at by the telling of tales; narrative creates the possibility for knowledge.[10] Thus, the argument that narratives are purely tropological constructs that arbitrarily assign causality to reality by creating narratives that adhere to their own literary logic, rather than accurately representing the events they purport to relate, and that they are hence unreliable cognitive guides, neglects the *productive* or *transformative* aspect of narrative. Narratives do not reflect reality; they produce it—or at least imaginatively reproduce it. This is all the more true in highly developed, technologically advanced postmodern societies in which reality is relentlessly encoded and transmitted in mininarratives in the form of advertisements, movies, videos, television programs, newspapers, cartoons, magazines, rag sheets, and of course novels, especially popular novels. Reality, that is, comes to us in the form of narrative. This is not to say that this was not the case in older, premodern societies: clearly storytelling, myths, and dances performed similar functions. However, consumer capitalism, technological developments, and the information explosion have intensified this process.

Similarly with knowledge: it is not arrived at by reflecting what is given; it is essentially a transformative act, one that works only by creatively remaking what is. The dynamic, sequential open-endedness of narrative thus makes it a privileged form for the communication of both knowledge and experience. Of course, this remaking of reality authorized by narrative can be liberating or repressive, or a hybrid of these elements. One of the most obvious examples of the productive capacity of narrative is the American Declaration of Independence, which, along with the Constitution, produced the United States as a political entity.[11] Among other things, this example indicates the power of narrative to transform reality by remaking it in ways that affirm, contest, or otherwise mediate hegemonic values and structures. To be an author, or, more generally, to *authorize* one's actions within historically defined limitations, is to be involved in essentially creative action. As we have seen, the narratives of Marx and Freud suggest the regenerative power of narrative to create and convey knowledge. While doing so in terms that are more strictly socially symbolic, much postmodern crime fiction, similarly, attempts to convey knowledge of the subject's position by representing it within the context of individual and collective social and cultural pasts.[12] What allows the possibility of seeing, of vision, of knowledge, then, is not the abolition of perspective, but the integration of these elements in narrative. As Nietzsche pointed out in *On the Genealogy of Morals:* "There is *only* a perspective seeing, *only* a perspective 'knowing'; and the *more* eyes, different eyes, we can use to observe one thing, the more complete will our 'concept' of this thing, our 'objectivity' be. But to eliminate the will altogether, to suspend each and every affect, supposing we were capable of this—what would that mean but to *castrate* the intellect?" (555).

Fictional narratives may not, in and of themselves, generate social change, but their *form* offers a model for narratives that, in their grasp of historical circumstances and forces, could ultimately inspire social transformation. Against the tendency of much contemporary theory to deny the possibility or worth of perspective—or, alternately, to fetishize it to the extent that all knowledge becomes a form of solipsism—some of the narratives analyzed in this book suggest just the opposite, that narratives create the possibility for understanding history. And what may be more important, all of them suggest the power of narrative fiction to intervene in history in ways that remain socially significant.

Notes

1. Since my argument is that modernism and postmodernism evolve out of the same cultural field, it is technically possible to argue that Poe's detective fiction is also postmodern, although I would see it as a proto-postmodernism. In this context, the term "postmodernism" is obviously more confusing than helpful. Yet I hope it is clear that although I argue that these texts have emerged out of the same cultural field, I do not mean to suggest that they are formally identical. Different combinations of elements, and different kinds of discourse, distinguish Poe's work from Pynchon's even though they are both mass-culture forms, both fictions of crime.

2. My position is similar to the one Fredric Jameson maps out in *Postmodernism, or the Logic of Late Capitalism,* but not identical. Whereas Jameson sees post-modernist reality as dominant, I believe that it is emergent, still inextricably linked with the structure and experience of modernity. Jameson gives postmodernity a kind of internal cohesion or integrity. To my mind postmodernity is still a nascent formation, coexisting with modernity. Ultimately, this difference of opinion can be understood as a disagreement about determination. Although Jameson gestures toward the necessity of preserving a sense of human agency, his use of French postmodernist theoreticians such as Baudrillard and Debord suggests an attraction toward the type of totalizing systems that in theory make human agency impossible.

3. In light of my argument, it would be more accurate to refer to postmodernity as "(post)modernity," but I have refrained from doing so because the constant repetition of the parentheses becomes tedious and overly insistent.

4. Fredric Jameson, one of the preeminent writers on postmodernism, seems to affirm this continuity (even if he denied it earlier) at one point in *Postmodernism, or the Logic of Late Capitalism* when he asserts: "I have already pointed out that Mandel's intervention in the postindustrial involves the proposition that late or multinational or consumer capitalism, far from being inconsistent with Marx's great

19th-century analysis, constitutes on the contrary the purest form of capital yet to have emerged, a prodigious expansion of capital into hitherto uncommodified areas" (35–36). Yet he remains somewhat ambiguous on this point: much of his argument could be read as a defense of the position that modernity and postmodernity are not continuous.

5. For more on the connections between Hammett's fiction and monopoly capitalism, and on the way in which Hammett's fiction can be read as an "antifascist fascist allegory" (217), see Carl Freedman and Chris Kendrick's stimulating essay "Forms of Labor in Dashiell Hammett's *Red Harvest,*" in *PMLA* 106 (March 1991).

6. Following Fredric Jameson, I use the terms "monopoly capitalism" and "consumer capitalism" not quite as synonyms, but as signifiers with the same referent; they are useful inasmuch as they call attention to different aspects of that referent—namely, late capitalism.

7. This is not the place to fully elaborate a theory of power, but the etymologies of "power" and "authority" are suggestive in terms of the argument I have been making. The *OED* traces the modern English noun "power" back to the Old French *poeir,* which is related to the modern French *pouvoir*—"to be able." Hence, the primary meaning of "power": "ability to do or effect something or anything, or to act upon a person or a thing." The etymology of "authority" is rooted in the Latin noun *auctoritas.* The primary meaning of "authority" is "power to enforce obedience." Or, more explicitly, "power or right to enforce obedience; moral or legal supremacy; the right to command, or give an ultimate decision." The fiction discussed in this chapter attempts to use the power of authority in order to expose and resist the workings of political power.

8. In "Language, Narrative, and Anti-Narrative" Robert Scholes pithily and usefully defines narrative in the following way: "Narrative is a sequencing of something for somebody" (*Critical Inquiry* 7, 1 [Autumn 1980], 209). This rather broad sense of narrative can stand as a point of departure for my argument concerning the relationship between narrative and history.

9. From the perspective of many writers, especially those from developing nations or marginalized situations within the developed world, Lyotard's notion that history is "unpresentable" is a luxury they can ill afford, for the denial of history amounts to a denial of identity and particular historical experiences. There is a sense, then, in which the denial of reality (and ultimately of history) found so often in the work of intellectuals from the developed world is a position that is facilitated by not being one of history's victims, for whom "the nightmare of history" is inescapable. For these intellectuals, a privileged place in an international, predominantly capitalist social and economic order enables the occlusion or even the negation of "the real." This point is dramatized in the contrast between Franz Fanon's work, which engages history, and the later work of Jean-François Lyotard, which elides it. This is not to suggest that an intellectual's position vis-à-vis the developed world wholly determines his/her response to the question of reality, but rather that this subject position is one of a number of crucial (and determining) factors.

10. As many people have observed, "narrative" and "knowledge" have the same etymological root: "Latin *narrare* to relate, recount, supposed to be for **gnarare,*

relates to *gnarus,* knowing, skilled, and thus ultimately allied to KNOW" (*OED*). I have quoted the above passage from Ross Chambers's *Story and Situation,* 70.

11. In my view, the United States also stands as a primary example of a politically ambiguous reality, one that is both liberating and repressive—a division written into the Constitution, with its acceptance of freedom for some but not for others.

12. An excellent example of this is Graham Swift's *Waterland,* which makes use of conventions from the murder mystery (among other genres) in order to explore both an individual history and a collective or regional one.

Works Cited

Achebe, Chinua. "An Image of Africa: Racism in Conrad's *Heart of Darkness.*" *Hopes and Impediments: Selected Essays.* New York: Anchor Books, 1989. 1–20.

Adorno, T. W. *Aesthetic Theory.* Trans. C. Lenhardt. Ed. Gretel Adorno and Rolf Tiedmann. London: Routledge and Kegan Paul, 1984.

Allen, Michael. *Poe and the British Magazine Tradition.* New York: Oxford University Press, 1969.

Althusser, Louis. "A Letter on Art in Reply to André Daspre." *Lenin and Philosophy and Other Essays.* Trans. Ben Brewster. New York: Monthly Review Press, 1971. 221–28.

Altick, Richard D. *Deadly Encounters: Two Victorian Sensations.* Philadelphia: University of Pennsylvania Press, 1986.

———. *The English Common Reader.* Chicago: University of Chicago Press, 1957.

Anderson, Perry. "Modernity and Revolution." *Marxism and the Interpretation of Culture.* Ed. Cary Nelson and Lawrence Grossberg. Urbana: University of Illinois Press, 1988. 317–33.

Arnold, Matthew. *Culture and Anarchy. The Portable Matthew Arnold.* Ed. Lionel Trilling. New York: Viking and Penguin, 1980. 469–573.

Atkins, John. *The British Spy Novel: Styles in Treachery.* London: John Calder, 1984.

Bakhtin, M. M. *The Dialogic Imagination.* Trans. Caryl Emerson and Michael Holquist. Ed. Michael Holquist. Austin: University of Texas Press, 1981.

Barthes, Roland. *Mythologies.* Trans. Annette Lavers. New York: Hill and Wang, 1985.

———. *Writing Degree Zero.* Trans. Annette Lavers and Colin Smith. New York: Hill and Wang, 1968.

Baudrillard, Jean. "The Precession of Simulacra." *Simulations.* Trans. Paul Foss, Paul Patton, and Philip Beitchman. New York: Semiotext(e), 1983. 1–79.

Benjamin, Walter. "One-Way Street." *Reflections.* Ed. Peter Demetz. New York: Schocken Books, 1986. 61–94.

———. "The Storyteller." *Illuminations*. Ed. Hannah Arendt. New York: Schocken Books, 1969. 83–109.

———. "The Work of Art in the Age of Mechanical Reproduction." *Illuminations*. Ed. Hannah Arendt. New York: Schocken Books, 1969. 217–51.

Bennett, Tony. "Marxism and Popular Fiction." *Popular Fictions: Essays in Literature and History*. London: Methuen, 1986. 214–27.

———, et al., eds. *Popular Culture and Social Relations*. Philadelphia: Open University Press, 1986.

———, and Janet Woollacott. *Bond and Beyond: The Political Career of a Popular Hero*. London: Routledge, 1987.

Berman, Marshall. *All That Is Solid Melts Into Air: The Experience of Modernity*. New York: Simon and Schuster, 1982.

Bernheimer, Charles and Claire Kahane, eds. *In Dora's Case: Freud-Hysteria-Feminism*. New York: Columbia University Press, 1985.

Birkenhead, Lord. *Rudyard Kipling*. New York: Random House, 1978.

Birkett, Sir Norman, ed. *Newgate Calendar*. London: Folio Society, 1951.

Bleier, Ruth. "Robe of Innocence or Klansman's Sheet." *Feminist Studies/Critical Studies*. Ed. Teresa de Lauretis. Bloomington: Indiana University Press, 1986. 55–65.

Bloch, Ernst. "A Philosophical View of the Detective Novel." *The Utopian Function of Art and Literature: Selected Essays*. Trans. Jack Zipes and Frank Mecklenburg. Cambridge, Mass.: MIT Press, 1988. 245–64.

Brantlinger, Patrick. *Rule of Darkness: British Literature and Imperialism, 1830–1914*. Ithaca: Cornell University Press, 1988.

Breuer, Josef. *Studies in Hysteria*. Boston: Beacon Press, 1950.

Brookner, Anita. *Hotel du Lac*. London: Cape, 1984.

Burgess, Anthony. *Tremor of Intent*. London: Penguin, 1966.

Cain, James M. *The Postman Always Rings Twice*. New York: Vintage, 1978.

Callinicos, Alex. *Against Postmodernism: A Marxist Critique*. New York: St. Martin's Press, 1990.

Carlson, Eric, ed. *The Recognition of Edgar Allan Poe: Selected Criticism Since 1829*. Ann Arbor, Mich.: Ann Arbor Paperbacks, 1970.

Cawelti, John G. *Adventure, Mystery, and Romance: Formula Stories as Art and Popular Culture*. Chicago: University of Chicago Press, 1976.

———. and Bruce Rosenberg. *The Spy Story*. Chicago: University of Chicago Press, 1987.

Chambers, Ross. *Story and Situation*. Minneapolis: University of Minnesota Press, 1984.

Chandler, Raymond. *The Big Sleep*. New York: Vintage Crime, 1988.

———. "The Simple Art of Murder." *The Art of the Mystery Story*. 222–37.

Charvat, William. *Literary Publishing in America*. Philadelphia: University of Pennsylvania Press, 1959.

Christie, Agatha. *An Autobiography*. New York: Dodd, Mead, and Co., 1977.

———. *Curtain*. New York: Pocket Books, 1976.

———. *Murder in Mesopotamia*. New York: Dell, 1936.

———. *The Murder of Roger Ackroyd*. New York: Pocket Books, 1971.

——. *Murder on the Orient Express.* London: Collins, 1934.

——. *The Mysterious Affair at Styles.* New York: Bantam Books, 1961.

——. *Sleeping Murder.* New York: Bantam Books, 1977.

Cixous, Hélène and Catherine Clément. *The Newly Born Woman.* Minneapolis: University of Minnesota Press, 1986.

Clark, J. et al., eds. *Working Class Culture: Studies in History and Theory.* New York: St. Martin's Press, 1979.

Collins, Wilkie. *The Moonstone.* New York: Signet Classic, 1984.

Conrad, Joseph. *Heart of Darkness and the Secret Sharer.* New York: Bantam Classic, 1981.

——. *Nostromo.* Harmondsworth, England: Penguin Modern Classics, 1979.

——. *The Secret Agent.* Harmondsworth, England: Penguin English Library, 1984.

——. *Under Western Eyes.* Harmondsworth, England: Penguin Classics, 1985.

Debord, Guy. *The Society of Spectacle.* Detroit: Black and Red, 1983.

Defoe, Daniel. *Moll Flanders.* Harmondsworth, England: Penguin English Library, 1978.

——. *Robinson Crusoe.* New York: Norton Critical Edition, 1975.

DeLillo, Don. *Libra.* New York: Penguin Books, 1991.

Denning, Michael. *Cover Stories: Narrative and Ideology in the British Spy Thriller.* London: RKP, 1987.

Dickens, Charles. *Bleak House.* Harmondsworth, England: Penguin Classics, 1985.

——. *Hard Times.* New York: Bantam Classic, 1981.

——. *Little Dorrit.* New York: Oxford University Press, 1982.

——. *Our Mutual Friend.* Harmondsworth, England: Penguin Classics, 1985.

Dostoyevsky, Fyodor. *Crime and Punishment.* Trans. David Magarshack. Middlesex, England: Penguin, 1975.

Doyle, Sir Arthur Conan. *The Complete Sherlock Holmes.* Two vols. New York: Doubleday, 1930.

Eagleton, Terry. *Criticism and Ideology.* London: NLB, 1976.

——. "Form, Ideology and *The Secret Agent.*" *Against the Grain: Essays 1975–1985.* London: Verso, 1986. 23–32.

——. *Literary Theory: An Introduction.* Minneapolis: University of Minnesota Press.

Eliot, George. *Middlemarch.* New York: Penguin English Library, 1965.

Eliot, T. S. "The Waste Land." *The Complete Poems and Plays.* New York: HBJ, 1952. 37–55.

Engels, Friedrich. *Socialism: Utopian and Scientific. The Marx-Engels Reader.* Ed. Robert C. Tucker. New York: Norton, 1978. 683–717.

Eysteinsson, Astradur. *The Concept of Modernism.* Ithaca: Cornell University Press, 1990.

Fiedler, Leslie A. *Love and Death in the American Novel.* New York: Stein and Day, 1982.

Flaubert, Gustave. *Madame Bovary.* Trans. Mildred Marmur. New York: Signet Classic, 1964.

Ford, Ford Madox. *The Good Soldier: A Tale of Passion.* New York: Knopf, 1951.

Foucault, Michel. *Discipline and Punish: The Birth of Prisons.* Trans. Alan Sheridan. New York: Vintage, 1979.

———. *The History of Sexuality: Volume I: An Introduction.* Trans. Robert Hurley. New York: Vintage, 1980.

Freedman, Carl. "Towards a Theory of Paranoia: The Science Fiction of Philip K. Dick." *Science-Fiction Studies* 11 (1984): 15–24.

———, and Christopher Kendrick. "Forms of Labor in Dashiell Hammett's *Red Harvest.*" *PMLA* 106 (March 1991): 209–21.

Freud, Sigmund. *Civilization and Its Discontents.* Trans. James Strachey. New York: Norton, 1961.

———. *Dora: An Analysis of a Case of Hysteria.* New York: Collier Books, 1963.

———. *Introductory Lectures on Psychoanalysis.* Trans. James Strachey. New York: Liveright Paperback, 1977.

———. "On the Mechanism of Paranoia (1911)." *General Psychological Theory: Papers on Metapsychology.* Ed. Phillip Rieff. New York: Collier, 1963. 29–48.

Friedman, Donald. Preface. *Illustrated Sherlock Holmes Treasury* by Arthur Conan Doyle. New York: Chatham River Press, 1986. vii–viii.

Gilbert, Elliott. "McWatter's Law: The Best Kept Secret of the Secret Service." *Dimensions of Crime Fiction.* Bowling Green, Ohio: Popular Press, 1976.

Godwin, William. *Caleb Williams.* New York: Norton, 1977.

Gramsci, Antonio. *Selections from Cultural Writings.* Cambridge, Mass.: Harvard University Press, 1985.

———. *Selections from the Prison Notebooks.* New York: International Publishers, 1971.

Green, Martin. *Dreams of Adventure, Deeds of Empire.* New York: Basic Books, 1979.

Greene, Graham. *The Human Factor.* New York: Avon Books, 1979.

Gregory, Sinda. *Private Investigations: The Novels of Dashiell Hammett.* Carbondale: Southern Illinois University Press, 1985.

Grossvogel, David I. "Agatha Christie: Containment of the Unknown." *Poetics of Murder.* Ed. Glenn W. Most and William W. Stowe. New York: HBJ, 1983. 252–65.

Hall, Stuart. "Notes on Deconstructing 'The Popular.'" *People's History and Socialist Theory.* Ed. Raphael Samuel. London: RKP, 1981. 227–40.

Hammett, Dashiell. *The Continental Op.* Ed. Steven Marcus. New York: Vintage, 1975.

———. *Five Complete Novels.* New York: Avenel Books, 1980. [*The Dain Curse, The Glass Key, The Maltese Falcon, Red Harvest, The Thin Man.*]

Hart, James D. *The Popular Book: A History of America's Literary Taste.* New York: Oxford University Press, 1950.

Hartman, Geoffrey H. "Literature High and Low: The Case of the Mystery Story." *Poetics of Murder.* Ed. Glenn W. Most and William W. Stowe. New York: HBJ, 1983. 210–29.

Haycraft, Howard, ed. *The Art of the Mystery Story: A Collection of Critical Essays.* New York: Simon and Schuster, 1946.

Herman, Edward S. and Noam Chomsky. *Manufacturing Consent: The Political Economy of the Mass Media.* New York: Pantheon Books, 1988.

Highsmith, Patricia. *The Mysterious Mr. Ripley.* New York: Penguin, 1985.

Himes, Chester. *Cotton Comes to Harlem.* New York: Vintage Crime, 1988.

Hofstadter, Richard. *The American Political Tradition.* New York: Vintage, 1948.

Holquist, Michael. "Whodunit and Other Questions: Metaphysical Detective Stories in Postwar Fiction." *Poetics of Murder.* Ed. Glenn W. Most and William W. Stowe. New York: HBJ, 1983. 149–74.

Horkheimer, Max. "The End of Reason." *The Frankfurt School Reader.* Eds. Andrew Arato and Eike Gebhardt. New York: Continuum, 1985. 26–48.

———, and Theodor W. Adorno. *Dialectic of Enlightenment.* Trans. John Cumming. New York: Continuum, 1986.

Howe, Irving. "The Culture of Modernism." *The Decline of the New.* New York: Harcourt Brace and World, 1963. 3–33.

Huyssen, Andreas. *After the Great Divide: Modernism, Mass Culture, Postmodernism.* Bloomington: Indiana University Press, 1986.

Jameson, Fredric. *Marxism and Form: Twentieth-Century Dialectical Theories of Literature.* Princeton, N.J.: Princeton University Press, 1974.

———. "Modernism and Imperialism." *Nationalism, Colonialism and Literature.* Minneapolis: University of Minnesota Press, 1990. 43–66.

———. *The Political Unconscious: Narrative as a Socially Symbolic Act.* Ithaca: Cornell University Press, 1981.

———. *Postmodernism, or the Logic of Late Capitalism.* Durham, N.C.: Duke University Press, 1991.

———. "Progress Versus Utopia; or, Can We Imagine the Future?" *Art After Modernism.* Ed. Brian Wallis. New York: New Museum of Contemporary Art, 1984. 239–57.

———. "Reification and Utopia in Mass Culture." *Social Text* 1 (Winter 1979): 130–47.

Jardine, Alice A. *Gynesis: Configurations of Woman and Modernity.* Ithaca: Cornell University Press, 1985.

Jones, Gareth Stedman. *Languages of Class: Studies in English Working Class History, 1832–1982.* Cambridge: Cambridge University Press, 1983.

Joyce, James. *Ulysses.* New York: Vintage, 1986.

Kafka, Franz. *The Trial.* Trans. Willa and Edwin Muir. New York: Vintage, 1969.

Kipling, Rudyard. *The Jungle Book.* New York: Doubleday, Doran and Co., 1932.

———. *Kim.* Harmondsworth, England: Penguin Classics, 1987.

Knight, Stephen. *Form and Ideology in Crime Fiction.* Bloomington: Indiana University Press, 1980.

Lacan, Jacques. "Seminar on 'The Purloined Letter.'" *Poetics of Murder.* Ed. Glenn W. Most and William W. Stowe. New York: HBJ, 1983. 21–54.

Lawrence, D. H. *Sons and Lovers.* Basingtoke: Macmillan, 1987.

Leavis, F. R. *The Great Tradition.* New York: New York University Press, 1963.

———. *Mass Civilization and Minority Culture.* Cambridge: Minority Press, 1930.

Le Carré, John. *The Honourable Schoolboy.* New York: Bantam, 1978.

———. *A Perfect Spy.* New York: Bantam Books, 1987.

———. *Smiley's People.* New York: Bantam Books, 1980.

———. *Three Complete Novels.* New York: Avenel Books, 1983. [*The Looking Glass War, A Small Town in Germany, The Spy Who Came in from the Cold.*]

———. *Tinker, Tailor, Soldier, Spy.* New York: Bantam Books, 1975.

Lukács, Georg. *The Meaning of Contemporary Realism.* Trans. John and Necke Mander. London: Merlin Press, 1979.

Lunn, Eugene. *Marxism and Modernism: An Historical Study of Lukacs, Brecht, Benjamin and Adorno.* Berkeley: University of California Press, 1982.

Lyotard, Jean François. "Answering the Question: What is Postmodernism?" *The Postmodern Condition: A Report on Knowledge.* Minneapolis: University of Minnesota Press, 1984. 71–82.

———. *The Postmodern Condition: A Report on Knowledge.* Minneapolis: University of Minnesota Press, 1984.

Macdonald, Ross. *The Drowning Pool.* New York: Garland Press, 1976.

Macherey, Louis. *A Theory of Literary Production.* Trans. Geoffrey Wall. London: RKP, 1978.

Mackenzie, John M. *Propaganda and Empire: The Manipulation of British Public Opinion, 1880–1960.* Manchester: Manchester University Press, 1984.

Mandel, Ernest. *Late Capitalism.* London: NLB, 1972.

Mangan, J. A. *Athleticism in the Victorian and Edwardian Public School.* Cambridge: Cambridge University Press, 1981.

Marcus, Steven. Introduction. *The Continental Op* by Dashiell Hammett. New York: Vintage, 1975. vii–xxix.

Marcuse, Herbert. *Eros and Civilization.* Boston: Beacon Press, 1974.

Márquez, Gabriel García. *Chronicle of a Death Foretold.* New York: Knopf, 1973.

Marx, Karl. *Capital. Karl Marx and Friedrich Engels: Selected Works,* Vol. Two. Moscow: Progress Publishers, 1969. 86–142.

———. *The German Ideology. The Marx-Engels Reader.* Ed. Robert C. Tucker. New York: Norton: 1978. 146–200.

———, and Friedrich Engels. *The Communist Manifesto.* Harmondsworth, England: Penguin, 1967.

Merry, Bruce. *Anatomy of the Spy Thriller.* Montreal: McGill-Queen's University Press, 1977.

Meyer, Nicholas. *The Seven Per Cent Solution.* New York: Ballantine Books, 1975.

Miles, Peter and Malcolm Smith. *Cinema, Literature and Society: Elite and Mass Culture in Interwar Britain.* London: Croom Helm, 1987.

Mill, John Stuart. *Autobiography.* Riverside Edition. Boston: Houghton Mifflin, 1969.

Miller, D. A. "The Novel and the Police," *Poetics of Murder.* Ed. Glenn W. Most and William W. Stowe. New York: HBJ, 1983. 229–325.

Miller, Perry. *The Raven and the Whale: The War of Words and Wits in the Era of Poe and Melville.* New York: HBJ, 1956.

Miller, William. *A New History of the United States.* New York: Dell, 1968.

Moretti, Franco. *Signs Taken for Wonders: Essays in the Sociology of Literary Form.* London: NLB, 1983.

Morgan, Janet. *Agatha Christie: A Biography.* London: Collins, 1984.

Most, Glenn W. "The Hippocratic Smile: John Le Carré and the Traditions of the Detective Novel." *Poetics of Murder.* Ed. Glenn W. Most and William W. Stowe. New York: HBJ, 1983. 341–65.

———, and William W. Stowe, eds. *The Poetics of Murder: Detective Fiction and Literary Theory.* New York: HBJ, 1983.

Muller, John P. and William J. Richardson, eds. *The Purloined Poe: Lacan, Derrida and Psychoanalytic Reading.* Baltimore: Johns Hopkins University Press, 1988.

Mullin, Chris. *A Very British Coup.* London: Hodder & Stoughton, 1982.

Nabokov, Vladimir. *Lolita.* Berkeley Medallion Books, 1977.

Ngugi wa Thiong'o. *Petals of Blood.* New York: Dutton, 1978.

Nietzsche, Friedrich. *On the Genealogy of Morals. Basic Writings of Nietzsche.* Trans. and ed. Walter Kaufmann. New York: Modern Library, 1968. 451–599.

Nolan, William F. *Hammett: A Life at the Edge.* New York: Congdon and Weed, 1983.

Ohmann, Richard. *The Politics of Letters.* Middletown, Conn.: Wesleyan University Press, 1987.

Orwell, George. "Rudyard Kipling." *A Collection of Essays by George Orwell.* New York: HBJ, 1953. 116–32.

Palmer, Jerry. *Thrillers: Genesis and Structure of a Popular Genre.* New York: St. Martin's Press, 1979.

Panek, LeRoy L. "The Naked Truth: The Origins of the Hard-Boiled School." *The Armchair Detective* 21,4 (Fall 1988): 363–75.

Paretsky, Sara. *Deadlock: A V. I. Warshawski Mystery.* Garden City, N.Y.: Dial Press, 1984.

Parry, Benita. *Conrad and Imperialism: Ideological Boundaries and Visionary Frontiers.* London: Macmillan, 1983.

Poe, Edgar Allan. *Complete Stories and Poems of Edgar Allan Poe.* New York: Doubleday and Co., 1966.

———. "The South Vindicated from the Treason and the Fanaticism of the Northern Abolitionists." *The Complete Works of Edgar Allan Poe.* Ed. James A. Harrison. Vol. VIII. New York: E. R. Dumont, 1902. 265–75.

Poirier, Richard. *A World Elsewhere: The Place of Style in American Literature.* Oxford: Oxford University Press, 1966.

Porter, Bernard. *The Lion's Share: A Short History of British Imperialism, 1850–1983.* New York: Longman, 1984.

Porter, Dennis. *The Pursuit of Crime: Art and Ideology in Detective Fiction.* New Haven: Yale University Press, 1981.

Pound, Ezra. "Hugh Selwyn Mauberley." *Collected Shorter Poems.* London: Faber and Faber, mcmlii. 203–14.

Pynchon, Thomas. *The Crying of Lot 49.* New York: Bantam Windstone, 1982.

Quinn, Arthur Hobson. *Edgar Allen Poe: A Critical Biography.* New York: D. Appleton–Century, 1941.

Radway, Janice A. *Reading the Romance: Women, Patriarchy and Popular Literature.* Chapel Hill: University of North Carolina Press, 1984.

Reed, Ishmael. *Mumbo Jumbo.* New York: Atheneum, 1972.

Rendell, Ruth. *The Lake of Darkness.* New York: Bantam Books, 1987.

Robbe-Grillet, Alain. *The Erasers.* Trans. Richard Howard. New York: Grove Press, 1964.

Said, Edward. Introduction. *Kim* by Rudyard Kipling. Ed. Edward Said. Harmondsworth, England: Penguin Classics, 1987.

———. *Orientalism.* New York: Vintage, 1979.

Sanford, Charles L. "Edgar Allan Poe." Ed. Eric W. Carlson. *The Recognition of Edgar Allan Poe: Selected Criticism Since 1829.* Ann Arbor, Mich.: Ann Arbor Paperbacks, 1970.

Sayers, Dorothy. *Strong Poison*. New York: Harper and Row, Perennial Library, 1987.

Scholes, Robert. "Language, Narrative, and Anti-Narrative." *Critical Inquiry* 7,1 (Autumn 1980), 204–12.

Seltzer, Mark. *Henry James and the Art of Power*. Ithaca: Cornell University Press, 1984.

Sherry, Norman. *Conrad: The Critical Heritage*. London: Routledge and Kegan Paul, 1973.

Simenon, Georges. *The Blue Room*. New York and London: HBJ, 1978.

Simpson, Lewis P. *The Dispossessed Garden: Pastoral and History in Southern Literature*. Baton Rouge: Louisiana State University Press, 1983.

Sinfield, Alan. *Literature, Politics and Culture in Postwar Britain*. Berkeley: University of California Press, 1989.

Stowe, William W. "From Semiotics to Hermeneutics: Modes of Detection in Doyle and Chandler." *Poetics of Murder*. Ed. Glenn W. Most and William W. Stowe. New York: HBJ, 1983. 366–83.

Sweezy, Paul. *The Theory of Capitalist Development*. New York: Monthly Review Press, 1956.

Swift, Graham. *Waterland*. New York: Washington Square Press, 1983.

Symons, Julian. *Bloody Murder: From the Detective Story to the Crime Novel*. London: Viking, 1985.

Thomas, Ross. *Briarpatch*. New York: Penguin, 1985.

Thompson, Jon. "Joyce and Dialogism: Politics of Style in *Dubliners*." *Works and Days* 5:2 (1987): 79–96.

Tolstoy, Leo. *Anna Karenina*. Ed. George Gibian. New York: Norton, 1970.

Volosinov, V. N. [and M. M. Bakhtin]. "Discourse in Life and Discourse in Art." *Freudianism: A Marxist Critique*. Trans. I. R. Titunik. New York: Academic Press, 1976. 93–117.

———. *Marxism and the Philosophy of Language*. Trans. L. Matejka and I. R. Titunik. New York: Seminar Press, 1973.

Walker, I. M., ed. *Edgar Allan Poe: The Critical Heritage*. London: RKP, 1986.

Wallis, Brian, ed. *Art After Modernism: Rethinking Representation*. New York: New Museum of Contemporary Art, 1984.

Waugh, Evelyn. *Brideshead Revisited*. Boston: Little, Brown, 1945.

Williams, Raymond. *The Country and the City*. New York: Oxford University Press, 1973.

———. *Keywords: A Vocabulary of Culture and Society*. New York: Oxford University Press, 1985.

———. *The Long Revolution*. New York: Columbia University Press, 1961.

———. *Marxism and Literature*. Oxford: Oxford University Press, 1978.

———. *Politics and Letters*. London: NLB, 1979.

———. *The Sociology of Culture*. New York: Schocken Books, 1981.

———. *The Volunteers*. London: Eyre Methuen, 1978.

———. "When Was Modernism?" *New Left Review* 175. 48–52.

Wilson, Angus. *The Strange Ride of Rudyard Kipling*. New York: Viking, 1977.

Worpole, Ken. *Dockers and Detectives*. London: Verso, 1983.

—————. *Reading by Numbers: Contemporary Publishing and Popular Fiction.* London: Comedia Group, 1984.

Ziff, Larzer. *Literary Democracy: The Declaration of Independence in America.* New York: Viking, 1981.

Index